The Book of Tests

Bruce M. Nash and Randolph B. Monchick, Ph.D.

THE BOOK OF TESTS

*The Ultimate Collection of Quizzes
to Help You Find Out
What You're Really Like*

DOLPHIN BOOKS
DOUBLEDAY & COMPANY, INC.
GARDEN CITY, NEW YORK
1980

Library of Congress Cataloging in Publication Data

Nash, Bruce M.
The Book of Tests

1. Personality tests.
I. Monchick, Randolph B., joint author.   II. Title.
BF698.5.N37   155.2 '8

ISBN: 0–385–15471–2
Library of Congress Catalog Card Number 79–6611
BOOK DESIGN BY BENTE HAMANN
First Edition

The following are the sources of the tests not especially created for this volume: The tests on pages 3, 27, 30, 39, 43, 45, 66, 72, 76, 79, 81, 84, 94, 106, 115, 125, 133, 161, 178, 245, 247, 253, 268, 272, 276, 294, 299, 310, 323, and 332 by Jane Sherrod Singer, M.A. Psychology and Education, University of California, 59 and 122 by Dr. Frank S. Caprio, 64 and 153 by David Gunston, 142 by Dr. P. Carbone, 172 by Sid Krupicka, 185 by Laurence Schwab and Karen Markham, 241 and 243 by Lisa Dahlberg, 260 and 334 by Jean Black, 341 by George Kezer, and 1, 6, 7, 9, 11, 12, 14, 17, 51, 53, 54, 56, 57, 61, 70, 88, 89, 92, 97, 100, 113, 117, 137, 135, 148, 156, 164, 168, 170, 174, 192, 220, 222, 226, 274, 281, 303, 305, 313, 326, 352 and 354, all courtesy Singer Communications, Inc., Anaheim, California; page 15 courtesy Dr. Zev Wanderer, Marina del Ray, California; page 21 by Janet Muchovej, courtesy *American Home;* 37, 215, and 347 courtesy Marilyn Lane and Dr. Syvil Marquit; 62 courtesy Dr. Frank S. Caprio; 110 copyright © 1978 by *Cleo Magazine,* courtesy *Cleo Magazine* and Singer Communications, Inc.; 126 by Myles Callum, reprinted with permission from The Saturday Evening Post Company © 1977; 141, 145 by Arline Brecher, 225 by Edward B. Camlin, 231 by Gwen Anne Yount, 238 by John South, 256 by Karen Fisher, 336 by Laurence Schwab and Dr. Fred Weaver, 360 by John Cooke and 289, all courtesy *NATIONAL ENQUIRER:* 144 courtesy Dr. Neil Solomon; 150 courtesy Alan Gessner, Ph.D.; 166, 229, 251, 287 courtesy Dr. Fred Weaver III, M.D., Consulting Director of the Institute for Creative Living, La Jolla, California, and Laurence Schwab; 195 courtesy Robert K. Alsofrom, Ph.D., P.A.; 212 courtesy Laurence Schwab and Karen Markham; 234 by Naomi Leiter, M.D., © 1970 LHJ Publishing, Inc., reprinted with permission of *Ladies' Home Journal;* 261 courtesy Gam-Anon National Service Office; 263 by Ellen Sherman, courtesy *GLAMOUR* magazine, © 1978 by the Condé Nast Publications, Inc.; 283 by Lee Fowler, © 1978 THE FAMILY CIRCLE, INC., reprinted from May 19, 1978, issue of *Family Circle Magazine,* reprinted with permission from the November 1978 *Reader's Digest;* 291 reprinted by permission of Hawthorn Books, Inc., from *How to Avoid a Nervous Breakdown* by Frank S. Caprio, M.D., and Francis Leighton, copyright © 1969 Frank S. Caprio and Francis Leighton, all rights reserved; 298 © American Bankers Association, 1975, reprinted with permission, all rights reserved; 314 by Beatryce Nivens, ESSENCE COMMUNICATIONS, INC.; 329 by Lawrence Smalheiser, Ph.D., from the book *Self Encounter* by Lawrence Smalheiser, Ph.D., condensed by permission of Price/Stern/Sloan Publishers, Inc., Los Angeles.

To Sophie and Jojo

Preface

Have you ever taken the time to find out what kind of person you *really* are? Are you an introvert or an extrovert? Do you have sex appeal? Are you a superbrain? Do you have charm? Are you happy or depressed? Are you a creative person? How easy are you to live with? Are you a junk-food "junkie"? How popular are you? Are you a nagger? How honest are you? . . . Chances are you've never made a complete assessment of yourself. Now for the first time, you can do so in the privacy of your own home. With the help of the carefully chosen tests in this book, you can learn more about who you are, why you act and think the way you do, and what you can do to modify your behavior and attitudes.

Using this book, you can explore virtually every dimension of your personal life—your mental health, marriage, friendships, love life, social relationships, mind, capacity for success, body, sex life, and much more. Some tests will confirm ideas you already have about yourself; others will open up new vistas for you as to the way you tick.

Although the tests in this book will provide you with insights as to what type of person you are, don't take the results of the tests *too* seriously. The tests merely suggest the general direction in which your behavior and attitudes are heading. Be aware of certain clues about you and your personality, but don't fret too much if the results of a particular test are not to your liking. You just might be having an "off day" when you take a test! Keep in mind that this is a book to be read and enjoyed. Have fun with it. Use it to discover yourself. You may be surprised to learn many things you never knew about yourself.

This is a book that is not just to be read, but also "played." You can go through the entire book one test after another, take all the tests in one particular section, or skip around from section to section taking the tests you find most interesting. However you use it, the book will provide you with endless hours of entertainment as you learn more about yourself.

Take the tests by yourself or with your spouse, lover, best friend, parent, child . . . whomever you choose. See how your answers compare. You'll find it an eye-opening experience to discover how compatible (or incompatible) you are with your mate, as well as with other family members and close friends.

Another interesting way to use this book is to take the same test at different times, then compare the results to see how you've changed. For example, take the test "Are You Depressed?" today; then a month later try it again. Maybe you'll have cheered up a bit by then!

Ready to have fun taking an in-depth look at yourself? Are you prepared for an entertaining and enlightening venture into self-analysis? All set? . . .

Acknowledgments

Our special thanks go to Kurt and Jane Singer, whose invaluable co-operation, contribution, and assistance made this book possible.

We wish to express our deepest appreciation and gratitude to Dawson Taylor, Gloria Caughlin, and Edith Schorah for their research assistance and generous devotion of time and resources.

We are extremely grateful for the contributions made by Dr. Frank S. Caprio, Laurence Schwab, Dr. Fred Weaver, Marilyn Lane, and the many other physicians, columnists, publishers, agencies, periodicals, authors, researchers, and corporations who unselfishly gave of their time and their material.

Finally, we are forever grateful for the efficient and speedy typing of Sophie Nash and Cheryl Seiple, without whom we would still be pecking away at the keys of our typewriter.

Contents

The Book of Tests

YOU
AND YOUR
TOTAL SELF

Taking Stock of Yourself

Every now and then it is a good idea to take stock of ourselves. One of the best ways to do it is to try to look at ourselves impersonally—that is to say, see ourselves as others see us; for example, like a personnel officer assessing an applicant for a job.

Here is a test to help. Answer "Yes" or "No" to the questions before turning to the scoring key at the end.

PERSON
1. Are you particular about physical freshness, your nails, hair, teeth?
2. Are your clothes suitable to the occasion, neat, clean, free from grease spots and dandruff, in good style, reasonably in fashion?
3. Are you particular about your undergarments, shoes, shirts, collars, and ties, stockings, comb, hair brush, makeup, scarf?
4. Nobody can help having a cold. But do you check bad habits, such as continual sniffing, clearing your throat, blowing your nose, and looking at the result?
5. Do you carry yourself well, head up, shoulders back, stomach in, not slouching and drooping along?

MANNERS

6. Do you admire politeness and courtesy in other people rather than think it "put on," "soft," "sissy"?

7. Would you put yourself to trouble and inconvenience to help somebody else?

8. Do you know how to behave on social occasions?

9. Are you polite when you are nervous or tired, or when people are irritating?

10. Is it your habit to be courteous, not just a party manner you assume when you want to give a favorable impression?

ATTITUDE

11. Do you find it easy to like and work well with most people rather than dislike them?

12. Do you think most people like rather than dislike you?

13. Would you consider other people before pleasing yourself?

14. Would you agree that you can be wrong and that criticism of you may be justified?

15. Can you regard people as people, without being prejudiced one way or the other by sex, age, race, or status with regard to you?

REACTIONS

16. Do difficulties and setbacks make you try harder rather than defeat you?

17. Do you go more than halfway to be friendly and approachable?

18. Are you quick to respond when someone expects to have your attention, help, sympathy, support, co-operation?

19. Would you be able to keep your temper if someone suggested that you did not know what you were talking about?

20. Are you sorry rather than exasperated when a friend lets you down?

SCORING

Count 5 marks for every "Yes." A total of 60 may be regarded as satisfactory. But, since this is an all-around personality test, you must score at least 15 marks in each section. Anything above 60 is good.

Keep this test by you. Try it again in six months.

How Well Do You Know Yourself?

Throughout the centuries, we have been admonished to "know thy-self" . . . and this means more than looking in the mirror while combing our hair. "Failures in self-honesty," says Dr. Albert Ellis, the noted psychotherapist, "are at the root of almost every emotional and mental disturbance." Here is a quiz that may give you some clues to your own ability to evaluate yourself.

1. Can you list five people who have greatly influenced you either positively or negatively:

    Yes _____   No _____

2. Do you think people are frank, honest, and forthright with you?

    Yes _____   No _____

3. Are you honest with your comments and criticisms of others?

    Yes _____   No _____

4. When you are involved with other people and things go wrong, do you sincerely feel *they* are usually in error?

    Yes _____   No _____

5. Can you laugh at yourself?

    Yes _____   No _____

6. Can you list your good and bad traits, your talents and your weaknesses?

    Yes _____   No _____

7. Have you ever stopped to ask yourself why you are engaged in the job or task you now have?

    Yes _____   No _____

8. Do you feel all emotions can be controlled?

    Yes _____   No _____

9. Do you sometimes have the feeling that other people are letting you down?

    Yes _____   No _____

10. Do you want to become thoroughly competent, adequate, talented, and intelligent in all possible ways?

    Yes _____   No _____

11. On the list you made for Question 6, did you give more negative points than positive ones?

Yes _____   No _____

SCORING

ANSWERS: (Give yourself a point for each correct answer.)

1. Yes.   If your answer is "No," you have a hint that you are not honest with yourself. Dr. Camilla Anderson calls people in our background "significant." We all have them. Such a list can give us great insight into why we think and act as we do. Parents usually head the list.

2. Yes.   While this may not always be pleasant, honest appraisals by your friends and associates are actually compliments to your own maturity. If people are afraid to tell us the truth about many things, it is a pretty good sign that we are also afraid to tell the truth about ourselves.

3. Yes.   Once you admit and verbalize your true feelings, you are on your way to self-honesty.

4. No.   Case studies have shown that people who constantly blame others for outbursts, arguments, and disagreeable moments seldom ask themselves, "What did *I* do that made the problem thicker?"

5. Yes.   If you can, says Dr. Gordon Allport of Harvard University, you can be fairly certain you know yourself.

6. Yes.   This is where a good friend should go over the list with you, and make comments. "If you do not have a friend from whom you can ask such help," says Dr. Frederick F. Gaudet, "that too may well be a sign that you are not being honest with yourself."

7. Yes.   A false sense of ambition, the prodding of others, working to live being confused with living to work or vice versa, may be making you miserable. Many people do not want more education, money, and the added responsibility of advancement. Advancement is not synonymous with success. It should be the result of a drive that comes from within. Were you honest in your answer?

8. No. The false belief that we can always control our emotions is too often a screen for lack of self-understanding. If you know what makes you angry, you will avoid the situation. If you recognize your needs for happiness, you will seek to answer them.

9. No. In all probability, when you feel people are letting you down, you have either failed to see yourself properly or you are shifting the responsibility to shoulders other than your own.

10. No. If you said "Yes," you may be in for heartaches and frustrations. To be all things is virtually impossible. Look to your strengths and develop them. Recognize, with frankness, your weaknesses and try to eliminate them.

11. No. If the number of negative traits greatly exceeds the positive ones, you are very likely showing a false modesty . . . or, and more critical, you fall into the category of people who are experiencing the greatest danger in the search for self-honesty: You are confusing honesty with self-castigation.

ANALYSIS:

0–3: You do not see yourself as you really are. Your image is distorted like a reflection in a warped mirror in an amusement park.

4–6: Many of your problems stem from the fact that you either kid yourself or have never taken the time for self-evaluation. The fact, however, that you have answered some of these points correctly shows you are on the right track. Honesty, says Mr. G. Hollowitz, a sociologist, is not something we win overnight. It is something we must slowly work toward.

7–9: You dare to face yourself frankly, and from this comes a calmness and self-assurance. Experiments show that people who possess a mature knowledge of themselves suffer from less anxiety than those who lie to themselves.

10–11: You have learned the secret of being true to yourself. Your reactions are mature and you are able to accept joy and grief, success and failure, love and hate without confusion or feelings of personal guilt. You are a person with an "open self," a term used by Carl Rogers, dean of U.S. psychotherapists.

Do You Think Enough of Yourself?

It is necessary for us to have the right ideas about ourselves. It is bad to imagine that we are all-important and to have an exaggerated idea of our abilities. On the other hand, it is not good to rate ourselves too low.

We have to try to strike the right balance. Here is a test for you. Answer "Yes" or "No" to the following questions before turning to the scoring key at the end.

1. Are you satisfied with what you are doing for a living?
2. Are you willing to tell people about yourself when they ask you?
3. Are you expecting to progress and improve your position in the years ahead?
4. Have you a definite ambition and definite likes and dislikes?
5. Do you know what you want to do with your life?
6. Do you take a pride in your appearance?
7. When you look in the mirror are you reasonably satisfied with what you see?
8. Do you feel fully capable of tackling your job and any problems?
9. Would you see a sudden responsibility as the chance to show what you can do?
10. Are difficulties, snags, and setbacks stimulating challenges to you?
11. Do you look forward to meeting people?
12. When you go out socially, do you expect to enjoy yourself?
13. Do you believe that most people like you?
14. Would you make the first approach and start a conversation?
15. Would you ask for an explanation of something you did not understand or did not know?
16. Can you hold your own in argument and discussion without getting cross, or feeling that you had better shut up because the other person must know best?
17. Would you stick to a decision and follow your own line if other people were doubtful about it?
18. Assuming somebody is unfriendly, or rude, or moody, you are able to carry on normally without allowing it to upset you?
19. Could you admit to a mistake without losing confidence in yourself?
20. Do you regard yourself as a useful, interesting character and think of yourself as worth knowing?

SCORING

Count 5 marks for every "Yes." A score of 70 and over is very good; 60 to 70 is good; 50 to 60 may be counted satisfactory.

Under 50 means you do not think enough of yourself.

If you feel inadequate, start by doing simple things in a small way. Be useful to somebody and gradually build up your confidence in yourself by taking on a little more. The best way to get to feel that you are of some real value in the world is to share activity with your friends and neighbors.

What Kind of Personality Do You Have?

Here is a list of forty adjectives or phrases. List the numbers of the twelve that you can honestly apply to yourself.

1. self-controlled	21. helpful
2. slow	22. scoffing
3. creative	23. outgoing
4. easily bored	24. easily hurt
5. peaceful	25. tactful
6. evasive	26. emotional
7. modest	27. lover of beauty
8. lazy	28. fearful
9. logical	29. alert
10. cynical	30. unimaginative
11. inquisitive	31. reverent
12. untidy	32. indecisive
13. sympathetic	33. dependable
14. stubborn	34. critical
15. prompt	35. truthful
16. self-centered	36. belligerent
17. consistent	37. sense of humor
18. always serious	38. introverted
19. adaptable	39. hard-working
20. fickle	40. conceited

SCORING

If your list of twelve adjectives and phrases includes eight odd-numbered and four even-numbered selections, you are a very normal person, well-adjusted and honest with yourself. If you have checked all the even numbers, the chances are you are a mouse. If all your answers are odd-numbered, we suspect you are either a saint, or fooled yourself when you took this quiz.

YOU
AND YOUR
INNER SELF

Do You Think Positively?

The way we think determines the kind of people we are. If our attitude is wrong, we think the wrong way. We become people who neither make the most of themselves nor get along with others.

One of the ways in which we can handicap ourselves is by thinking negatively instead of positively. We can help ourselves by taking the positive line.

This test will show you how you stand. Answer "Yes" or "No" to the questions before turning to the scoring key at the end.

1. Is your response to people generous and wholehearted? Are you quick to take part, join in, share activity with other people?
2. Do you often become enthusiastic?
3. Do you offer to do things for people?
4. Do people frequently ask your advice and opinion and choose you to do things for them?
5. Do you say "Yes" more often than you say "No"?
6. Are you more interested in all that is happening around you than in your own self, personal feelings, and troubles?
7. Say you are not feeling so good. You could have been disappointed about something, or you are not well. Are you the type who says to yourself: "Never mind. I'll go along and forget it," or, "I'll work it off"?
8. Would you blame yourself for a failure, rather than put the blame on outside circumstances, bad luck, or somebody else?

9. Are you quick to forgive and forget and make allowances, rather than the kind of person who nurses hurts and nourishes a grievance?

10. Would you prefer to be admired for sound common sense rather than for your strong-mindedness?

11. Would you go a bit more than halfway to reach a workable agreement?

12. Would you take the long, rather than the short, view if this meant putting up with temporary discomfort?

13. Can you work reasonably well with people you dislike and with those who dislike you?

14. Are you able to distinguish between useful criticism and the type of destructive criticism that is not worth bothering about?

15. Do you recognize when people are flattering you and do you take this into account?

16. Do you realize when you are allowing people to influence you, maybe unfairly or unwisely?

17. Do you tackle problems calmly and systematically, taking enough time to think them through from start to finish, considering all the advantages and disadvantages, unpleasant as well as pleasant?

18. Is it always your decision, not the line of least resistance or what you think will win popularity or admiration?

19. Would you discount an idea or inspiration that came to you at a moment of anger, irritability, emotion, fear, or fatigue, and think again?

20. Would you think there was something wrong with you if everybody agreed with you?

SCORING

Count 5 marks for every "Yes." A score of 70 and over is very good; 60 to 70 is good; 50 to 60 is satisfactory. Under 50 is not satisfactory.

The positive thinker is a realist. He accepts people as they are. This means that he does not expect too much, or the impossible, from anyone, including himself. He is a fighter because he refuses to allow disappointment and even bad health to stop him from sharing activity with people.

He always makes up his own mind but since he is ready to allow others the same freedom this does not prevent him from getting on with them.

How Suspicious Are You?

One of the worst habits we can develop is that of imputing bad motives to others. True, we have to be reasonably guarded, especially with strangers. But we should be prepared to give others the benefit of the doubt by assuming that they mean well until we prove the contrary.

This is important because the attitude we reveal to others has a lot to do with the way they feel about us. Try this test and check on yourself. Answer "Yes" or "No" to the questions before turning to the scoring key at the end.

1. Are you prone to think that people dislike you?
2. Do you think that family and friends talk about you among themselves?
3. Do you take a long time getting to know people?
4. Do you have to know them a long time before you trust them?
5. People are being specially kind and attentive. Are you wondering what they want?
6. Are you slow about forgetting an injury?
7. Do you believe that every man has his price?
8. Do you believe that most people behave themselves only because they are afraid of being caught?
9. Do you believe that most married couples would be unfaithful if they had the opportunity and thought they could get away with it?
10. The only way you can be sure that people are doing their work properly is to supervise them all the time. Do you think this is true?
11. Would you never employ anyone, not even a man to dig the garden for a couple of hours, unless he or she were recommended by someone you knew?
12. You are on your way to catch a bus. A local carpenter and his mate arrive to do a job for you. Would you put off going out rather than leave them alone in the house?
13. Something that belongs to you is not in its usual place. Is your first reaction "Someone has taken it," rather than that it must have been mislaid?
14. You are snuggled down in bed. Suddenly you start wondering whether you locked all the doors. Would you get up and recheck?
15. Do you dislike lending anything?
16. Have you ever weighed a packed product?
17. You need to ask the way in a strange city. A police officer is nowhere in sight. Would you ask more than one person?

18. A friend makes an excuse to cancel an appointment. Would you think that, really, it was because he did not want to come?
19. Do you carry any kind of lucky charm?
20. Do you think to yourself, "I'm not really surprised," when a friend lets you down?

SCORING

Count 5 marks for every "No." A score of 60 to 70 is satisfactory. If you score more than 70 you are too gullible and overanxious not to give offense. If you score under 60 you are an uncomfortable person to live with.

Are You a Strong Character?

People's ideas of a strong character vary. Physical size and strength have nothing to do with it. The frailest and most delicate of men and women are numbered among the world's strongest characters.

Aggressiveness often denotes weakness, being a compensation for fear or inferiority. The domineering, bossy type may really be trying to gratify a sense of self-importance.

Here is a test to enable you to assess your strength of character. Answer "Yes" or "No" to the questions before turning to the scoring key at the end.

1. Can you make up your own mind?
2. Would you stick to your decision if it were unpopular?
3. Assuming a job were long and hard, monotonous, or unpleasant would you stick at it until it was completed?
4. Can you be patient (while another reconsiders, for example) and wait?
5. Can you say "No" (to another drink or second helping of food, for example) and mean it?
6. Do you believe that when you lose control of yourself you are letting yourself down?

7. Can you keep your composure without becoming rattled or upset when someone is moody or dislikes you?

8. Are you ready to own up to a mistake, admit you were wrong, apologize?

9. Would you refuse to take advantage of someone inexperienced or in a weaker position?

10. Do you feel you want to help anyone who is weak, less fortunate, or inexperienced on his or her own?

11. Does it hurt you (more than being hurt yourself) to see someone you are fond of being hurt?

12. Do you hate to think you are not pulling your full weight?

13. Do you like being independent and doing things for yourself rather than relying on others?

14. At the same time, are people prone to rely on you?

15. Is your word your bond as far as is humanly possible?

16. Do you put other people's wishes and feelings (in matters of sexual satisfaction, for example) before your own personal desires?

17. Do you like to see other people getting on?

18. Are you perfectly happy to stand back and let somebody else have all the attention and praise?

19. Can you be fair to people who are unfair to you?

20. Are you a good loser?

SCORING

Count 5 marks for every "Yes." A score of 70 and over is good; 60 to 70 is satisfactory; 50 to 60 may be reckoned fair. Under 50 is poor.

The strong character knows his own mind and is prepared to stand by it. Although he knows his rights, he also recognizes his responsibilities and the rights of other people.

As a thoroughly grown-up, generous-hearted person he feels that other people are important to him. A desire for their happiness and well-being makes him consider their feelings so as not to hurt or injure them.

Do You Organize Well?

It's easy to get into a mess. Most of us have to fight the tendency to push unwanted things out of sight rather than to get rid of them.

There are many people who just drift along, getting into bigger messes, living in the vague hope that one day they'll sort themselves out. Are you one of those people, or are you a good organizer? Here's a test to tell. Answer "Yes" or "No" to the following questions:

1. Do you plan your days, deciding what you'll try to get done and in what order?
2. Do you tackle one job at a time?
3. Can you manage to cope with an unexpected visitor without looking bothered or confused?
4. Do you have regular housecleanings in which you dispose of unwanted possessions?
5. A job badly needs doing. Would you stay at home and get it done, rather than keep on putting it off because you like going out with friends?
6. Do you believe a stitch in time saves nine, and apply the maxim to every aspect of your life?
7. Do you automatically replenish when things get used up or worn out?
8. Do you arrange to give yourself sufficient time to complete jobs and get places?
9. Do you plan journeys so as to do them the best and easiest way?
10. Do you know when your important financial commitments fall due, and budget your spending to meet them?
11. Could you lay hands easily on all the data and documents necessary to deal with your business and personal affairs?
12. Do you keep an appointment book?
13. Are you careful about seeing that you don't promise to take on more than you can handle?
14. Do you make a note of names, addresses, telephone numbers, and important dates?

SCORING

Score 5 points for each "Yes" answer. A score of 50 or over is good, and 40 to 50 is satisfactory. From 30 to 40 is fair, under 30 is poor.

When we organize ourselves efficiently, we make life easier for ourselves as well as for other people. A good way to start is to aim at becoming methodical.

Are You Assertive Enough?

Are you assertive enough to enjoy life to its fullest or obtain the goals you've set for yourself? Take this simple test and find out:

1. When a person is blatantly unfair, do you usually say something about it?

   Yes _____   No _____

2. Are you always careful to avoid trouble with other people?

   Yes _____   No _____

3. Do you avoid social contacts for fear of doing or saying the wrong thing?

   Yes _____   No _____

4. If a friend betrays your confidence, do you tell him how you feel?

   Yes _____   No _____

5. If you had a roommate, would you insist that he or she do a fair share of the cleaning?

   Yes _____   No _____

6. When a clerk in a store waits on someone who has come in after you, do you call his attention to the matter?

   Yes _____   No _____

7. Do you find that there are very few people with whom you can be relaxed and have a good time?

   Yes _____   No _____

8. If someone who has borrowed five dollars from you seems to have forgotten about it, would you remind him?

   Yes _____   No _____

9. If someone keeps on teasing you, is it difficult for you to express your annoyance or displeasure?

   Yes _____   No _____

10. If someone keeps kicking the back of your seat in a movie theater, would you ask him to stop?

    Yes _____   No _____

11. If a third person butts into your conversation with a friend, do you express your irritation?

Yes _____   No _____

12. In a plush restaurant, if you ordered a medium steak and found it too rare, would you ask the waiter to have it cooked some more?

Yes _____   No _____

13. If your landlord failed to make certain necessary repairs after promising to do so, would you insist upon it?

Yes _____   No _____

14. Would you return a faulty garment you purchased a few days ago?

Yes _____   No _____

15. If someone you respect expresses opinions with which you strongly disagree, do you venture to state your own point of view?

Yes _____   No _____

16. Are you usually able to say "No" if people make unreasonable requests of you?

Yes _____   No _____

17. Do you protest out loud when someone pushes in front of you in a line?

Yes _____   No _____

18. Are you able to express love and affection openly?

Yes _____   No _____

SCORING

1. Yes	10. Yes
2. No	11. Yes
3. No	12. Yes
4. Yes	13. Yes
5. Yes	14. Yes
6. Yes	15. Yes
7. No	16. Yes
8. Yes	17. Yes
9. No	18. Yes

13–18:   If you gave the right answers for thirteen or more questions, Dr. Zev Wanderer, the author of the test, says: "You're assertive enough, but you may want to carry out self-correction in areas where you gave wrong answers."

7–12:   You need to be slightly more assertive, but basically you have the right attitude toward people and situations.

1–6:   "You're probably not getting anywhere near the benefits that life has to offer. You might even need some professional help as the result of suppressing your perfect right to meet people on an equal footing.

"Remember that being more assertive is NOT a sign of aggressiveness."

Are You an Individualist . . . or Just One of the Crowd?

It's been said that there's little scope for individuality today, that all of us are necessarily part of a group or class, and that there are few opportunities to plow an individual furrow, as it were.

But it's not true. The individual with the courage to voice a personal opinion or follow a particular rainbow is as much a part of our society as ever—though today's individual is usually a little more subtle about it.

Are you an individualist? Or are you just one of the crowd?

To find out, answer the following questions:

1. How many of your close friends and family have opposing political convictions to your own?
   a. Only one or two—most are the same.
   b. About half have different opinions.
   c. You've never asked.

2. Do you consider that people with conservative taste in clothes, etc., are more boring as a rule than casual or eccentric dressers?
   a. No—clothes mean nothing so far as an interesting personality is concerned.

b. You think people with conservative tastes are usually more interesting. They don't need clothes to speak for them.

c. Yes, you think people who dress in a conservative fashion are usually quite boring.

3. A person you dislike has invited you to a lush and expensive champagne party to celebrate a sudden large windfall. Do you . . .

a. Go and enjoy the champagne—but steer clear of the host all evening?

b. Swallow your dislike and make polite conversation just for the one evening?

c. Write a short note of refusal?

4. When someone in authority quotes a personal view that is violently opposed to your own, do you . . .

a. Bite your tongue and say nothing?

b. Speak up at once and explain your own conviction?

c. Put your opinion tentatively and if the reaction looks as if it might be a violent one, gradually change the subject?

5. If you are giving a party, do you . . .

a. Invite as many different types as possible so that the party will have spice and interest?

b. Invite only those types you know will get along well together?

c. The question doesn't arise for you, because most of your friends are similar types anyway.

6. If you could wave a magic wand and be blessed with one of these talents or gifts, which would you choose . . .

a. Creative or artistic talent?

b. The talent for making money?

c. A talent for making friends?

7. At the firm's annual luncheon you chat disrespectfully for some time with a middle-aged lady you assume to be one of the clerks. You discover later she is the managing director's wife. Do you . . .

a. Make a fast getaway, totally embarrassed and confused, and spend a sleepless night going over the things you've said?

b. Apologize briefly, continue talking on less dangerous topics—then forget the whole thing?

c. Try to laugh your way out of it—explaining that you can't imagine how you came to make such an unforgivable mistake—but enjoy the joke with your friends afterward?

8. You hear some rather shocking facts about the morals of a friend. Do you . . .
   a. Ignore the gossip, telling those who mention it to you to mind their own business?
   b. Listen quickly, saying that you don't think it could be true—then keep it to yourself?
   c. You wouldn't be able to resist passing it on—but only to close, nonmalicious friends.

9. Do you find . . .
   a. You quote the views of experts you've read in the newspapers when talking of a special subject?
   b. You prefer to give your own opinions rather than "borrowed ones"?
   c. You rarely give opinions, other people always seem to have more confidence in their own ideas than you?

10. When buying gifts for other people, do you . . .
    a. Choose something interesting that you like?
    b. Consider carefully the person's personality and give something you feel he or she will like?
    c. Play safe and buy useful and sensible gifts?

11. Answer "True" or "False" to these five statements.
    a. It's better to stay quiet than offend other people with an outrageous idea.
    b. One should be able to express one's personality adequately without wearing ridiculous clothes or growing hair to extreme lengths.
    c. We shouldn't be afraid of hurting others if we are sure of our facts.
    d. It's always best when abroad, or away from home, to remember, "When in Rome, do as the Romans do. . . ." etc.
    e. People who prefer to be alone most of the time must have inadequate personalities.

SCORING

Study your score chart, then count up your marks. The number you score will tell you how you rate on the individualist stakes.

1.	a–2	b–3	c–1
2.	a–2	b–1	c–3
3.	a–2	b–1	c–3
4.	a–1	b–3	c–2

5.	a–3	b–2	c–1
6.	a–3	b–1	c–2
7.	a–1	b–2	c–3
8.	a–3	b–2	c–1
9.	a–2	b–3	c–1
10.	a–3	b–2	c–1

11.
a—True—1		False—3
b—True—1		False—3
c—True—3		False—1
d—True—1		False—3
e—True—1		False—3

Between 38 and 45:   You are an individualist, all right, but sometimes you tend to forget that other people exist! You are so busy plowing your lonely and noble furrow, so busy giving opinions and thinking only of yourself, that you have no time to listen to others. You could be missing out. It's not necessary to join the crowd to benefit, but other people have something to teach all of us. So don't be quite so self-centered—you may have quite a lot to gain if you simply join the rest of us on occasion.

Between 30 and 37:   You are an individualist. You are not afraid of voicing opinions, or being different, or of being the sort of person you are. Sometimes you forget that other people don't feel as you do, and your bluntness and honesty does sometimes cause others embarrassment. On the whole, though, you "do your own thing" without hurting anyone. Well done.

Between 20 and 29:   You are a bit too concerned about your own image really to be an individualist. You are too terrified of being laughed at or derided to go against the majority opinion. You are too kindhearted, also, to assert yourself against others. You are frightened of upsetting people and are anxious to be liked. Don't worry—your goodheartedness will endear you to other people.

19 and under: You really should have a bit more courage. You go along with the crowd too often, never give an opinion, never follow your own instinct or intellect. You are unhappy when you have to make your own decisions; you like them to be made for you. You're almost too conformist to be true.

How Liberated Are You?

If you are a woman, do you desire protection and guidance from men? Do you consider yourself independent and feel comfortable making your own decisions? Do you deal with people as human beings, or do you expect men to behave one way, women another?

If you are a man, do you like a woman to take care of you and agree with you most of the time? Do you expect a woman to take responsibility for her own life and not look to you for answers? Do you respond to people in the context of their sex—or simply as other people with needs and feelings similar to yours?

Take our quiz and see where you stand. Circle the choice that comes closest to what you would do—not should do—in the following situations.

1. Sally and Howard, both divorced within the past year, have been dating for three weeks. Howard, fifty, was married for twenty-six years and has never been sexually intimate with any woman other than his ex-wife. Sally, forty-two, has enjoyed sexual relationships with men other than her ex-husband and finds Howard very desirable. For the tenth time, they have been sitting on her couch, kissing and touching, and he has just jumped up to go home. She should:
   a. Let him go home.
   b. Take his hand and lead him into the bedroom.
   c. Ask him to have another drink in hopes of further developments.
   d. Talk with him about her interest in having a sexual relationship.

2. Bob, glad to be a bachelor since his divorce three years ago, is deeply concerned about his two daughters, ages five and nine. They are living with his ex-wife, Ann, whom he has always suspected of being mentally ill. The last two times he came to visit, Ann refused to allow the girls out of the house and kept him locked out. He initiated a court action to protect his visitation rights. This morning the school called him at his office, informing him that the younger child arrived with a black eye that both girls say the mother inflicted. He should:
   a. Think seriously of remarrying in order to provide a better home for the children.
   b. Confront Ann and continue to visit and call frequently to check on the children.
   c. Seek custody now.
   d. Suggest that his ex-wife and children enroll in a family therapy program with him.

3. Al earns a comfortable income, but Joan consistently spends more than he makes. Right now he's ten thousand dollars in debt and she's talking about remodeling the basement. He's approaching fifty and wants to start saving for his retirement. They've had some friction about money over the years; she secretly wishes she had married a wealthier man. He should:

   a. Cancel all her charge accounts and dole out a weekly household allowance in cash.
   b. Suggest she get a job to handle the extra household expenses.
   c. Get a second job or a better job to earn more money.
   d. Suggest that they go to a marriage counsellor.

4. Fresh out of college, Marc has landed his first job as a secretary for a fortyish woman lawyer. She is constantly reaching over and squeezing his cheek or giving him a hug. Last week, as he was leaning over the filing cabinet, she patted his bottom as she passed. This is a very important stepping-stone in his career, and the last thing he can do now is quit this job. He should:

   a. Sit down and tell her how he feels.
   b. Make some remarks about her being ''middle-aged'' and hope she gets the message.
   c. Push her hand away next time and tell her he doesn't like that.
   d. Grit his teeth and keep quiet.

5. Lucy and Frank are the parents of five-year-old twins who just started school. Lucy's ecstatic about her new full-time job selling cosmetics for a department store. The family's short on money, and she loves the contact with other people. Frank's pretty uptight about coming home to a sitter and two hungry kids three nights a week while his wife works until nine. He should:

   a. Cook the family meal and eat with the kids.
   b. Cook the family meal, eat with the kids, and keep her plate warm.
   c. Feed the kids sandwiches but wait for his dinner until Lucy gets home.
   d. Insist that she refuse the after-six shift, even though it will probably mean losing her job.

6. Alice is very upset. Late this afternoon she saw her husband enter a motel with another woman. She realized that she and Mel weren't as close as they used to be, but he insisted that his big promotion was the reason for his unavailability. Tonight, when she confronted him, she was stunned by his reply. He said that he was no longer in love with

her, that he planned to continue with his outside relationship, and that he didn't want a divorce for the sake of the kids. She should:

a. Get a divorce.

b. Suggest they see a marriage counselor.

c. Accept the situation and hope it eventually blows over.

d. Get involved with activities outside the home, which might include having an affair.

7. Bill, Jr., has invited his parents to spend their two-week vacation at his apartment in sunny Florida. It's been two years since he finished his internship as a surgeon and accepted a position at a hospital two thousand miles from home. Marge and William, who have been looking forward to the reunion for months, are shocked when they arrive. Their son is living openly with another man who is clearly his lover. Marge and William should:

a. Express their fears and anger, then try to accept the situation.

b. Leave at once and break off all contact with him if he doesn't renounce his lover.

c. Accept the situation without comment.

d. Strongly suggest that he see a psychiatrist.

8. Jane and Bernice have been good friends since they met on the job five years ago. Jane was already engaged at the time, and is now happily married to Ed. Ed has tried to get along with Bernice, but finds her absolutely intolerable. He thinks she's pretentious, pushy, and a female chauvinist who's always putting men down. He should:

a. Tell Jane how he feels, and ask that she try to see Bernice when he's not around.

b. Put his foot down and tell Jane to get rid of Bernice.

c. Tell Bernice how he feels about her attitude and his difficulty in dealing with them.

d. Keep his feelings to himself.

9. Vivacious Marilyn enjoyed the attentions of many men before she married quiet, lovable Stan. She's happy in every way except one: He's a slam-bam, thank-you-ma'am lover. She wants sensuous foreplay and tender care during lovemaking. She should:

a. Tell him what she wants him to do when they're in bed.

b. Accept him the way he is.

c. Guide him nonverbally by showing him what she wants in bed.

d. Start a discussion about both their needs and how they can best satisfy each other.

10. Roger and Emily, both past sixty five, have been keeping company for several months. They have been formal and courteous, although their passions run deeper. At last he's proposed marriage and she's thrilled. However, the reduction in their Social Security checks caused by their new status would impose a grave financial hardship. They should?

   a. Live together.

   b. Get married anyway.

   c. Forget about marrying, but enjoy the physical intimacy they desire.

   d. Continue as they have been.

11. Jean is an advertising executive earning a hefty thirty thousand dollars a year. She's just begun to date a commercial artist whose income is half that amount. He's forced to budget carefully while she's able to spend freely. As far as the costs of their evenings out are concerned, she should:

   a. Let him figure it out.

   b. Take care of her share of the tab when the bill arrives.

   c. Help to reach a joint decision about where they are going, and how the expenses are to be divided.

   d. Get used to going out less since he can't afford it.

12. Barb and Hal, both in their thirties, have settled in their hometown of Detroit since they married seven years ago. Barbara, a fireball of a salesperson, has just been offered the position of sales manager of the Chicago office. Hal's the assistant manager of a bank, earning about 60 per cent of her prospective income. He should:

   a. Agree to her commuting—her company will send her home on the weekends.

   b. Go with his wife to Chicago and find a new job.

   d. Let her go and try out the job, then move if she's satisfied.

SCORING

Circle the answers that you gave, then add to find your total score in the columns below.

QUESTIONS	a	b	c	d
1.	1	4	2	8
2.	1	2	8	4
3.	1	2	0	4
4.	16	4	8	2
5.	4	8	2	1
6.	4	16	2	8
7.	4	0	2	1
8.	2	0	4	1
9.	8	2	4	16
10.	4	1	2	0
11.	2	8	16	4
12.	2	8	1	4

If your score was 12–37,
you are a conservative person who sees clearly defined roles for each of the sexes. Women are the weaker, less capable sex. Men are the natural decisionmakers, the ones who carry burdens and assume responsibility. To you, the man is the head of the household, the breadwinner, the competitor. A woman is meant to be a wife and mother, to care for the home and the kids, and to defer to her husband's authority.

Your attitude is probably based on your early upbringing, and reinforced by an environment in which most of your friends, family members, and neighbors share this point of view. You do not stray far from the fold, and generally find it easier to go along with the group then take independent action that might arouse criticism. You will often resist doing what you secretly want to do because "the hassle just isn't worth it."

Your dealings with the opposite sex are characterized by conflicts that are rarely verbalized. You have resentments that you feel unable to express because "that's the way men and women are." You might find it very helpful to talk openly about your real feelings, and to listen to what the opposite sex has to say. You may discover there's more common ground than you think.

If your score was 38–62,
you tend to make decisions based on traditional role concepts, but you also take situations into account. You feel that women need to be taken care of and that men should shoulder that responsibility, but you recognize that individuals have needs that do not always fall within their role definitions. You would feel understanding toward a woman who wanted a career as long as she didn't neglect her family. You would be able to accept a divorce if it was in the best interests of most family members.

You have strong opinions and heavily rely on your own judgment. However, you modify your traditional attitude with pragmatic flexibility. When there is a problem to solve, you tend to take action and to speak up for yourself when necessary. In the end, you usually come up with solutions that are fair compromises between your principles and the needed result.

Because you see clear role definitions between men and women, you tend to judge people and form expectations of them based on their sex. You are basically an understanding person, but such a demand for adherence to roles sometimes makes you insensitive to the feelings of others, as well as your own real needs. Rather than simply doing what you "should" do in a given situation, you might find it more rewarding to ask yourself what your real feelings are.

If your score was 63–87,
you reject the role definitions of the past and applaud men and women who are brave enough to try something new. You regard women as people with the same need for achievement and a sense of personal identity that men possess; you don't see marriage and motherhood as their only appropriate destinies. As far as you're concerned, men are people with the same right as women to be human and unsure, and to have their feelings taken into consideration. You don't think the financial support of the family has to be the responsibility of the male. You view a relationship between a man and a woman as a partnership between two adults, each of whom is responsible for making it work through communication and compromise.

As a freethinker you tend to observe a situation and form an opinion based on people's feelings, rather than assumptions about the feelings they ought to have as "male" or "female." You are impatient with others who aren't as open as you are, and resent attitudes you consider to be unjust. It takes the ability to stand alone to be a liberated man or woman, and you are probably a fighter in other ways as well. In fact, you may actually enjoy a good fight—your liberationist attitude may have elements of rebelliousness against a restraining parent. In any event, you take command of your own life, and don't go along with the crowd.

If your score was 88–112,
yours is a very humanistic view of life. You are not influenced by society's traditional role models, and treat everyone as a unique individual. You assess a person according to his or her sensitivity to others, and feel concern for those who seem unable to respond openly. In any given situation, how people feel is always the key issue to you. You are a great believer in sitting down and talking things over. You try to deal with your own feelings immediately by expressing them directly. If you are upset with your husband, you will tell your husband, not your neighbor. Conversely, you are almost always available to hear someone else's view.

You get along with the opposite sex because you get along with just about everybody. You recognize that most people are comfortable in the sexual roles society has designated for them and respect their needs. Nevertheless, you personally do not have a desire to be part of the norm. You probably lead a very unconventional life, but most people simply accept it as "your way." They tend to view you as a relaxed and loving person, sense your tolerance, and are tolerant of you. You extend kindness and understanding, and usually you are treated in the same way.

How Humble Are You

The famed English bishop Edward Reynolds made his comment about humility with this simple statement: "The fullest and best ears of corn hang lowest toward the ground." People who flaunt their personalities are usually bores. Humility, compassion, and understanding are the characteristics of the great men and women throughout history.

This test will help you evaluate your ego, but the results will be of no value unless you do soul-searching and answer with honesty and candor.

1. Which of the shapes below appeals to you the most?

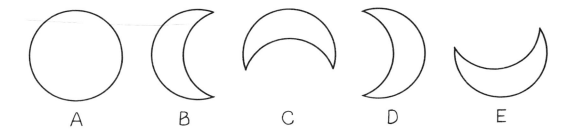

A　　　　B　　　　C　　　　D　　　　E

Answer the following questions "Yes" or "No":

2. Are material things, such as clothing, house, and car your primary interests in life?

    Yes _____   No _____

3. When telling a story, do you exaggerate the details?

    Yes _____   No _____

4. If you feel you are the victim of an injustice, do you plot revenge?

    Yes _____   No _____

5. Is it difficult for you to ask others for advice?

    Yes _____   No _____

6. Are your successes almost entirely due to your own hard work and abilities?

    Yes _____   No _____

7. Do you often look at yourself in the mirror?

    Yes _____   No _____

8. Do you have only a few acquaintances with whom you wish to associate?

    Yes _____   No _____

9. Do you think older people have outdated ideas?

    Yes _____   No _____

10. Is it difficult for you to admit an error or to apologize?

    Yes _____   No _____

11. When things go wrong, is the cause usually someone else's error?

    Yes _____   No _____

12. Do you have secret doubts about people of other races, creeds, or religions?

    Yes _____   No _____

SCORING

Psychologists have proven under clinically controlled tests using many volunteers that similar personality types tend to show preferences for the same shapes.

1.   a–0 point: Those who chose the full circle usually agreed, when questioned in more detail, that they were generous, materialistic, and outgoing, but often their generosity was to gain attention, to be the center of the stage.

b–2 points: This was the selection of many testees who stated they were forward-looking and ambitious and that their acts of humility were basically moves to be successful.

c–3 points: The comment of the testees who chose this crescent often mentioned a desire to be protective to those around them but, in turn, they wanted respect and gratitude. This indicates compassion but not humility—"freedom of pride."

d–1 point: This shape seems to be most often checked by the aggressive personality—strong with push. They tend to resent their past rather than to be grateful for it.

e–4 points: The selection of this shape by a man who was named by almost unanimous choice by his coworkers in a large firm as having the most humility summed up this crescent: "I do not wish to be above, behind, or in front of anyone. I want to be a solid, good person, eternally grateful. Too, this crescent reminds me of a smile, which I hope I give all my fellow men."

2–12.   Score 2 points for each "No" answer, Questions 2 through 12. (Highest possible score on this test is 26.)

ANALYSIS:

20–26:   This is an excellent score. "Sense shines with double luster when it is set in humility." (William Penn)

10–19:   This is an average score made by most of us who, being human, have earthly pride, vanity, and prejudices.

0–9:   People with this score have lots of room for improvement in their attitude toward themselves and toward others. It always helps to put yourself in the other fellow's position.

Are You an Easy Victim?

They say "there's one born every minute," meaning that many of us are so naïve that we'll believe almost anything we're told. Others, however, are less gullible to the point of never taking anything on face value. To find out which category you fall in, try this fun test.

1. Which of the two abstract designs below do you think best describes your normal daily life pattern?

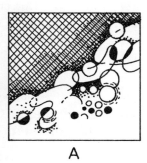
A

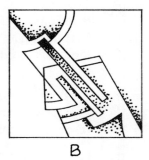
B

2. Do you buy food, clothing, gadgets, etc., on the basis of newspaper or magazine ads?
   a. Hardly ever, and only for known products at a good price, such as sales, etc.
   b. Sometimes, provided the magazine or newspaper is one of high standards.
   c. Often.

3. Are you influenced by your reaction to the salesperson?
   a. No. On the merits of the product.
   b. Sometimes I succumb to pleasantries or the "hard sell."
   c. Yes. I have a strong reaction of like or dislike that leads me to buy or to refuse.

4. Do you have a strong urge to help those less fortunate than you?
   a. Yes.
   b. Sometimes.
   c. No. I leave that to governmental agencies or established philanthropic organizations.

5. When salespeople come to your home do you listen to their pitches?
   a. Only if I invited them.
   b. Never.
   c. Yes. I find most of them interesting and a pleasant interruption.

6. Honestly, are you influenced by flattery?
    a. It makes me feel better.
    b. I usually question the motives.
    c. Flattery will get people nowhere with me.

7. When someone of the opposite sex you've just met tells you they love you, do you let down your resistance?
    a. No. I expect a trial period.
    b. Yes. I believe in love at first sight.
    c. Yes, because I want his (or her) love and warmth.

8. If a person who seems well educated and charming offers you a safe way to double your money quickly, such as in real estate or in an at-home occupation, would you sign up?
    a. No—on principle!
    b. Perhaps, after I had thought it over and talked to others.
    c. Probably if the person mentioned big names, such as financiers, movie personalities, and professional men and women who had made the same investment.

9. When you are traveling in an unfamiliar area, do you pick up strangers?
    a. Yes.
    b. No.
    c. Sometimes, if they look all right.

10. When you sign a contract, do you read every sentence and ask if you don't understand the wording?
    a. No. I assume it is legal and sound.
    b. Definitely.
    c. Only if it's very important.

11. Do you believe everything you read?
    a. Yes.
    b. Only if I've read the same elsewhere.
    c. No. Reporters and writers are biased.

12. Are you insured?
    a. Yes.
    b. No. It's too expensive.
    c. Only on major items.

13. When people need material help such as loans, or physical assistance like using your car, do you help?

     a. If it is feasible.

     b. Only if there is a very real need.

     c. Yes, because it's hard to say "No."

14. On important matters, do you seek an opinion?

     a. Yes.

     b. No.

     c. Sometimes.

15. If you work closely with a person who has a severe personality problem can you help him or her?

     a. Yes. With love and patience.

     b. Yes, if he or she sincerely wants to change.

     c. Yes, with the help of experts.

16. If a person promises something, do you believe him or her implicity?

     a. It depends on who is promising.

     b. Yes. People keep their promises.

     c. No. I am skeptical.

17. If your current pattern of life were shattered, have you got unused talents, monetary reserves, or willing friends to fall back on?

     a. No.

     b. Many.

     c. Perhaps.

18. Do you do things in a slipshod way, hoping you'll get by with it?

     a. Sometimes.

     b. No. Anything worth doing is worth doing well.

     c. Shortcuts are my forte.

SCORING

1. a–6; b–2. The life patterns of those who are vulnerable and easy targets are the confused design a, which lacks the "straight and narrow" arrangement of design b.

2. a–2; b–2; c–6	8. a–2; b–4; c–6	14. a–6; b–2; c–4
3. a–2; b–4; c–6	9. a–6; b–2; c–4	15. a–6; b–4; c–2
4. a–6; b–4; c–2	10. a–6; b–2; c–4	16. a–4; b–6; c–2
5. a–2; b–2; c–6	11. a–6; b–4; c–2	17. a–6; b–2; c–4
6. a–6; b–4; c–2	12. a–2; b–6; c–4	18. a–4; b–2, c–6
7. a–2; b–6, c–6	13. a–4; b–2; c–6	

ANALYSIS

90–108:   You leave yourself wide open for disappointments and emotional injuries because of your childlike belief in people and the validity of your own snap judgment. Your so-called friends probably leech on you because you're a delightful target for unscrupulous wheeler-dealers. If you like being the fall guy, that's your problem. But you also have responsibilities to your associates and family.

72–89:   You are probably ruled more by your heart than by your head. You are sentimental and open, very easily swayed by a strong argument and yearn to please. You give little or no thought to your own welfare. Good clear pre-evaluation will very likely temper your ultimate decisions in the future.

52–71:   You temper your actions with logic. You are sometimes victimized but seldom drastically hurt. Successes when you make an emotional gamble or snap decision outweigh losses.

36–51:   Friends and associates probably think you're as "hard as nails." You never take chances and live strictly by your head, thus stifling your heart. You'd do well to ponder the statement, "It is better to have loved and lost than never to have loved at all" along with another proverb: "Nothing ventured, nothing gained."

Are You Self-confident?

The worn-out phrase "Are you a man or a mouse?" is erroneous and deceptive. Mice have self-confidence. Self-confidence comes from an inner peace with one's self and a conscientious evaluation of strengths and weaknesses. By building strengths each of us gains greater self-confidence. Use this test as a beginning point.

1. Which of the three drawings shown below do you like the best?

   a _____   b _____   c _____

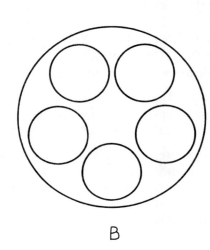

A   B   C

2. Answer the following questions "Yes" or "No":

   a. If you were turned down three times for jobs or by colleges, would you doubt your own ability?

   Yes _____   No _____

   b. Do large crowds confuse you and frighten you?

   Yes _____   No _____

   c. Is your present wardrobe filled with shabby clothing?

   Yes _____   No _____

   d. Do you constantly look at yourself in mirrors?

   Yes _____   No _____

   e. Is your posture erect?

   Yes _____   No _____

f. Do you often have the feeling that people gossip about you?

Yes _____   No _____

g. If approached by a member of the law-enforcement agencies, does your heart beat faster?

Yes _____   No _____

h. Among strangers in a restaurant, bus, or street, do you feel that some stare or laugh at you?

Yes _____   No _____

i. If you won or were given a free ticket to a country unknown to you, would you be afraid to go alone?

Yes _____   No _____

j. Do you think you could make love to most people of your choosing?

Yes _____   No _____

k. Do you often have unpleasant dreams?

Yes _____   No _____

l. When a problem arises, can you usually solve it on your own?

Yes _____   No _____

m. Do you have money saved for emergencies, that "rainy day"?

Yes _____   No _____

n. Do you feel your parents loved you?

Yes _____   No _____

o. Do you believe you should learn something new every day?

Yes _____   No _____

p. Would you rather take the loss than return a purchase?

Yes _____   No _____

q. Do you feel that you often fail in your endeavors?

Yes _____   No _____

r. Do people often ask you for advice?

Yes _____   No _____

SCORING

1. If you selected drawing a, you probably have more self-confidence than if you selected b or c, both of which indicate a "closing up" and seclusion from the outside world. Drawing c indicates more complexity of personality than b, which is orderly and self-contained but lacking the push, ambition, and drive of a. (a–10; b–4; c–0)

2. Self-confident answers to the Yes-No questions:
    a–No; b–No; c–No; d–No; e–Yes; f–No; g–No; h–No; i–No; j–Yes; k–No; l–Yes; m–Yes; n–Yes; o–Yes; p–No; q–No; r–Yes (2 points for each answer that agrees with research findings)

    YOUR SCORE _____

40–46: No problem with self-confidence here. People look to you for leadership and inspiration. Probably, however, some folks think of you as being rather cocky and overbearing. But, in the words of the German poet Goethe, "To do everything he is asked to do, a man must overestimate himself."

20–38: This is the average range and indicates a person who has strengths and weakness in his self-confidence. Through this test you can locate your fears, evaluate their validity, and correct them if you wish.

6–18: You are a timid, insecure person who needs the leadership and guidance of those around you.

0–4: This is a rare score, but if you fall in this range you need help from a wise person, perhaps a psychiatrist, doctor, or member of the clergy. Life must be full of fear for you.

Are You Plugged into Life?

*A quiz to help you find out
if you're as young as you could be*

Who are the people we look up to today as interesting representatives of our time? Very often they are the ones who live with energy and verve no matter what their age. People who remarry—or marry—beyond the time we consider the marriage age. Men who start a new career when they might be retiring to play golf. Women who go back to work when their children reach college. Mothers who return to school to continue an education they dropped fifteen years earlier. Today it's no longer appropriate to "be your age." What matters more is being able to tune into current, contemporary youthful ideas, comfortably. To be able to adjust to a new idiom, whether it's a style of living, dressing, entertaining, or updating personal ideas about relationships.

Psychologists tell us we stand to benefit by having a youthful mind, just as doctors have proved we gain by maintaining a young physique. To approach life in this fashion is to live it in a crescendo. There is no feeling of the younger years being better or more exciting than the older years. Maturity doesn't bring limitations, only continuing expansion as we grow with new concepts and thought fed through the younger generation's pipeline.

Now may be the time to ask yourself: Are you as young as you could be? You can check yourself out in this intriguing quiz worked out by a well-known psychologist. Answer all the questions, circling the answer closest to your feeling.

1. A friend suggests you might want to go to a lecture session on environmental problems. You feel:
   a. I'm interested in the subject but won't attend the lectures because I'm not doing anything to cause pollution.
   b. When I understand all the problems I might be able to inform others intelligently and effect a change, so I will go to these lectures.
   c. This is a problem for industry, if it is a real problem.

2. Your recently divorced daughter comes to you because she has had a party invitation and has found out that her ex-husband has been asked as well. You tell her:
   a. Call the hostess, give her your regrets.
   b. It's not the end of the world. Go to the party and decide to enjoy it.
   c. The hostess should know better than to invite you both.

3. It occurred to you recently that almost every day you learn or read
    something about women's lib. You believe:
    a. It's just a passing phase because at rock bottom what women really
        need and want is a conventional family life.
    b. The more the subject is discussed the better. Women are achieving
        significant benefits from this movement.
    c. I belong to another generation so it really has no place or
        importance in my life.

4. You are invited to attend an encounter-group session where each person
    promises to express his real feelings openly about each person in the
    room. You decide:
    a. To decline regretfully because you feel you might hurt the feelings
        of others in the group.
    b. To accept eagerly and look forward to a refreshing experience.
    c. To refuse because you think these sorts of group meetings are too
        experimental and of little value.

5. A friend tells you she is considering plastic surgery to look younger.
    You say:
    a. It doesn't fool anybody.
    b. You're in good health, have a happy life, so why bother to change
        things?
    c. It's a great idea. It will not only make you look better, but you will
        feel better, too.

6. You've always felt you should do more exercise but somehow you
    haven't gotten around to it. You hear a health spa is now operating in
    your neighborhood. You think:
    a. It's important but I don't have the time for this right now.
    b. My friends are used to me the way I am so I don't have to bother
        improving my shape.
    c. I'll look into it. It gives me the chance I've been looking for.

7. How do you face the prospect of a major move?
    a. Do your best to resist it and find a way to stay where you are.
    b. Decide to approach it by hanging onto everything you have now
        and re-creating exactly the same atmosphere in the new place.
    c. Look forward to it and seize the opportunity to review and change
        things about the way you live now.

8. Your best friend is very concerned because her only daughter wants to marry someone totally outside the middle-class professional world in which she was brought up. Your opinion is:
   a. Two people from such different backgrounds are headed for disaster but you know there's nothing she can do about it.
   b. There is a lot to be said for life outside the conventional middle-class professional world.
   c. It's the man who matters, not the job.

9. You are on a fund-raising committee intent on getting together a large sum for underprivileged children. There is a suggestion that a charity ball would be the best idea. You decide:
   a. There are so few opportunities for elegant, old-fashioned evenings nowadays, why not support the suggestion?
   b. To voice a protest pointing out that this sort of opulent evening is incongruous and not a very economical way of raising money.
   c. Lobby strongly among the committee members and come up with a workable and acceptable alternative.

10. In thinking about romantic love and getting older you feel:
    a. As you grow older your need to experience this emotion diminishes.
    b. Love continues to be a part of life as long as you are alive—it's a vital part of well-being.
    c. It's really an emotion we all experience best when we're young.

11. You notice a slight decline in energy but a physical checkup proves you are fit. How do you react?
    a. I realize I must expect this to happen as I get older but I'll try to continue as before.
    b. I consider the possibility that my flagging energy may mean I'm bored and in a rut.
    c. I understand I must slow down even though I don't want to.

12. Your daughter is leaving for college and you feel something should be said about coed dormitory arrangements. Your view is:
    a. Young people should be very selective about their relationships, realizing that there are emotional as well as physical involvements.
    b. That youth is a time for exploring life and living arrangements. Parents obviously don't have all the answers, as divorce statistics indicate.
    c. Young people today are going off on the wrong track and headed for trouble.

13. When you go to bed at night, do you:
    a. Watch TV until you fall asleep?
    b. Prepare yourself mentally for a good tomorrow by thinking how well you're going to feel when you wake up?
    c. Feel unable to sleep as well as you'd like because you have so many problems?

14. A friend is reaching the compulsory age of retirement and is wondering how to approach this change. You say:
    a. Carry on with your career in some form or other.
    b. Plan for your new lifestyle as carefully as you planned your career.
    c. Go right ahead and do all the things you've always wanted to do.

15. You know that it's time for you to give a party to return many invitations you've received. Your immediate thought is:
    a. To sit down and plan something totally original and different from any other kind of party you've had before.
    b. To consider which of all the parties you've given before was the most successful and duplicate it.
    c. To copy a successful party idea from a friend.

16. You love furs and furry textures and a decorator has told you of a source for obtaining a tigerskin rug, something you've always wanted for your bedroom. Do you:
    a. Discount the idea of any fur skin despite your inclinations and opt for a new rug or throw in a fluffy, shaggy wool?
    b. Tell him you can't bring yourself to buy a skin of an animal that is an endangered species but ask him to find you a rabbit rug or throw instead?
    c. Go ahead because tigers and other animals are killed daily and your buying something will have no effect on the over-all situation?

17. Your niece's idea of marriage is to sign a legal contract and forget about any other kind of ceremony. This is precipitating a family upheaval. Your view is:
    a. It's her life; she ought to do what she wants.
    b. The family ought to be able to work out some sort of compromise.
    c. She ought to be convinced that traditional marriage is still valid and that she'll regret not going through with a conventional ceremony.

18. You are going through your clothes closet one day and suddenly realize you've been wearing the same style of clothes for some years. You look

around your house and consider that your taste in decorating has remained pretty constant, too. Do you:

a. Feel that you ought to break out and make some drastic alterations in both?

b. Consider that it's right to hold onto continuity, it helps create an image that is individual?

c. Feel you'd like to make some changes but that it's all too much of an effort and not really that vital since you are quite happy with both your clothes and your house?

SCORING

You have the possibility of getting a total score of 54 points. Add up your score now and see how young you really are.

Questions 1–4   _____ a's $\times$ 2 = _____

   _____ b's $\times$ 3 = _____

   _____ c's $\times$ 1 = _____

Questions 5–6   _____ a's $\times$ 1 = _____

   _____ b's $\times$ 2 = _____

   _____ c's $\times$ 3 = _____

Questions 10–14 _____ a's $\times$ 2 = _____

   _____ b's $\times$ 3 = _____

   _____ c's $\times$ 1 = _____

Questions 15–18 _____ a's $\times$ 3 = _____

   _____ b's $\times$ 2 = _____

   _____ c's $\times$ 1 = _____

ANALYZING YOUR SCORE
40 or more:

Flexibility is the key to youthfulness, and this quality is very much within you. You move along with the changing tide. As new evidence presents itself, you update your views, and this keeps you lively and young. You are an activist, state firmly what you stand for—typical habit of the younger generation. You are aware of social problems, have an understanding of how they should be approached in current times. To other people you give an image of strength and activity, which helps you to blend successfully with any group of any age. You come away with something of value from any person-to-person encounter, and you pass this on to others in a free-thinking, forward-moving, positive way. You deserve congratulations. You are very probably as young as you could be.

If you scored between 25 and 40:

With a little nudge from your psyche you can be younger. The results of this quiz indicate that you are wavering toward youthfulness, but sometimes going in the opposite direction. Why not get back into the mainstream, try new experiences, and explore alternatives? It's probable that you have given up on some of the things you wanted to have in your life because it's too much trouble to keep trying. Perhaps it's time to rethink. Gather up some new force within you. Enroll in that exercise class, or get restimulated with a new interest—painting, perhaps, or a handicraft that you've always wanted to do. Often by spending some energy you can be refueled with energy. Keep thinking of the more interesting, liberated, and richer life that is waiting for you as soon as you start to think young again.

If you scored under 25:

Because some of your life attitudes and ideas are rooted in habit and routine, check yourself. Are you judging a situation on an opinion you formed two or more years ago? Well, maybe you ought to review your ideas. Life is dynamic, and just because it is ever changing you should be ready to adapt, too. This is what keeps a person up-to-date, vital and alive, energetic and attractive, physically and mentally. Changing old habits may bring on feelings of insecurity, but try to remember how you fought this when you were twenty—and survived. Accept the challenge of being younger in outlook. You have the maturity of experience to bring it off successfully—and it's certain you can enjoy a rosier life all around you.

How Honest Are You?

Although most people agree with the old saying, "Honesty is the best policy," many of us indulge in small acts of dishonesty. We excuse our behavior in terms of tact or today's way of living. Most of us go along with the wit who said, "Honesty pays—but it doesn't pay enough to suit a lot of people." Take this test to find out how honest you really are.

1. You meet a scientist who specializes in a subject you have never heard of. When he begins to talk about his work, you would:
   a. Tell him immediately that you know nothing about his specialized field.
   b. Try to look wise and nod agreement now and then.
   c. Switch the subject to something you know about.

2. You see a child steal a 25-cent bar of candy from a counter. You would:
   a. Follow him outside and give him a lecture.
   b. Do nothing.
   c. Make him put it back.

3. You are asked to do a job, but you are not satisfied with your performance. When someone publicly praises you, you would:
   a. Accept the compliment.
   b. Say that you will return later and try to do a better job.
   c. Tell the person later that you realize you did sloppy work.

4. If a casual acquaintance asks your age, you:
   b. Subtract or add to suit your convenience.
   b. Imply politely that it is none of his business.
   c. Tell your exact age.

5. You wish to sell a chair with a slipcover that hides a tear in the upholstery. You would:
   a. Tack down the slipcover and say the chair is in good condition.
   b. Tell the buyer to examine the chair.
   c. Tell the prospective buyer about the rip.

6. You accidentally break an ashtray in a friend's home, but no one sees you. You would:
   a. Send a replacement later with a note of apology.
   b. Tell your hostess and offer to replace it.
   c. Hide the pieces and say nothing.

7. You find a wallet on the street. It contains ten dollars but no identification. You would:

    a. Give it to a police officer.

    b. Keep the money.

    c. Donate the ten dollars to your church or to charity.

8. You are returning from a foreign country with one hundred dollars more in merchandise than customs allows. You would:

    a. Ask a stranger without a full quota to declare to carry the article through customs for you.

    b. Declare and pay customs on the articles.

    c. Smuggle the article in among your clothing.

9. You are undercharged a dollar in a restaurant. You would:

    a. Pay the amount shown on your check.

    b. Leave the waitress an extra-large tip.

    c. Ask the waitress to recheck the bill.

10. You have helped a friend study for an exam. But when you two sit down to take it together, an answer you knew very well has slipped your mind. You would:

    a. Leave the answer blank.

    b. Glance at your friend's paper for the answer you once gave him.

    c. Discuss your mental lapse with the examiner later.

11. When driving or walking you are aware that you unintentionally went through a red light. When a police officer makes you stop, you would:

    a. Tell him his eyesight needs checking.

    b. Admit you were in the wrong.

    c. Say the signal changed when you were in the middle of the intersection.

12. In the drawing on the next page, a motel is built on an island (a), which is in the middle of a river. The island is connected to the mainland by bridges 1, 2, 3, 4, and 6. Bridges 5 and 7 cross the two forks of the river but they are not connected to the island. Several guests tried to plan a walk from the motel that would take them over each of the seven bridges only once and bring them back to their motel. Can you map their route?

    a. I cannot map the route.

    b. I can map the route in five minutes or less.

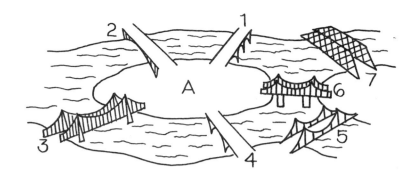

How Fearful Are You?

Feeling a little skittish? Heart pounding when a branch rubs against your window? Afraid of that little old lady sitting on the park bench? Well, these are symptoms of fear. It has been wisely said, "Early and provident fear is the mother of safety," but some of us, provoked by news hysteria, ugly rumors, and traumatic stories are so encased by fear that we cease to function happily. This test will help you know yourself and give you insights into how to control unnecessary anxieties.

In the following situations, please select the response that is nearest your own.

1. You are going for a routine physical checkup. You
    a. regard your visit as one of those things everyone should do.
    b. are sure the doctor will find something wrong with you.
    c. look forward to your visit because you always probe him/her about new medical findings and methods.

2. You return to your home and find the door slightly ajar. You
    a. chide yourself for not closing it correctly and enter.
    b. go to the nearest phone and call the police.
    c. arm yourself with something—a stick, a brick, your purse, or a briefcase—open the door, and peer cautiously in.

3. You are invited to a night dinner that involves your going through a section of town infamous for muggings, rapes, and other crimes. You
    a. refuse the invitation.
    b. accept because you feel secure with your information about the use of police whistles and physical-defense techniques.
    c. never give danger a thought and head for the dinner.

4. You pass an old house with bars on the windows. There are indications of activity inside. Your first reaction is
    a. an interest in the old building and its occupants.
    b. an uneasy feeling that a prisoner might be held inside.
    c. the thought it should be torn down to make way for a new building.

5. You are walking down a dimly lit street and become aware that a man is rapidly overtaking you. You
    a. walk faster in an effort to stay ahead.
    b. move aside to let him pass.
    c. make an evasive move of some kind, such as turning at the next corner, going into a cafe.

6. You are with a group of people who are obviously "brains." Their conversation revolves around subjects you know little about. You
    a. ask questions in order to learn.
    b. try to switch the conversation to topics you can talk about.
    c. sit in dread, fearing someone will address a remark you way.

7. You are tramping through an area where people have told you repeatedly there are no poisonous snakes. One suddenly slithers onto your path. You

a. pick up a rock and kill it.

b. stop and let it cross.

c. beat a hasty retreat.

8. You are walking or driving down a street and notice a police car cruising, slowly behind you. You

a. wonder if they are going to pick you up for something you've done.

b. feel secure with the knowledge police are on patrol.

c. consider the police car as just a normal part of traffic.

9. You have an expensive ring. You

a. wear it all the time.

b. never wear it but stash it away in a safe place.

c. wear it only when you are sure you and it will be safe.

10. Each time you go to bed you

a. do so with the apprehension you will be disturbed by nightmares.

b. look forward to sweet dreams.

c. sleep soundly.

11. When each birthday rolls around you

a. look forward to the day.

b. feel depressed because you're one day nearer death.

c. check it off as just another day of the year.

12. In reviewing the attitudes of your parents, you

a. think one or both were fearful of people, places, or things.

b. feel they were almost daredevils.

c. think they brought you up to be cautious but not afraid.

13. In your thinking, insurances (accident, fire, etc.) are

a. wise investments.

b. a waste of money.

c. something you've never considered.

14. You have a hunch the time is ripe for a love affair. You

a. improve your physical attractiveness, rehearse your come-on lines, and look forward to the happening.

b. make up some excuses and avoid the situation.

c. approach the love affair as a matter-of-fact situation.

15. You have been working for a company for several years. With little notice, the company goes out of business. You

a. feel you can find another job that is as good, if not better.
b. are petrified by your future bleak prospects.
c. take a vacation until your money runs out.

16. You are invited to a reception given for a famous person. You
a. accept without hesitation.
b. feel inadequate and decline.
c. go with a nervous stomach and uneasiness.

17. You win a free trip to some exotic foreign place, such as Morocco, Hong Kong, or Turkey. There is nothing to stand in the way of your going. You
a. start your preparations immediately.
b. remember the books and movies about crime and intrigue in that faraway place and turn in your ticket.
c. try to get another person to go with you for safety's sake.

18. You are alone in your home. A stranger raps on the door, explains he needs help, and asks to use your phone. You
a. tell him your phone is out of order.
b. let him in to use your phone.
c. tell him to wait outside while you make the call for him.

19. Your area has certain natural hazards, such as occasional earthquakes, tornadoes, floods, and tidal waves. You
a. live in constant fear of such a catastrophe.
b. move to another part of the country.
c. learn all you can about what to do if—.

20. Take a minute to study the picture on the next page.

You
a. have an uneasy, upset feeling after looking at it.
b. are reminded of an exciting movie, TV show, or book that you enjoyed.
c. look at the picture realistically and question if only two buildings could be shattered as depicted.

SCORING

DON'T BE AFRAID OF SCORING

1.	a–4; b–2; c–6	11.	a–6; b–2; c–6
2.	a–6; b–2; c–4	12.	a–2; b–6; c–6
3.	a–2; b–4; c–6	13.	a–6; b–6; c–6
4.	a–6; b–2; c–6	14.	a–4; b–2; c–6
5.	a–2; b–6; c–4	15.	a–6; b–2; c–6
6.	a–6; b–4; c–2	16.	a–6; b–2; c–4
7.	a–2; b–6; c–2	17.	a–6; b–2; c–4
8.	a–2; b–6; c–6	18.	a–2; b–6; c–4
9.	a–6; b–2; c–4	19.	a–2; b–2; c–6
10.	a–2; b–6; c–6	20.	a–2; b–6; c–6

WHAT YOUR SCORING MEANS:

100–120: You are so fearless you may be lacking in the normal sense of survival. You think life is beautiful and nothing can hurt you or yours. In some cases, one's fears can be overcome by careful planning and well-founded knowledge, such as knowing how to cope with emergencies, such as an earthquake. But, as in situation 13, a person is less fearful when he is protected by insurance, but stupidly fearless when he thinks insurance is a waste of money, or if he has given it no thought. "When using your needle you move your fingers delicately and with wise caution. Give attention—do not take things by the point."

80–98:   You are above normal in your ability to control your fears. You are matter-of-fact in your attitudes and generally unemotional. You live Franklin Roosevelt's famous statement: "The only thing we have to fear is fear itself." Hang in there and show your self-confidence with others.

58–78:   You get the shudders now and then. You're cautious and tread uneasily in many situations. If you can pinpoint where you feel least secure, you can easily see through the shadows in your life that envelop you. Put yourself in the position of believing in yourself and in the basic goodness of others.

48–56:   "There is great beauty in going through life without anxiety of fear. Half our fears are baseless and the other half discreditable." You are the sort of person who needs to find a fearless person who will take you by your hand for a while and then let you go on your own, step by step. Get on a bus with a friend, take a trip with a neighbor! Talk with people. Find something you fear to do and then do it. Know deep in your heart that nothing can frighten you as much as you are frightening yourself.

YOU
AND YOUR
SOCIAL SELF

How Kind Are You?

Kind people are always welcome and always well liked.

The reason why there are not as many kind people as there might be is that being kind means putting others first.

This often requires effort, time, and trouble, which many of us prefer to use selfishly.

Try this test to see whether you are a kind person. Answer "Yes" or "No" to the questions before turning to the scoring key at the end.

1. Are you sufficiently interested and concerned to inquire about people?
2. Do you remember names and faces and associate them successfully?
3. Do you remember the bits of news people tell you about themselves and their families?
4. Do you make a note of birthdays and special days so that you remember in time?
5. Are you quick to show appreciation, offer sympathy, praise, and congratulate?
6. Do you enjoy amusing children and looking after pets?
7. Would you go out of your way to help a stranger?
8. Are you quick to offer hospitality?
9. Would you try to ensure that everybody felt comfortable and nobody felt out of it?
10. Do you do your fair share of the cleaning up and the domestic chores generally?

11. Does it hurt you to see someone in trouble, unhappy, lonely?

12. Would you do something about it if you could?

13. Even if this meant putting yourself to trouble and inconvenience, such as missing an appointment, or shouldering a responsibility?

14. Are you there when the family and your friends need active or moral support?

15. Are you quick to offer to do things without being asked?

16. Are you kind to everybody, not just to those people you wish to impress?

17. Can people rely on you to keep your word and your promises?

18. Can your friends trust you not to discuss them with other people?

19. Are you quick to fit in when people want to change the subject, be quiet, be left entirely alone, or, conversely, when they want company?

20. Are you slow to impute bad motives as well as being quick to forgive and forget?

SCORING

Score 5 points for every "Yes." A score of 70 is good; 60 to 70 may be counted satisfactory. If you score less than that you are not a kind person.

To be kind we have to like people enough to care about what is happening to them and how they are feeling.

It implies having enough imagination and sensitivity to put ourselves in other people's shoes, so that we are not only ready to help them, but are also prepared to make allowances for them.

Are You a Lively Person?

Lively, vital people enjoy their lives. They are forward-looking and outward-looking, welcoming change, new people, different experiences.

To be like this is to live life to the fullest and to take advantage of every opportunity that comes our way.

Here is a test you can try on yourself. Answer "Yes" or "No" to the questions before turning to the scoring key at the end.

1. Would you rather be out and about among people than stay at home on your own?
2. Is it almost a natural reflex for you to say "Yes" when you are asked to go somewhere or do something?
3. On the other hand, would you join in and have a go and share activity with people without waiting to be asked?
4. Is it usual for people to remember you, your face, and your name?
5. Do strangers show interest in desiring to meet you and talk to you?
6. Is it easy for you to get to know people and become friendly?
7. Do you look forward to social occasions because you know you will enjoy them?
8. Do you keep up with fashion and like trying new things and doing something different?
9. Do you like to hear and know about all that is going on around you?
10. Are you often enthusiastic?
11. Are you interested in most of the things that interest people generally?
12. Do you enjoy conversation with a wide variety of people?
13. Is it easy for you to find something to talk about?
14. Do you find it easy to put across your point of view and sell your ideas to people?
15. Do people often look to you to start the ball rolling, to take the initiative, and to show leadership?
16. Are setbacks, rebuffs, and difficult people stimulating challenges rather than depressing obstacles?
17. Are you much more interested in the present and the future than in what has happened in the past?
18. Do you become so interested and enthusiastic that you quite forget to be self-conscious?
19. Are you the type with plenty of energy who does not tire easily?
20. Do you enjoy good health?

SCORING

Count 5 points for every "Yes." A score over 70 is very good; 60 to 70 is good, and 50 to 60 is satisfactory. From 40 to 50 may be counted fair, but under 40 is not satisfactory.

Your general health is important to vitality. But also this quality is a matter of temperament and disposition; some of us are naturally extroverted, while others tend to be more withdrawn.

If your score is low, try to improve by becoming more interested and outward-looking. Lively, vital people are always intensely interested in others and in everything going on around them.

Are You Stimulating to Others?

When we come in contact with a stimulating personality, it is like stepping out of darkness into a bright room.

How do such people do it? They obviously enjoy every minute of their lives. What makes them so interested and so interesting?

This test may help to reveal to you the secret of the stimulating personality. Answer "Yes" or "No" before turning to the scoring key at the end.

1. You are interested in a wide variety of things, as well as specially interested in one of two things?
2. You like trying out new ideas and new methods of doing things?
3. You are not afraid or self-conscious of being and sounding really enthusiastic?
4. Within reason, you are ready and willing to drop what you are doing at the moment to take part in a surprise activity, like a motor drive, or a picnic, or a shopping expedition?
5. You like all kinds of people and you like people as people, instead of hand-picking your friends because you share the same social background or work in the same office?
6. It is exciting to meet new people, attend social functions, be expected to take part?
7. Mistakes and failures do not depress you for long because there are so many other interesting things to do?

8. You are too interested learning and too keen on doing things yourself to bother about pleasing everybody and being criticized?

9. You like asking questions and finding out the answers?

10. You are ready to take the initiative and lead the way?

11. You are willing to shoulder responsibility?

12. You can encourage the waverers and fainthearts?

13. You like seeing that everybody has a good time?

14. You always have plenty to talk about and you enjoy talking, especially friendly arguments and discussions?

15. Conversely, you equally enjoy listening to other people?

16. You like to have people calling casually on you, and make it obvious that they are welcome at any time?

17. You find it easy to fit in and take pot luck?

18. You never mind looking silly when it is all in the cause of good fun?

19. You are extra quick off the mark with sympathy, congratulations, offers of help?

20. You believe that you still have a lot to learn, and know that you are learning something every day, especially about people?

SCORING

Count 5 points for every "Yes." A really stimulating personality will score an easy 100, but 70 and over may be regarded as good; 60–70 is satisfactory; 50–60 is fair.

This test is designed to demonstrate an outstanding type of person. The standard is high.

Keen interest outside oneself in life, in people, and in the outside world is what is needed here. Keep the test by you so that you can try it again.

Are You Really Such a Nice Person?

Most of us regard ourselves as nice people. When our relations with other people go wrong and we are finding it difficult to get along pleasantly with them, there is always the tendency to put the blame on the other fellow.

Before we do this, it might be a good thing if we took a closer look at ourselves. Here is a test to help you do this. Answer "Yes" or "No" to the questions before turning to the scoring key at the end.

1. Are you really so delighted to see your friends and neighbors becoming more prosperous and rising in the world?

2. Do you like people for their personal qualities, not for their status or what they can give you?

3. Can you listen to other people being praised without wanting to put in a disparaging word?

4. Do you like most of the people you meet, rather than managing to find things to dislike about them?

5. Are you good about allowing other people their fair share of notice and attention?

6. Do you praise and encourage people's efforts rather than criticize and disparage them?

7. Are you one to gloss over people's mistakes, rather than draw attention to them by making fun, or talking about them to those who were not present at the time?

8. Do you make a habit of saying "Thank you," and showing your appreciation for affection and kindness, rather than taking people for granted?

9. Are you quick to sympathize when people are ill or in any trouble and do what you can to help?

10. Are you tactful and careful not to hurt or embarrass people with what you say to them, or about them?

11. Can people trust you to be loyal and respect their confidences?

12. Do you consider other people's wishes and feelings, not merely do what you feel like doing?

13. Generally speaking, is it your practice to fit in and adapt yourself to others because you want them to enjoy themselves?

14. Can you control your moods so that you are not pleasant one day and unpleasant the next?

15. Can you keep your temper when people do not agree with you?

16. Are you willing to admit when you are wrong and apologize?

17. Would you admit that you were prejudiced and had been unfair?

18. Are you slow to blame but quick to forgive and forget?
19. Are you fair and conscientious about shouldering your share of responsibility, work, expenses?
20. Are you particular about your person and your personal habits?

SCORING

Count 5 points for every "Yes." If you can score over 70 you are truly a nice person; 60–70 means that you are quite nice; 50–60 implies that you can be nice but it would be wise not to depend on it. If you score under 50, your chief concern is yourself. You are nice only when it suits you.

Are You Socially Minded?

You have to be socially minded to get along with people. You have to be able to fit in with them reasonably.

Their little ways should not spark off moods or temper in you.

Try this test by answering "Yes" or "No" to the questions. Then turn to the scoring key at the end.

1. Do you tend to like people rather than dislike them?
2. Do you think that most people like you, rather than dislike you?
3. Can you take people as they come without bothering unduly about what they may think of you?
4. Have you enough poise not to be upset when someone is difficult or rude to you?
5. If you lost your temper in public would you regret it, feeling that you had let yourself down?
6. Are you naturally tactful, not the type who enjoys using blunt or offensive language?
7. Can you be courteous, even kind, to those you do not like very much?
8. Do you hate hurting people?
9. Do you consider other's wishes before you think of yourself?
10. Can you agree to differ and yet remain on friendly terms?

11. Are you quick to apologize when you know you are in the wrong?

12. Are you able to say that you're sorry without resenting having to do so?

13. Can you enjoy a joke against yourself without being annoyed or embarrassed?

14. Do you enjoy talking about subjects not of direct personal interest to you?

15. Do you enjoy listening to other people as much as you do talking yourself?

16. Can you see somebody else holding the stage without feeling resentful?

17. Do you keep your promises to do things with other people?

18. Are you quick to offer your sympathy, help, and co-operation?

19. Do you like sharing activity rather than being on your own?

20. When you go out socially, do you expect to enjoy yourself?

SCORING

Count 5 points for every "Yes." A score over 70 is good; 60–70 is satisfactory; 50–60 is fair. Under 50 is poor.

Being socially minded means being interested in people and things outside ourselves. This implies being much less concerned with ourselves and what others think about us.

This is the way to be relaxed and comfortable with people, and therefore more socially minded.

Do You Irritate Others?

Do you irritate others? "Some people don't realize they've developed attitudes that are reflected in behavior patterns that irritate others," says Dr. Frank Caprio, noted psychiatrist and author. "But it is usually possible to overcome these habits once you realize you have them." This test is designed to help you. For each of the following questions, select the answer that comes closest to your feelings.

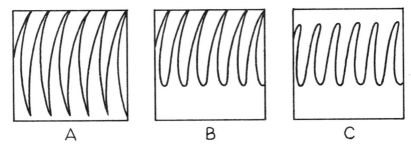

1. Above are three drawings. Which one appeals to you most: a, b, or c?

2. How would you describe people you find most difficult to deal with:
   a. Oversensitive.
   b. Bad-tempered.
   c. Selfish.

3. Complete this statement with the phrase you find most appropriate: Everyone needs friends, but even the best of friends
   a. Tend to take advantage of friendship.
   b. Are not to be trusted too far.
   c. Can at times be a burden.

4. People who strongly object to profanity under any circumstances are:
   a. Stuffy and should be avoided.
   b. Have a right to their feelings and should be tolerated.
   c. Are behind the times and should be told so.

5. When you are having marital problems, do you find it best to:
   a. Keep it to yourself.
   b. Tell as many people as possible to get their advice.
   c. Confide in one close friend.

6. Most of us find certain kinds of people unpleasant. Which would you most try to avoid:
   a. People who think they know it all.
   b. People who are prejudiced and opinionated.
   c. People who can't take this criticism.

7.   To get ahead in the world, one needs to:
      a.   Step on a few toes now and then.
      b.   Speak softly and carry a big stick.
      c.   Overlook an awful lot.

8.   If the following three comedians were appearing on television at the same time, which would you most likely choose to watch:
      a.   Don Rickles.
      b.   Phyllis Diller.
      c.   Red Skelton.

SCORING

1.   a–3; b–2; c–1
2.   a–1; b–2; c–3
3.   a–1; b–3; c–2
4.   a–1; b–2; c–2
5.   a–1; b–3; c–2
6.   a–1; b–2; c–3
7.   a–3; b–2; c–1
8.   a–3; b–2; c–1

ANALYSIS:

20–24 points: You are prone to be tactless, to assert yourself rather harshly at times, and to disregard the sensibilities of others. Much of this behavior probably results from thoughtlessness rather than malicious intent, but it is still having an adverse effect on those around you.

14–19 points: You have the good sense to "bite your tongue" occasionally rather than irritate someone needlessly. Yet you also have the courage to speak your mind when the time is opportune and the issue important.

8–13 points: By going to extremes in an attempt to avoid irritating others, you could be accomplishing the opposite result. Be careful not to present yourself in an overly-ingratiating manner. Take a stand from time to time, and try to temper your anxiety with good sense.

Just How Popular Are You?

We all like to think of ourselves as being popular, but it may well be that we are deluding ourselves to a great extent.

Answer the following questions truthfully and you will then be wise to yourself, perhaps for the first time in your life!

Tick a. or b. according to choice, and then check your score at the end.

1. a. Are you really a good loser?
   b. Or do you only pretend to take all defeats and setbacks in the proper spirit?

2. a. Do you break your word at times?
   b. Or is your word your bond, as the saying goes?

3. a. Are you invariably late for appointments?
   b. Or do you do your utmost to be on time?

4. a. If someone asks you for a loan, do you give it freely?
   b. Or are you prone to lecture the person first?

5. a. You are part of a foursome; the boy or girl with your friend is something of a pain in the neck. Do you try to turn it into a twosome?
   b. Or do you see it through to the bitter end for your friend's sake?

6. a. Are you inclined to boast?
   b. Or do you leave that to the others?

7. a. Do you enjoy deflating people, possibly calling it "debunking" them?
   b. Or do you feel that one should live and let live in that respect?

8. a. Do you believe that everyone is concerned only with No. 1?
   b. Or do you feel that there are quite a few unselfish people in this world?

9. a. If you can't think of anything nice to say to a person, do you hold your tongue?
   b. Or do you feel that people should know the truth about themselves, no matter from what corner it comes?

10. a. Someone is telling the same old joke for the umpteenth time; do you forcibly remind them of the fact?
    b. Or do you grin and bear it?

SCORING

ANSWERS

Score 5 points for each correct answer.

1.–a	6.–b
2.–b	7.–b
3.–b	8.–b
4.–a	9.–a
5.–b	10.–b

Maximum score is 50 points.

If you have genuinely scored 40–50 points, then you need never worry about not being popular.

A total of 25–35 points means that you're not doing everything in your power to make people like you: possibly you are much too independent-minded.

A total of 20 points or under would indicate that you're likely to wind up being exceedingly unpopular if you don't change your ways really soon!

Do You Have Charm?

Do you have charm? You can find out very easily by taking this quick and simple test.

1. Which of the three drawings below attracts you the most: a, b, or c?

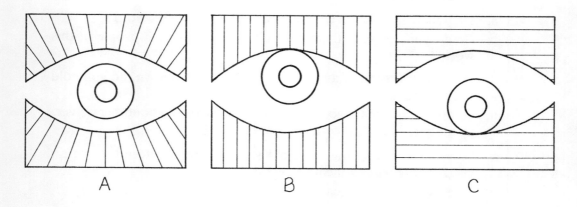

A   B   C

2. Someone you don't recognize is staring at you from an adjoining table in a restaurant. Do you:
    a. Lean over and ask, "Do I know you?"
    b. Complain to the waiter.
    c. Nod at the person staring and go on with your meal.

3. There's an uncomfortable pause in the conversation at a dinner party where you are a guest. Do you consider it your responsibility to think of something to say to break the silence:
    a. Always.
    b. Sometimes.
    c. Never.

4. Which of the following best represents your idea of a "charming" woman:
    a. Jackie Onassis.
    b. Phyllis Diller.
    c. Carol Burnett.

5. When you were younger, did you have:
    a. No desire,
    b. Some desire,
    c. A great desire . . . for a theatrical career?

6. After a heated discussion do you:
    a. Often.
    b. Occasionally.
    c. Never . . . think of things that you might have said?

7. Some people have a habit of using their hands while talking. Do you consider this:
    a. Expressive.
    b. Offensive.
    c. Acceptable, if not overdone.

8. If someone tells a joke and you fail to see the point, do you:
    a. Laugh anyway.
    b. Try to change the subject.
    c. Ask to have the joke explained.

SCORING

1.	a–3; b–2; c–1	5.	a–1; b–2; c–3
2.	a–3; b–1; c–2	6.	a–1; b–2; c–3
3.	a–3; b–2; c–1	7.	a–3; b–1; c–2
4.	a–1; b–3; c–2	8.	a–3; b–1; c–2

ANALYSIS:

21–24 points: You're a real charmer, one who brightens every room. No one will feel left out of any gathering while you're around to keep the party bubbling.

15–20 points: You show many of the attributes that add up to a charming personality. You seem to have a fine sense of judgment when it comes to saying and doing the right thing.

8–14 points: You might not charm the apples off a tree, but at least they'll be ripe by the time you pick them. You value meaningful relationships. And when you're being charming, you really mean it.

Are You Really "in Touch"?

Are you really "in touch" with other people? Linked to them by the unique, heartwarming medium of touch itself?

For the touch—loving, kind, meaningful, warm, humane—is indeed a very special way of expressing affection or friendliness, understanding or sympathy that may go far deeper than mere words.

Or are you held back, as so many of us are, by timidity, inhibitions, even fear? Is there at the back of your mind the feeling that outward show of feeling expressed in even the simplest of physical terms—the touch—is a dubious sign of weakness?

Psychiatrists are so unanimous in their faith in what they call the remedy of "touchingness" for so many of our ills today that it is well worth our everyday consideration to see how far we ourselves are benefiting from it.

There is nothing new in this, of course. Christ always healed by touch. The healing power of "the laying on of hands," as it is called, cannot be explained simply by autosuggestion.

There is, in fact, abundant evidence that if we recoil from truly being "in touch" with those close to us in this way, we may well be extremely foolish. Equally, we may be aware of a thing in principle, but afraid to show our real feelings openly.

Either way, we need to look afresh at the ever-present problem of our basic failure to communicate with others, and see if we can better be "in touch" with those who need our outward gestures as well as our inward feelings to support them.

Here are some penetrating questions along these lines.

Each time you can truthfully answer "Often" you score 10 points.

Each time you can truthfully answer "Sometimes" you score 5 points.

Each time you can truthfully answer "Never" you score 1 point.

1. In ordinary life, do you hold hands with any adult?
2. Do you get down on the floor and romp with your (or any) young children?
3. Do you generally shake hands with older relatives or friends?
4. When helping someone on with a coat, do you finish the process with a light, friendly pat or pressure on the arms or shoulders?
5. As a rule, are you the sort of person who would lightly ruffle a youngster's hair as a gesture of affection, pride, or joy?
6. Are you yourself the recipient of the single but especially meaningful touch that invariably evokes an atmosphere of love or devotion?
7. Is it likely to sadden you if another person says: "Don't touch me!"?
8. When approaching a sick person, is your instinct to grasp one or both of the person's hands in your own, whether or not you actually do so?
9. Do you yourself react favorably to a squeeze of the arm?
10. Are you the sort of person another can readily put an arm around?
11. Do you enjoy the sort of party games where everyone is expected to link hands or arms?
12. Do young children (or animals) readily climb onto your lap?
13. Have you a warm, firm, friendly, but not oppressive handshake?
14. In conversation, do you lightly pat your listener's wrist or arm to emphasize a significant or amusing point?
15. On the occasions when you feel like it, do you actually put a protective arm around someone—a child or an adult—instead of stifling the instinct?
16. Do you ever envy the freedom and simplicity with which Latin people embrace each other?

17. As everyone knows, there are kisses and there are kisses, but when you kiss someone, whatever the person's age, do you really mean it?
18. Do you think there is something beneficial in literally giving someone a pat on the back?
19. Are your own hands expressive in touching other people?
20. On the whole, do you think people generally regret missing opportunities for being "in touch" like this when they might so easily have been?

SCORING

Now add up your total of marks.

Anyone who scored 150 or more is clearly aware of the magical language of touch, and needs no further advice.

If you scored over 100 but under 150, you are really hesitating on the borderline between being truly "in touch" with your fellow human beings and being proudly and unwisely aloof. Why not let your instincts rule your actions for a change? The chances of rebuff are much slighter than you imagine, and the benefits to be gained and bestowed are enormous. Try it and see!

If your score was under 100, you cannot truly be said to be "in touch" at all. Love, kindness, friendliness, sympathy, understanding—none of these is much good unless you show it. You probably feel some or all of these, yet you hold back in their simplest physical demonstration, thus making the world a poorer place. Ponder the recent words of a doctor on this very subject: "Touch has its own magic. It can express love and ease pain, and can give mankind its humanity."

How Bossy Are You?

Some people just can't help being pushed around. They're the milquetoasts of the world—men and women who let people tread all over them and still come up smiling. At the other end of the personality scale are the do-it-my-way-or-else types who insist on giving all the orders. Just where do you fit in this scale?

1. When you were growing up, were there people who bossed you around?

a. many.

b. few.

c. none.

2. Do you enjoy starting an argument when you feel quite sure you will win?

a. never.

b. sometimes.

c. often.

3. Do you have a strong feeling that if you don't control others they will take advantage of you?

a. with some people.

b. with most people.

c. no.

4. Do you expect others to be on time but expect them to wait for you if you are late?

a. no.

b. always.

c. usually.

5. When you need something to be done you

a. do it yourself.

b. tell others to do the job.

c. ask others if they will help you.

6. Do you welcome the ideas of others?

a. no; their ideas are usually a waste of time; mine are tried and true.

b. yes; I let them try out their ideas.

c. sometimes; when we can try out their ideas together.

7. Do you feel it is important for you to know what everyone at home, on the job, in your social circle is doing?

a. yes; I like to keep an eye on my family, friends, and associates.

b. no; what they do is their own business.

c. no; but I'll listen if they want to talk.

8. On your sexual adventures you

a. like to be petted, snuggled, and made to feel comfortable.

b. enjoy the mutuality of romantic moments.

c. take the lead and expect your companion to go along with your sexual game.

9. You
    a. have many keys and personally lock up your home, belongings, office, etc.
    b. leave most doors, desks, and drawers unlocked.
    c. give your keys to people whom you consider responsible.

10. You like to wear or to display in your living quarters
    a. medals, pins, trophies, and awards that show your distinction.
    b. nothing that draws attention to yourself.
    c. ordinary, comfortable attire and things around you that fulfill a function.

11. When you drive a vehicle or walk on the street you
    a. expect others to get out of your way.
    b. adjust your strategy to that of others.
    c. let other people have the right of way.

12. You use the words "Please" and "Thank you"
    a. on social occasions.
    b. often and with a sincerity of meaning.
    c. seldom to my family or associates because they're doing what they're supposed to do.

13. Have you ever been a member of a "secret" group?
    a. yes, as a child.
    b. yes, as a teen-ager or adult.
    c. never.

14. When you want something done you
    a. use your hand or fist to emphasize your desire.
    b. casually express your wishes.
    c. make your wants known and answer any questions necessary.

15. When in a crowd you
    a. are willing to wait your turn.
    b. push to be first.
    c. step back to avoid the rush and come in last.

16. If you had your choice about organizing a group of people to get a project going you would
    a. give everyone a job and see that he or she does it.
    b. let the group select their own jobs and report progress to you.
    c. tell someone else to take over the job of getting it done.

17. If you were to choose an animal for a pet you would prefer
   a. an animal that you can easily train to do tricks, such as an obedient dog.
   b. an animal that is an independent thinker, such as a cat.
   c. an untrainable animal, such as a goldfish.

18. If a business associate or family member were to get into a problem with the law you would
   a. never have anything to do with the person again.
   b. try in every possible way to help.
   c. let matters run their course while maintaining your friendly relationship.

19. The most important things in life to you are
   a. possessions.
   b. ideas.
   c. family relationships and friends.

20. Which of the drawings below attracts you the most, a, b or c?

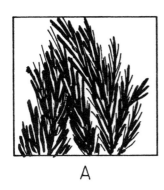
A

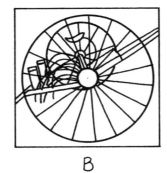
B

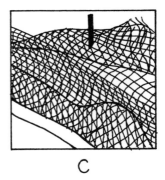
C

SCORING

HOW TO SCORE:

1. a–6; b–4; c–2	8. a–4; b–2; c–6	15. a–4; b–6; c–2
2. a–2; b–4; c–6	9. a–6; b–2; c–4	16. a–2; b–4; c–6
3. a–4; b–6; c–2	10. a–6; b–2; c–4	17. a–6; b–4; c–2
4. a–2; b–6; c–4	11. a–6; b–4; c–2	18. a–6; b–4; c–2
5. a–2; b–6; c–4	12. a–6; b–2; c–4	19. a–6; b–2; c–4
6. a–6; b–2; c–4	13. a–2; b–6; c–2	20. a–2; b–6; c–4
7. a–6; b–2; c–4	14. a–6; b–2; c–4	

WHAT YOUR SCORE MEANS:

100–120:   You are bossy and wear yourself out. You are a born leader, even if it kills everyone around you. You butt your head against stone walls and wonder why you have a headache. Think your life through. Have you had to stand up to domineering parents, associates? Had to "fight out of" difficult situations? Life is easy and beautiful. Relax. Enjoy.

90–98:   You have executive qualities. You can dominate but are not overly domineering. You expect to be heard and obeyed. You demand respect. Use your talent of strong guidance wisely.

58–78:   You have a fine ability to work with others. You are not a milquetoast personality. You listen, lead, and take care of those around you. One of the greatest assets is the ability to listen and to learn.

40–56:   You are a happy person, willing to serve. Your inner fulfillments are many. "Blessed are the meek: For they shall inherit the earth."

How Tactful Are You?

Tact is a must if you want to live happily and amicably with others. You can test your tact by placing a tick against the way you would react to the following situations. Then turn to the scoring key at the end.

1.   Somebody is rude to you.
   a.   It hurts you. You show it. You talk about it to others.
   b.   You are rude back.
   c.   You refuse to be upset and pass on to nicer people.

2.   You overhear someone speaking unfavorably of you.
   a.   Turn a deaf ear but treat him with cutting politeness the next time you meet.
   b.   I've caught you! Right! We'll get this straight now!
   c.   He could be letting off steam. It might even be a case of the cap fitting. So keep quiet. Use it to examine yourself, perhaps to adjust something that is wrong.

3. Someone is lying, or, worse still, telling half truths.
   a. Say nothing, but tell everyone behind their back that they are unreliable.
   b. A public showdown!
   c. Try to throw true light on the situation. Ask questions like: "How well do you know . . . ? Were you actually there . . . ? Did you actually hear . . . ?" Possibly, you can say: "That's not what I was told," or "I didn't get that impression," or "You can't have understood correctly."

4. Someone starts telling you something told him in confidence.
   a. What can I do except listen?
   b. Tell others about it, including what was said.
   c. Say: "Please don't go on. I'm sure that was said in confidence, I'd rather not know, and I'd be careful about repeating it if I were you."

5. Someone is talking. You have heard it before.
   a. Get ready to change the subject as soon as he pauses to take a breath.
   b. Say bluntly: "You've told us that before."
   c. Give him a fair hearing. After all, he's proud of it, or likes it, or thinks that it is funny. Try to lead the conversation by getting him interested in what others have to say.

6. Someone is insisting on a viewpoint that you can prove wrong.
   a. Right is right, even when the matter is trifling. You may keep your temper and remain polite, but you are determined to make him admit that he is wrong.
   b. Loud-voiced protests. Ridicule. You imply, possibly say: "Only a fool thinks that!"
   c. Let it pass, hoping that one day he will have more sense. If it is important, suggest that other people think differently and that it is as well to take this into account. Meanwhile, agree to differ.

7. Someone is difficult. Irritability is building up inside you.
   a. Say politely but exasperatedly: "That is enough! I won't discuss it!"
   b. Explode!
   c. Try to excuse yourself. Failing that, try to listen with only half an ear so that he irritates you only half as much.

8. People like someone you dislike.
   a. Drop hints that you regard this person as untrustworthy.
   b. Try to force the issue by criticizing or by showing him up.
   c. Leave people to decide for themselves.

9. You meet someone who has had a bad failure or been let down.
   a. A kind manner but a "too bad you were not up to it" or a "I could have told you" air.
   b. Do you good to get it off your chest. **Tell me all about it.**
   c. A natural manner, plus extra kindness. If he wants to tell you, you listen sympathetically. Otherwise, no questions.

10. You visit a friend who is much more seriously ill than he thinks he is.
    a. The bedside manner. The lowered voice. You avoid meeting his gaze and find it difficult to talk.
    b. Overhearty cheerfulness in the "you will be up in next to no time" approach.
    c. As natural as you can be. Think out beforehand interesting items about the people you both know and interests you share.

SCORING

Count 10 marks for every ticked c. A score of 80 and over is good; 70–80 is satisfactory; 60–70 is fair. Under 60 is not satisfactory.

To be tactful we have to develop the habit of considering other people's feelings first.

Next, we need poise. This comes from experience in meeting and dealing with people.

Also, by watching how they behave we can learn from them and, sometimes, profit by avoiding their mistakes.

Does Prejudice Rule Your Life?

Of course you are willing to listen to all sides of every proposition. You are open-minded and judge every situation on the basis of its true worth. Naturally you hold no illogical biases and use your clear head rather than your confused emotions. In fact, you are not a victim of prejudice. Or are you? This quiz may give you some surprises. Almost all of us are influenced by preconceived ideas and feelings.

1. Do you believe that minority groups are inferior?
    a. no.
    b. yes.
    c. some.

2. Do you think that the youth of today are lacking in moral fiber?
    a. yes.
    b. some.
    c. no.

3. Do you tend to form permanent judgments about people on the basis of their clothing or physical characteristics?
    a. yes.
    b. no.
    c. sometimes.

4. Do you believe people are evil because they do not attend religious services?
    a. yes.
    b. no.
    c. some.

5. Are you prone to contradict others on the basis of what you think is true?
    a. yes.
    b. no.
    c. occasionally.

6. In your estimation, are recipients of welfare lazy?
    a. yes.
    b. no.
    c. some.

7. Laws that have served us well in the past, such as those that prohibit abortion and homosexuality, should serve us well now and in the future?
    a. yes.
    b. no.
    c. probably.

8. Do you dislike police officers, judges, teachers, and/or others who represent authority?

a. yes.

b. no.

c. sometimes.

9. Do you think that certain nationalities should be barred from the country by immigration laws?

a. no.

b. some.

c. many.

10. Do you harbor a feeling of intellectual or social superiority because you belong to a certain organization, club, or group, such as a fraternity, sorority, or country club?

a. no.

b. secretly.

c. decidedly.

11. Would you taste a new food if told it were made of something unfamiliar such as chocolate-coated ants, yak eyes, or fillet of snake?

a. yes.

b. doubtful.

c. no.

12. Do you consider travel by air dangerous?

a. no.

b. yes.

c. sometimes.

13. Do you feel you must stick with your political party even if you do not agree with their past actions?

a. no.

b. most of the time.

c. yes. -

14. Do you prefer to talk rather than to listen?

a. sometimes.

b. no.

c. yes.

15. Is it difficult for you to understand why others have chosen their dates or mates?

a. no.

b. yes.

c. sometimes.

16. Do you think the referee is wrong when he makes a decision against your team?
    a. sometimes.
    b. yes.
    c. no.

17. Do you feel your family and close friends are right in their actions?
    a. never.
    b. usually.
    c. always.

18. Are you opposed to the political or religious views of others who differ with you even if you are not sure what the implications of those views are?
    a. no.
    b. yes.
    c. sometimes.

19. Do you think your way of life should be the pattern for others?
    a. yes.
    b. some aspects.
    c. no.

20. In your opinion, were the "good old days" better than the present?
    a. no.
    b. in some respects.
    c. yes.

SCORING

HOW TO CHECK YOUR SCORES:

1.	a–2; b–6; c–4	11.	a–2; b–4; c–6
2.	a–6; b–4; c–2	12.	a–2; b–6; c–4
3.	a–6; b–2; c–4	13.	a–6; b–4; c–2
4.	a–6; b–2; c–2	14.	a–4; b–2; c–6
5.	a–6; b–2; c–4	15.	a–2; b–6; c–4
6.	a–6; b–2; c–4	16.	a–4; b–6; c–2
7.	a–6; b–2; c–4	17.	a–6; b–2; c–6
8.	a–6; b–2; c–4	18.	a–2; b–6; c–4
9.	a–2; b–4; c–6	19.	a–6; b–4; c–2
10.	a–2; b–4; c–6	20.	a–6; b–2; c–6

WHAT IT MEANS:

40–48:   Those who rate this score have a remarkably open mind, free from prejudice to the point of being almost superhuman. They may appear to friends as too universal and impractical.

50–58:   This score indicates a person who investigates before he makes a decision, which is open to revision. In general, these people do not have unwarranted fears and suspicions.

60–79:   Those who rate this score have set minds in certain areas of living, which they tend to use as self-protective devices. Because they are often insecure, they feel they are right and better than others.

80–98:   Scorers in this range usually verge on prejudice. Their reactions are often based on isolated bits of information or the attitudes of their associates. When they cultivate their curiosity and listen to reason, they often find their attitudes fallacious.

100–120: This score indicates those whose lives are ruled by prejudices. Generally they feel they have the one and only answer to everything and that everyone is out of step but them. Unfortunately, these people are not popular with others, but in their self-assurance, they may not realize this dismal fact.

Do You Make People Feel Guilty?

The founders of modern psychology—Freud, Jung, and Adler—identified feelings of guilt that plague many personalities. Their findings have been substantiated by other eminent doctors.

Today it is generally recognized that the feeling of guilt is a destructive force in a person. However, only recently have tests been devised that locate the giver of guilt, the person who makes people squirm.

Select the answer that is nearest to your reaction in each of the following situations. Be honest.

1. At the last minute a friend cancels an appointment because of an emergency. You would say:
    a. Take good care of yourself.
    b. I had planned something special just for you.
    c. We'll plan to meet later.

2. During a meal, a guest slides a piece of lettuce onto the table. You would:
   a. Jump up and clean it off.
   b. Ignore the situation.
   c. Tell the person not to worry.

3. You meet a friend who is wearing a new suit. You would say:
   a. You made a wise choice.
   b. Did you buy it on sale?
   c. I could never afford anything as expensive as that.

4. Your date (or mate) is late meeting you for a luncheon appointment. You would:
   a. scowl, look at your watch, and say nothing.
   b. smile and say hello.
   c. express your displeasure.

5. You are in a romantic mood but your spouse is unresponsive. You would:
   a. wait for another time.
   b. slam the door and walk away.
   c. accuse your mate of being frigid or impotent.

6. When a person disagrees with you, you usually tell him or her that:
   a. it is a matter of ignorance.
   b. everyone has a right to an opinion.
   c. he or she comes from a poor background.

7. You must exchange a purchase. You would:
   a. explain it doesn't meet your needs.
   b. apologize for the inconvenience.
   c. say the clerk high-pressured you into buying it.

8. A neighbor's child accidentally breaks your window. You would:
   a. ask him or her to pay or work off the cost.
   b. peer out the window each time he or she is around.
   c. punish the child.

9. You forget a social appointment. You would say:
   a. It was your error.
   b. Something unexpected came up.
   c. I decided you didn't want to see me.

10.   A family member forgets your birthday. You would:
    a.   laugh it off.
    b.   give him or her nothing on his or her birthday.
    c.   remind the person how much you love them.

11.   A child in your family brings home bad grades. You would:
    a.   spank the child.
    b.   hire a tutor.
    c.   talk about the bright members of the family.

12.   Generally speaking, you:
    a.   give praise when it is deserved.
    b.   find fault.
    c.   say nothing one way or the other.

SCORING

1–b; 2–a; 3–c; 4–a; 5–c; 6–c; 7–c; 8–b; 9–c; 10–c; 11–c; 12–c

Give yourself 1 point for each of the above, except 2 points each for getting 5, 6, 10, or 11. These four situations are more heavily weighted since they strike at ego, background, and sex.

After totaling your points, see the paragraph below relating to your score.

YOUR SCORE:

14–16 points: You are unmerciful with others. You take a delight in making people feel guilty and, worst of all, it is likely that you are a victim of a guilt feeling yourself.

8–13 points: This is a "thoughtless" score. It is doubtful if you realize that you instill guilt feelings in others, but you have a tendency to strike where it hurts the most.

3–7 points: Your methods of control are not as tactful as they could be. However, you create no great problems and you live with yourself nicely.

0–2 points or less: Excellent unless you missed on question 5. In this case, your marriage is heading for trouble.

What Kind of a Snob Are You?

A moderate dose of snobbery never hurt anyone. We are all snobs in one way or another and often in several ways. The questions here ask: What kind of a snob? And is the dose too heavy?

Snobbery, an offshoot of both pride and knowledge, can be fun—if kept in bounds. List your answers, using the alphabet a, b, c, etc.

1. You would like to spend your vacation:
    a. at an international festival of music or art.
    b. at a famous resort.
    c. in a metropolitan city.
    d. on a study tour.
    e. on a camping trip.
    f. on your own yacht.

2. Given a choice of records, you would first play:
    a. primitive music from Africa.
    b. Caruso's arias.
    c. popular tunes.
    d. Carl Sandburg reading his poetry.
    e. football.
    f. a symphony.

3. If money were no question, you would like to collect:
    a. ceramics by Picasso.
    b. furniture owned by European royalty.
    c. ashtrays from famous restaurants.
    d. rare books.
    e. pieces from famous explorations.
    f. rare stamps and coins.

4. When reading a newspaper, you generally first read:
    a. reviews by critics.
    b. gossip columns.
    c. comic page.
    d. editorial and features page.
    e. sports pages.
    f. business section and stock-market pages.

5. You would like your friends to see you:
   a.   at a modern dance performance.
   b.   in the second row on opening night at the opera.
   c.   at a political rally.
   d.   at a lecture.
   e.   at a tennis match or a football game.
   f.   buying a mink coat in an exclusive store.

6. You would like to tell your friends you have met:
   a.   Ernest Hemingway.
   b.   Queen Elizabeth.
   c.   Nancy Sinatra.
   d.   Albert Einstein.
   e. · Muhammad Ali.
   f.   Aristotle Onassis.

7. You would prefer to play:
   a.   charades.
   b.   bridge.
   c.   poker.
   d.   chess.
   e.   Ping-Pong.
   f.   roulette.

8. You would prefer to eat:
   a.   in a small restaurant with atmosphere.
   b.   in the dining room of a major hotel.
   c.   a good meal at sensible prices.
   d.   any place with a good conversationalist.
   e.   a picnic lunch by a roaring river.
   f.   in your hotel suite, being served by room service.

If you have four or more a. replies, you are probably an artistic snob. You are most comfortable with artists and will have to watch that you are not too impatient with those who do not share your interests.

Four or more b. replies indicate that you are a social snob, a name dropper, and a social climber. Balance your desires by doing good for those who are less fortunate than you. You will find that many whom you may think are "beneath you" have great talents and virtues.

Four or more c. answers: Hah, we caught you. You think you are not a snob, but just an average, normal person! You are, however, a snob about snobbery.

Four or more d. answers hint broadly that you are an intellectual snob. Mental improvement and increased knowledge are to be admired, but, like the artistic snob, watch that you do not frighten people away from you, or you'll find your tomb in the dark corner of some library.

Four or more e. answers and you are a sports snob. This is fine if you don't bore your friends by quoting football scores and racing results.

Four or more f. answers label you as a probable financial snob. If this is true, curb your desires to flash your money around and to judge everything in terms of its price. Remember: Money isn't everything . . . just almost!

It is likely that you scored two or three in several groups. This does not mean that you're not a snob. It merely shows that you are a "well-rounded" member of snobbery.

Are You a Nagger?

In our culture, the word "nagging" is usually applied to wives. Yet there are husbands who nag, children who constantly demand, and teachers who pick at students in their classrooms. Nagging is different from complaining. A chronic complainer fusses about such things as health, weather, food, taxes, and living environment. Naggers needle others in order to get what they want done or think should be done. This test may give you some insights as to whether or not you nag too much.

1. Please answer honestly. Which of the two drawings below do you think best describes, in general, your personality? This question requires serious thought.

   a _____   b _____

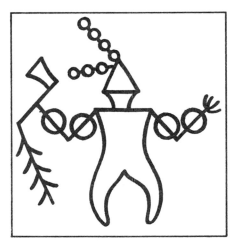

A   B

Please answer the following questions:

2. Are you aware of the abilities, talents, and intelligence of those with whom you deal, either at home or on a working level?

Yes _____   No _____

3. Are you happy with your life?

Yes _____   No _____

4. Are you mindful of a time schedule for yourself and for others?

Yes _____   No _____

5. Does it serve your own purposes to make others feel inferior?

Yes _____   No _____

6. Do you often criticize the grooming and appearance of others?

Yes _____   No _____

7. Do you repeatedly mention the things you do not have?

Yes _____   No _____

8. If you have a request, can you back up that request with several definite, sensible reasons for wanting it carried out?

Yes _____   No _____

9. When you make a request, do you wait until you think the moment is right?

Yes _____   No _____

10. Is it easy for you to do favors for family, friends, and associates— things beyond the call of duty?

Yes _____   No _____

11. If you want something done, can you usually think of at least three ways of accomplishing it?

Yes _____   No _____

12. Are you as polite to members of your family as you are to strangers?

Yes _____   No _____

13. Are you prone to compare negatively those in your family or on the job with someone else you know or knew?

Yes _____   No _____

14. If you are repetitious in your demands, do you think it is a way of getting a constructive point across?

Yes _____   No _____

SCORING

1. Under psychological testing conditions, those who selected a. did not nag but got things done with understanding and co-operative attitudes. Those who selected b. often admitted they nagged because they had no other way of solving their problems. Nagging seemed to be their way of making people work for them. (a–0; B–10)

2.	Yes–0; No–10	9.	Yes–0; No–10
3.	Yes–0; No–10	10.	Yes–0; No–10
4.	Yes–0; No–10	11.	Yes–0; No–10
5.	Yes–10; No–0	12.	Yes–0; No–10
6.	Yes–10; No–0	13.	Yes–10; No–0
7.	Yes–10; No–0	14.	Yes–10; No–0
8.	Yes–0; No–10		

YOUR SCORE

100–140:   Those testees in this bracket are prone to nag. They want what they want when they want it and have little tact or sense of emotional timing.

50–90:   This score is rated by those who nag when they feel a cause is right. Many times, however, they do not set the proper standards for themselves in order to gain attention and respect.

0–40:   Testees in this bracket were not rated by their families or friends as being naggers. In general, they were understanding people.

Are You an Extrovert or an Introvert?

Psychologists name three types of people when defining our relationships with others. There is the extrovert, who is the life of every group. Then there's the introvert, who keeps his thoughts to himself. And between them is the ambivert, who shares the traits of the other two.

This lively quiz will help you learn what kind of "vert" you are. Just select the response you think is nearest your own.

Once you know what type you are, you can adjust your personality to what you want to become; or stay as you are and be happy about it. It takes all kinds to make a world.

1. A friend invites you to a barbecue. When you arrive, she is not there and you don't know any of the guests. You would:
    a. introduce yourself.
    b. stay on the sidelines until someone else breaks the ice.
    c. step in as acting host or hostess until she returns.

2. A traffic officer stops you and says, "This is Moosetown, not a racetrack. I'll see you in court." As he writes the speeding ticket, you would:
    a. swallow hard and wait for the ticket.
    b. tell him to make it light because you'll never speed again.
    c. try to bluff him out of the ticket.

3. You have extra money to spend on clothing. You would:
    a. select only items that blend with your present wardrobe.
    b. buy some far-out new styles.
    c. shop for apparel that would give a new spark to what you now have.

4. At a dinner party, one guest monopolizes the conversation. You would:
    a. try to shut him up by taking over the floor yourself with a sort of "can you top this?" attitude.
    b. retreat into your own thoughts.
    c. encourage others to express themselves.

5. A person is given a promotion that you had hoped would be yours. You would:
    a. go to the boss and tell him or her how you feel.
    b. try to analyze how this sort of thing can be avoided in the future.
    c. accept the decision as something beyond your control.

6. You are asked to make a speech before a civic group. You would:
   a. be shy and refuse.
   b. prepare a speech and read it.
   c. jump at the chance to be heard.

7. You enjoy a field of specialized knowledge, such as minerology or astronomy. You would:
   a. willingly discuss it when asked.
   b. make a point of bringing the conversation around to the subject whenever possible.
   c. feel reluctant to speak of your pet interest.

8. When you evaluate your role in life, you honestly think:
   a. everything would be fairly difficult for others without you.
   b. you are indispensable.
   c. you could be replaced with relative ease.

9. Assume the pay is the same for all the jobs listed below and you have the talents required. You are asked to become involved in the movie-television business. You would prefer:
   a. to be a scriptwriter and work at home.
   b. to be an actor in an important role.
   c. to be the director-producer on the set.

10. Your boss has just given an order that you know will result in the loss of money for the business. You would:
    a. talk to him or her directly and explain the flaws as you see them.
    b. follow the orders because a boss is a boss.
    c. explain your thinking to someone close to the boss, hoping he'll hear it sooner or later.

11. You have an entertainment fund for your friends. You would:
    a. be reluctant to use it.
    b. spend it all on one gala affair.
    c. budget for a number of small dinners, shows, games, etc.

12. You are late in arriving for a group affair, such as the theater. Your reserved seat is in the front row. You would:
    a. stand in the rear to avoid disturbing others.
    b. take your seat because it is your place.
    c. wait for an intermission or pause and then take your seat.

13. You are an unknown in the presence of a celebrity. You would:
    a. maneuver yourself into a position where you most likely will be introduced.
    b. hope to catch his or her eye and be singled out.
    c. slip away as soon as possible.

14. Suppose you are corresponding with a person who will vacation in the same country where you once enjoyed yourself. You would write something like:
    a. "I had a super time in Nutslandia. Came home with a tan and suitcases full of native clothes."
    b. "The people and the customs of Nutslandia are fascinating. Everyone tried successfully to make our stay pleasant."
    c. "The experiences in Nutslandia make one think to evaluate our standards. Even if one feels a bit out of place at first, the feeling soon wears off."

15. Suppose you were physically handicapped and found yourself in the company of other newly handicapped people. You would:
    a. shrink from them.
    b. be more than willing to share your experience to overcoming your own problem.
    c. answer questions if and when asked.

16. If money were no object and you were buying a new car, you would:
    a. select a sleek, expensive foreign make.
    b. buy a conservative, tried-and-true, no-frills, long-lasting model.
    c. purchase a sensible car with all the added comforts, such as air conditioning, tinted glass, clock, radio, stereo hookup, etc.

17. You are going to an important affair with your date or mate. You hope she or he will:
    a. be more attractive than you, thus taking attention away from you.
    b. be less attractive than you.
    c. be on a par with you in appearance, wit, and demeanor.

18. You tell a joke on yourself. You would:
    a. usually come out on top as sort of a hero or heroine.
    b. verbally paint yourself as the victim of your own stupidity.
    c. tell it as it was with no self-editorializing.

19. You hit your thumb with a hammer or stub your toe. You would:
    a. let everyone know how much it hurts, ask for first aid and sympathy.

b. suffer in silence.

c. ask others to fill in for you until you can take care of the injury.

20. Shown below are three line drawings of people. Which best describes your normal mood toward life?

A   B   C

SCORING

1. a–4; b–2; c–6
2. a–2; b–4; c–6
3. a–2; b–6; c–4
4. a–6; b–2; c–4
5. a–6; b–4; c–2
6. a–2; b–4; c–6
7. a–4; b–6; c–2
8. a–4; b–6; c–2
9. a–2; b–6; c–4
10. a–6; b–2; c–4
11. a–2; b–6; c–4
12. a–2; b–6; c–4
13. a–6; b–4; c–2
14. a–6; b–4; c–2
15. a–2; b–6; c–4
16. a–6; b–2; c–4
17. a–2; b–6; c–4
18. a–6; b–2; c–4
19. a–6; b–2; c–4
20. a–6; b–4; c–2

WHAT YOUR SCORE MEANS:

100–120: You have an extroverted leadership personality, outgoing, vocal, fearless on the surface. You are great in any field of salesmanship, politics, on the stage, in the pulpit. You can talk yourself out of most situations. You may seem rude to others.

80–98: You are mildly extroverted. You need to be the center of attraction but aren't blustery. You give joy to the world. Don't worry if some of your gestures are turned aside or misunderstood.

58–78:   You are thoughtful but secure in your behavior. You are willing and able to take on the role of leadership or followship . . . to be onstage or to be part of the audience.

40–56:   You have an introverted personality. For the benefit of others, let your talents and your ideas break through. You've got a lot to give.

How Responsive Are You?

The amount of satisfaction we get from life depends on what we put into it. Some of us "sit back" and wait for it to come to us, while others expect other people to give it to them. We derive little, if any, satisfaction and interest if we do not respond to life and its demands on us and are not equally responsive to those around us. Here is a test to try. Answer "Yes" or "No" to the questions before turning to the scoring key at the end.

1. Do you enjoy meeting people?
2. Do you find it easy to talk and to be friendly?
3. Are there always plenty of things you can talk about?
4. Are you sufficiently interested to remember what people say about themselves and their interests?
5. Are you good at remembering faces and names?
6. Do you usually associate the right face with the right name?
7. Do you miss people when they are not around and inquire after them?
8. Are you good at getting on with different types of people?
9. Would you be quick to help a stranger and the shy or socially awkward person?
10. Are you patient with old people and good with children?
11. Are you quick to spot any jobs that need doing and offer to help?
12. Do you seem to know instinctively when somebody wants to be friendly?
13. Do you "warm up" in a friendly convivial atmosphere so that you are at your best in the social sense?
14. Do you go out expecting to enjoy yourself and in the frame of mind to help the fun along?
15. Are you often enthusiastic?

16. Are you an encourager of new ideas and activities?

17. Are you a patient, sympathetic, interested listener?

18. Are you good at sensing when people are tired, or not well, and want to be quiet?

19. Are you good at sensing when the atmosphere is getting strained and changing the subject?

20. Do you hate seeing people unhappy and want to do something about it?

SCORING

Count 5 points for every "Yes." A score over 70 is good; 60–70 may be counted satisfactory. In this test, under 60 is not satisfactory.

If you have a low score, it could be that you are too much concerned with yourself to bother about anything else. You could, for example, be seeing everything that happens around you strictly in relation to yourself and its effect on *me*.

This attitude develops an insensitivity to other people so that you may hurt or antagonize them without realizing it; or you can miss something important, like an opportunity or a new development.

How Do You React to Life's Problems?

We can make things harder for ourselves by the way we react. For example, we may act unwisely on impulse, or in an unguarded manner through emotion, leaving ourselves open to misunderstanding or a bad mistake.

Or we can feel that we have to react in a way that will save face, regardless of what we should really do.

Sometimes we just do not bother to think, and make no attempt to understand ourselves, let alone other people.

Try this test by putting a tick against the way you would react to the following situations. Then turn to the scoring key at the end.

1. You are tired and fed up:
    a. Get irritable, impatient, bad-tempered. Take it out on other people.

b. Ask yourself why. Try to understand yourself and keep yourself in hand. Is there something you can do about it, like taking it easy, varying routine, doing something different for a break and a change?

c. I must be ill even though the doctor says there is nothing wrong. No one appreciates me. They ought to sympathize more.

2. You are among unfriendly people:

a. I can be just as unfriendly.

b. Stay polite, helpful, approachable. If they choose to change their attitude I will meet them more than halfway.

c. There must be something wrong with me.

3. You are being flattered and you know it:

a. Impatience. Embarrassment. For goodness sake, cut it out!

b. How much do you want to borrow? Enjoy it and be amused without taking it seriously.

c. How lovely if they meant it. But of course they don't.

4. You are disappointed in someone or something:

a. It is somebody else's fault, or somebody else has been favored.

b. What went wrong? If it is just one of those things, accept it with good grace. Learn from a mistake or error of judgment.

c. Everything I do goes wrong; or something always happens to spoil it.

5. There is a misunderstanding:

a. If that is how you feel, we are through!

b. Let us try to discuss it quietly. I am ready to listen to you if you will listen to me.

c. Perhaps if I pretend not to notice, it will blow over.

6. You know you are being unreasonable, perhaps expecting too much:

a. I don't care. This is what I want. I won't settle for less.

b. Sorry, I must be a bit on edge. Give me time to think it over.

c. It is your fault!

7. Somebody else is being unreasonable:

a. You are wrong and you are going to admit it.

b. Sorry, I cannot agree. Shall we leave it for the time being? Or shall we agree to differ?

c. Have it your own way. Anything to keep the peace.

8. A friend is in trouble:
    a. Too bad and I'm sorry, but trouble comes to us all in turn. You have to put up with it.
    b. I'd just like to say how sorry I am. Can I do anything?
    c. Keep out of sight because they won't want to see anybody. And there's nothing I can do.

9. You have to make an important decision:
    a. What I want to do. Or whatever is quickest and easiest. Or what friends want me to do.
    b. Take enough time to think it out. Keep a cool head. Weigh up the points for and those against. Listen to competent advice. Take the long view. Stick to what I decide.
    c. Run around asking everyone what they would do. Postpone deciding for as long as I possibly can. If possible, get someone else to decide for me.

10. You have to refuse a loved one or a close friend:
    a. Sorry, but that is how it is. If you don't like it, you'll have to do the other thing.
    b. I know you like me too much to want me to do something that I honestly feel I cannot do, or should not do.
    c. Because it is you, I will do it. But it is against my better judgment, so do not blame me if anything goes wrong.

SCORING

Count 10 points for every ticked b. A score of 70 is good; 60–70 is satisfactory; 50–60 is fair; under 50 is poor. Keep this test by you and use it from time to time to check on yourself.

How Are Your Speech Habits?

Our chief means of communication with people is through the medium of speech. The way we speak, our manner as we speak, the words we use, and our tone of voice give people a favorable or an unfavorable impression.

Slovenly, ungrammatical speech usually handicaps us in a career. An abrupt manner of speaking hurts or angers people. A pleasant voice indicates a pleasant person.

Here is a test to try on yourself. Answer "Yes" or "No" to the questions before turning to the scoring key at the end.

1. Do you make a habit of using your lips and tongue actively, and speaking clearly and distinctly?
2. Do you regard it as important to speak grammatically?
3. Do you pitch your voice correctly so that you neither squeak nor growl, and can go on talking without any sense of strain?
4. Do you refrain from mumbling and dropping your voice at the end of sentences?
5. Are you voice-conscious, aware of nice voices in other people, and do you seek to improve your own?
6. Are you precise in your choice of words, and in keeping to the point, so that your meaning is not lost?
7. Do you look at the person to whom you are talking, or who is talking to you?
8. Do you allow the person to finish what he or she wants to say?
9. Do you listen so that you really know what he or she is talking about?
10. Do you show pleasure when you meet and greet people?
11. Have you a friendly, approachable manner?
12. Can you control moody feelings so that you are not talkative one day and silent the next?
13. Do you avoid depressing, gloomy, morbid subjects?
14. Do you avoid keeping on about your troubles?
15. Do you try to cheer up people when they tell you about their troubles?
16. Are you quick to express praise, appreciation, sympathy, congratulations, affection?
17. Do you hold back that clever wisecrack and swallow that smart retort when they may hurt somebody?
18. Do you curb any tendency to be sarcastic?

19. Do you refrain from spiteful and malicious gossip and discourage it in others?

20. Do you try to be kind and encouraging in all your remarks?

SCORING

Count 5 points for every "Yes." A score of 70 or over is good, and 50 to 65 may be counted satisfactory. Under 50 is not satisfactory.

You can improve your speech by reading aloud. Make a tape recording from time to time, and listen to yourself. It would help to join a discussion group or drama club.

Your manner and your type of conversation will depend largely on your emotional attitude. If you like people, you will not want to hurt them, and it will be natural to be kind and encouraging.

YOU
AND YOUR
LOVE LIFE

How's Your Love Life?

Before you change your toothpaste, try this fun quiz. It's designed to help you evaluate and understand your love life and your ability to put it in life's proper perspective.

1. When you meet a person for the first time, you wonder:
   a. if he or she should be cultivated as a friend.
   b. how this person would react in bed.
   c. how you can "pick" his or her brain to better your own interests.

2. When a member of the opposite sex gives you a present, you hope it is:
   a. something practical.
   b. something elegant that will enhance your personal appearance.
   c. something you can both enjoy.

3. When you talk to people you usually look:
   a. away.
   b. into their eyes.
   c. at their mouth.

4. When you come across a sexy magazine, you:
   a. throw it away.
   b. read it because it really turns you on.
   c. find it vaguely amusing.

5. You consider lovemaking:
   a. a positive statement of love.
   b. a negative act.
   c. fun.

6. If you found your love life unsatisfactory while married you would:
   a. change partners.
   b. discuss the problem with your doctor.
   c. find a new hobby, such as sports.

7. You think lovemaking should be:
   a. for mutual satisfaction.
   b. only to carry on the family tree.
   c. enjoyed whenever the mood is right.

8. You:
   a. have a lurking fear of love.
   b. enjoy lovemaking with the right person.
   c. keep looking for novel ways to express your needs.

9. When you become involved in lovemaking, you are happiest when:
   a. the other person is satisfied.
   b. both of you relax with the feeling of fulfillment.
   c. you have been satisfied.

10. You feel current sex education:
    a. lowers moral standards.
    b. is healthy, wholesome.
    c. is great because it encourages greater freedom.

11. You think there should be:
    a. no taboos in lovemaking.
    b. many taboos which, if broken, should be punished.
    c. scientifically established taboos.

12. If you were invited to spend a weekend at a nudist camp, you would:
    a. refuse because the idea is vulgar.
    b. accept for the excitement of it.
    c. accept or decline for the same reasons you would any other invitation.

13. When you buy clothing, you look for:
    a. practical attire.
    b. clothing that displays your body beautiful.

c.   the latest fashions.

14.   Your urge for lovemaking is strongest:
      a.   when the lights are low and the mood romantic.
      b.   any time.
      c.   on a set schedule.

15.   When you give a gift to an attractive person, you:
      a.   feel happy you made the gesture.
      b.   expect to be thanked physically.
      c.   do it because you think he or she expects it of you.

16.   When you take a shower, you:
      a.   enjoy having him or her with you.
      b.   like to have him or her soap your back.
      c.   want to be alone.

17.   If you were choosing a perfume or aftershave on the basis of its name would you buy:
      a.   Spring Breezes.
      b.   Love Potion.
      c.   Just for You.

18.   You resolve quarrels with your lover by:
      a.   an unemotional discussion of the issues.
      b.   walking away until the scene has cooled down.
      c.   forgetting the incident in the flames of passion.

19.   You prefer to sleep:
      a.   in a warm, well-blanketed bed.
      b.   in unironed sheets that smell of sunshine.
      c.   between satin sheets.

SCORING

1.   a–4; b–6; c–2
2.   a–2; b–6; c–4
3.   a–2; b–4; c–6
4.   a–2; b–6; c–4
5.   a–4, b–2; c–6
6.   a–6; b–4; c–2
7.   a–4; b–2; c–6

8.   a–2; b–4; c–6
9.   a–2; b–4; c–6
10.   a–2; b–4; c–6
11.   a–6; b–2; c–4
12.   a–2; b–6; c–4
13.   a–2; b–6; c–4
14.   a–4; b–6; c–2

15.   a–4; b–6; c–2
16.   a–6; b–4; c–2
17.   a–2; b–6; c–4
18.   a–4; b–2; c–6
19.   a–4; b–2; c–6

98–114:   You're far too preoccupied by sex. You miss the many other wonderful things around you. Your attitude is a parallel to those who live to eat rather than eating to live. Cool down—or go to see a doctor.

78–96:   You have more urge than good sense. Don't measure your masculinity or femininity by conquests alone but rather by contentment and peace of mind. You may be insecure in other facets of life.

56–76:   You have a wholesome, normal attitude toward sex. Changing times do not mortify you nor do they cause you to cast aside your own values. You know the difference between sex and love.

40–54:   You are fearful of sex and negatively disposed even to consider the subject. Even if you do not wish to join those who feel that physical love can be beautiful, rewarding, kind, and magnificent, give yourself the chance to consider the possibility.

What's Your Score in the Love Game?

One famous author wrote: "Some say that the spirit of romance is dead," yet another writer assures us: "Romance has been elegantly defined as the offspring of fiction and love." Certainly most of us regard the past as romantic.

Do you think that romance lingers on in this materialistic age? Are you essentially practical-minded, or do you believe in the exciting, thrilling, poetical aspects of the love game?

To find out how you rate as a romantic, place a tick against a, b, or c, then check your score at the end.

1. When the man in your life gives you a present, do you prefer it to be:
   a. tights or cosmetics?
   b. a book or a record?
   c. a bouquet of flowers?

2. If he gives you a small photograph of himself, do you:
   a. push it in a drawer?
   b. keep it in your handbag?
   c. sleep with it under your pillow?

3. What kind of nightie do you wear when no one will be seeing you?
   a. a pretty, flimsy one.
   b. no nightie.
   c. any old one.

4. Which hairstyle would you favor when going to a party with the man in your life?
   a. piled on top.
   b. short and straight.
   c. in ringlets or flowing loosely.

5. When your boyfriend or husband offers to take you to a show on your birthday, would you choose:
   a. a ballet performance?
   b. a good film?
   c. a serious play?

6. If you are cooking a meal for him for the first time, which dish would you choose for the main course:
   a. roast duck with orange?
   b. lamb chops?
   c. scampi?

7. When a strange man is introduced to you, do you prefer him to:
   a. shake your hand?
   b. kiss your hand?
   c. nod and express a greeting?

8. When your man accompanies you for an evening's dancing, what do you like him to wear:
   a. a well-cut dark suit with plain shirt and tie?
   b. casual shirt and jeans?
   c. a colored cord suit with gay shirt and floppy tie?

9. If you are moving into a new home temporarily, which would you prefer:
   a. a houseboat moored on a pleasant river?
   b. a fully-fitted caravan on a site?
   c. an apartment in a high-class block?

10. What do you enjoy reading best:
    a. love stories?
    b. poetry?
    c. thrillers or humorous books?

SCORING

1. a–1; b–2; c–3
2. a–1; b–2; c–3
3. a–3; b–1; c–2
4. a–2; b–1; c–3
5. a–3; b–2; c–1
6. a–2; b–1; c–3
7. a–1; b–3; c–2
8. a–1; b–2; c–3
9. a–3; b–2; c–1
10. a–2; b–3; c–1

SCORE 22–30.

You're a real romantic at heart and this makes the merry-go-round of love and marriage more exciting. But don't get too carried away by flights of fancy and forget the more practical side of living.

SCORING 15–22.

You enjoy a few romantic flutters occasionally, but tend to be materialistic. Remember you're only young once, and a spot of romance does brighten up life. Read a few love stories and borrow some exciting ideas to liven up your image.

SCORE 10–15.

Well, isn't life dull for you? Try to be far more imaginative. Create some interesting illusions to make your boyfriends rave about you. No man goes crazy about a prim, practical girl, so try to relax and enjoy life more. Study the girls who simply ooze romance and acquire some of their expertise.

How Good a Lover Are You?

As every woman knows, it takes more than a handsome hunk of beefcake to make a good lover. Over and above pure physical attractiveness, a man must have a blending of other qualities. First of all, he must have feelings. Not just urges and impulses, but also subtler feelings of tenderness and affection. And, further, he must be free to express these feelings to his beloved. (The strong, silent type may look nice on a movie screen, but he's a bore in the boudoir.)

The good lover—if he is to last long—must be perceptive, too. He must be sensitive to the moods and emotions of his mate. And he must be able to respond spontaneously.

He must possess a basic respect—both for himself and for his beloved. Needless to say, the self-conscious lady-killer with his compulsive conquests is motivated not by love but by neurosis. Whenever the man-woman relationship becomes a competition, love is lost in the battle.

In love, as in life, there is a time to speak and a time to be silent, a time to be bold and a time to be tender, a time to lead and a time to follow. Each attitude has its proper time, and the true lover, without taking thought, will have a sense of this ebb and flow.

A lover must also be able to laugh. Even at himself. A love affair without any laughter would soon sink into a slough of despond.

Now, of course, love is always a mutual feeling. And the man who leaves one lady cold may be another's ideal. One woman's mate is another woman's poison. Thus, in the next quiz, we do not try to grade you against any single inflexible standard. Rather, the test is designed to discover what kind of lover you are. It is a test of quality, not quantity.

At first glance the questions may seem silly to you, and very remote from the subject of love. But this is because the test is planned to peep beneath your conscious attitudes into the deeper trends that pattern your character and your behavior.

If you want to learn something about yourself, answer each question honestly "Yes" or "No." If you find yourself unable to give such a clear-cut reply to some question, mark it as "No."

The quiz is addressed to gentlemen, privately. But the ladies may give it to any man who is willing. (And if he is not willing, she may answer the questions as she thinks he would reply—though such a proxy may contain a large margin for error or argument.)

One last word of warning: Generally your first quick response to a question will be most revealing. Mulling them over too much often muddles things up.

This quiz will analyze your love ability.

A. 1. For your personal car would you choose a Cadillac over all other American makes?

Yes _____   No _____

2. Are you better than average at making long-range plans and following through on them?

Yes _____   No _____

3. Suppose you are a member of a local civic or professional club. Would you like to be elected president of it?

Yes _____   No _____

4. In general do you believe that men are more intelligent than women?

Yes _____   No _____

5. Would you be willing to switch to a different line of work that would be half as much fun but twice as much pay?

Yes _____   No _____

6. Are you adept at convincing other people to see things your way?

Yes _____   No _____

7. If you achieved some unusual success in your hobby, would you like to be publicized in the newspapers and magazines?

Yes _____   No _____

8. If at first you don't succeed, do you try and try again?

Yes _____   No _____

B. 1. Do you try to avoid heated arguments?

Yes _____   No _____

2. On important matters do you usually seek out the advice of your friends?

Yes _____   No _____

3. Do you make a conscientious effort to save money?

Yes _____   No _____

4. Do you dislike giving orders to subordinates and servants?

Yes _____   No _____

5. If you are going to a movie, do you prefer to have a friend along for company?

Yes _____   No _____

6. Do you go out of your way to do favors for others?

Yes _____   No _____

7. When dining with friends in a restaurant, do you prefer to know what they intend to eat before deciding what you will order?

Yes _____   No _____

8. Do you like to be liked even by people whom you do not like?

Yes _____   No _____

C. 1. If you have a report to write, would you prefer to do it yourself rather than collaborate with two associates?

Yes _____   No _____

2. Do you dislike it when someone whom you've just met, deliberately calls you by your first name?

Yes _____   No _____

3. In a game of charades do you much prefer the guessing part to the acting part?

Yes _____   No _____

4. Do you avoid tight belts, starched collars, or snug garters?

Yes _____   No _____

5. Are you more astute than most at analyzing character?

Yes _____   No _____

6. Do you enjoy a group of two or three persons more than a get-together with eight or ten people?

Yes _____   No _____

7. Do you prefer reading to bridge, gin rummy, or canasta?

Yes _____   No _____

8. Are you your own severest critic?

Yes _____   No _____

SCORING

DIRECTIONS:

Give yourself credit for each group in which you answered "Yes" to five or more questions. For example, if you answered "Yes" to six questions in group A, four in group B, and five in group C, your score is AC. Now read on to find the category that corresponds to your own score letters. Then study your analysis.

A.

You are the direct and dominating lover. You are the modern descendant of the old (and now outmoded) school of treat-'em-rough-and-tell-'em-nothing.

In the man-woman relation, you strive to keep the upper hand. You make the decisions, assume the responsibilities. You hate to take "No" for an answer, and you can be a most persistent suitor. You are an impatient Romeo, disliking subtleties and stalling.

You take pride in your sexual prowess. And—in your salad days, at least—you vastly enjoy the chase and the conquest. Sometimes, however, you are not too discriminating in your choice of women. You are likely to be attracted by a pretty face or figure—neglecting to note that the surface beauty camouflages a shrew or a *shnook*. Moreover, you are not overly sensitive in your personal relations and may sometimes alienate the fair lady without ever realizing what you are doing.

In the love relation, the lady is not likely to complain of your ardor. But she may wish for more tenderness and sensitivity to her moods. You are attractive to many women—and with the right one you are capable of a long-lasting relationship.

B.

You are the affectionate, not the aggressive type. It is likely that women have played an important part in your life and that you have come to depend on them. Some of them may want to "mother" you.

You are not primarily interested in sexual exploits—preferring the quiet, comfortable atmosphere of a steady relationship. You are capable of tenderness, but shy away from direct assertiveness. It is not unlikely that at some time you have "loved and lost" because of your disinclination to fight to win your lady love. No taming of the shrew for you.

In your intimate relations you tend to be gentle. You are sensitive to the moods and needs of your partner and anxious to please.

You have some tendency to overidealize your love—and this can lead to rude disillusionment. But you are resilient enough to recover from such a letdown.

You are casual and comfortable with women. They like to have you around. You like them too—and would feel unhappy if you were for long without a lady love.

C.

You are the aloof lover. This seeming coolness and reserve either strongly attracts or drastically repels women—depending on their own makeup.

To the casual observer it might appear that the women seduce you, rather than vice versa. But this is not quite true—since you use subtle and invisible maneuvers to lure them in.

You may be more interested in sex than in love. At any rate you seldom openly express real feelings of affection. And, too, you seem to have some fear of a really intimate entanglement.

You can be very charming, and you secretly like to test your powers of attraction. Sometimes it seems that you are more interested in proving your attractiveness than you are in actually making love. With the right girl, you'll "love and honor" but will balk at "obey."

A B.

Your love life would seem to be somewhat beset with inner conflict. Although you have a strong wish to conquer and dominate women, you do not feel really free to assert yourself, for you also have a need to be agreeable and appeasing with the woman you love.

It may be that you shift from one mood to the other. If your partner's moods are flexible, the result may be a pleasant variety.

On the other hand, you may put one aspect of your character out front and hide the other half from public view. The trouble with this is that the hidden half will have a tendency to pop into view in moments of intense intimacy. Thus if you have wooed a woman boldly, she may be disconcerted to find you turning soft and boyish at the final crucial moment. Or some teasing lass may be taken aback when, dropping your cloak of sweet reasonableness, you unexpectedly punch her one.

Happily you are not likely to linger long at either of these extremes, but will live a love life that blends both the dominating and the dependent aspects in a relationship of give-and-take.

A C.

Although we don't want to cry "Wolf! Wolf!" still it must be noted that the most successful lady-killers from Casanova to Cellini have had characters similar to yours.

While this does not necessarily make you a rake, it does suggest that you have tendencies toward loving and leaving. A reluctant lady presents a challenge to you. You like to test your powers just for the hell of it. But you are somewhat reluctant to enter into a truly intimate and long-lasting relationship. In the matter of give-and-take, you have a hidden urge to take more than you give. Many women find this quite attractive—a fact we will leave to sexologists for explanation.

Now we don't mean to paint too melodramatic a picture of you. It is quite likely that your actual behavior is all that Emily Post and the Marquis of Queensberry could ever ask for. But this is due to your own self-discipline, which safely subdues the gypsy in your soul.

B C.

You approach the love relationship with shyness or, maybe, just plain caution. You seem to be seeking the perfect, but nonexistent, Juliet.

You evade or avoid the overbold ladies, yet you seldom summon up enough boldness of your own to pursue the more elusive lasses. When you do find a woman who is not too hot, not too cold, you approach her with much sensitivity and considerable reserve. But for all this, you do have a large capacity for affection and tenderness.

You have more trouble finding a suitable mate than do many of your fellow men. But you are patient and persistent in the search.

The women you woo may wish, at first, that you would be more direct and outspoken. But as time goes by they discover the hidden warmth behind your cautious facade. It's just that you take it slowly.

A B C. OR NO LETTER

With apologies we admit that we cannot fathom you. Either you are an ideally well-balanced fellow (in which case you won't worry about what our analysis might be), or else you did not answer with enough care and candor (in which case you might recheck your replies).

Does Your Partner Love You?

Love means many things to many people. How do you know if he or she loves you?

It's easy to say, "I love you," but living the role of a lover is quite another matter. This quiz will give you some tips that are more revealing than picking petals off daisies.

1. In our daily life, most important decisions are made:
   a. jointly.
   b. by my partner.
   c. by me.

2. The dress standard and general grooming of my partner has:
   a. remained about the same.
   b. deteriorated.
   c. improved.

3. My partner usually reacts to my efforts:
   a. with stony silence.
   b. with negative criticism.
   c. with praise.

4. In my opinion, my partner:
   a. is more concerned about himself (or herself) than about me.
   b. focuses most of his (or her) attention toward my happiness and well-being.
   c. looks out for the welfare of us both.

5. In the back of my mind, I feel my partner:
   a. is searching for affection from someone other than myself.
   b. has put aside past romantic ties.
   c. still has memories of another love.

6. When I am ill or feeling down, my partner:
   a. becomes angry and/or upset.
   b. is especially attentive and tender.
   c. leaves me alone until I feel better.

7. Being human, I have some "sore points," perhaps about physical flaws or past mistakes. My partner:
   a. listens to my woes.
   b. holds them over my head constantly.
   c. might bring them up when angry.

8. My partner and I:
   a. handle money about the same.
   b. argue over spending.
   c. argue because I am extravagant.

9. When it comes to our mutual associations with people:
   a. he (or she) can't stand to be around most of my associates.
   b. he (or she) likes most of them.
   c. he (or she) endures them with reservations.

10. My date (or mate):
    a. feels free to invade my privacy in such ways as opening my mail and reading my diary.
    b. never pries into my private belongings or private life.
    c. sometimes asks to see items, such as checks or mail, or to know my activities.

11. When it comes to schedules, such as mealtimes, work, or appointments, my partner:
    a. seldom keeps me waiting.
    b. nearly always has an excuse to be late.
    c. is usually a wee bit ahead of time.

12. In our home life, my partner:
    a. expects me to do the major part of all the different kinds of work.
    b. is adjustable and likes to share home responsibilities.
    c. does the lion's share.

13. My partner seems to enjoy:
    a. praising me to others.
    b. comparing me unfavorably to others.
    c. telling jokes or making remarks that embarrass or belittle me.

14. In our lovemaking:
    a. he (or she) seems to be preoccupied by his (or her) own fulfillment.
    b. we find deep mutual satisfaction.
    c. he (or she) sometimes sacrifices his (or her) satisfaction to please me.

15. When our needs for solitude, amount of rest, or working schedule vary, my partner:
    a. complains.

   b. is understanding of my pattern.

   c. suffers in silence.

16. My date (or mate):

   a. except in a rare case of emergency, keeps me informed about his (or her) schedule so I won't worry.

   b. goes on his (or her) own way, leaving me in the dark.

   c. is consistent in his (or her) routine.

17. When my date (or mate) is with a member of the opposite sex, he (or she):

   a. is pleasant and charming.

   b. is prone to play the role of a sex symbol.

   c. retires into his (or her) social shell.

18. When I honestly evaluate our relationship, I think my partner:

   a. thinks of me primarily as a worker.

   b. is primarily concerned with me as a lover and/or parent of our offspring.

   c. considers me as a helpmate, friend, and lover.

19. In my considered opinion, I think my partner:

   a. lacks ambition.

   b. is highly motivated to be a great success at any price.

   c. works to get ahead at a normal, healthy pace.

20. Of the three abstract drawings below I think our love relationship is best described by the "feeling" I get when I look at: a, b, or c.

A

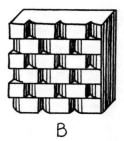
B

C

SCORING

HOW TO SCORE:

1.	a–6; b–4; c–4	11.	a–6; b–2; c–6
2.	a–4; b–2; c–6	12.	a–2; b–6; c–4
3.	a–2; b–2; c–6	13.	a–6; b–2; c–2
4.	a–2; b–4; c–6	14.	a–2; b–6; c–4
5.	a–2; b–6; c–4	15.	a–2; b–6; c–4
6.	a–2; b–6; c–4	16.	a–6; b–2; c–2
7.	a–6; b–2; c–4	17.	a–6; b–2; c–4
8.	a–6; b–2; c–2	18.	a–2; b–4; c–6
9.	a–2; b–6; c–4	19.	a–2; b–2; c–6
10.	a–2; b–6; c–4	20.	a–4; b–6; c–2

WHAT YOUR SCORE MEANS:

100–120: You can be pretty sure your partner loves you in a deep, satisfying way. You probably noticed the questions did not mention gifts or remembering birthdays, because these are the frosting on the cake, nice but not necessarily the gesture of real love such as being there when needed. Love is a two-way bridge.

80–98: You have racked up a better-than-average assurance that he (or she) loves you. Some people lack the ability or are too shy to show their true feelings in the little everyday ways. Hang in there and let your own warmth and consideration be examples to your partner.

58–78: This rating is a little tricky. Better evaluate whether or not you are inspiring the respect and friendship that are the bases of love. If you are sticking with your partner with the idea of changing him (or her), forget it. But it might be profitable for the two of you to have a rational evaluation of your time together.

40–56: This is a no-love score. You are building scars for yourself if you persist in being around your partner. There are some people, however, who seem to enjoy being used, and you may get your kicks out of being misused.

Will He Love You Forever?

Some women have that special quality that keeps their man devoted for decades. Are you one of them? This quiz will tell you.

1. Your mate acts stupidly and you are furious. Do you:
   a. enjoy the luxury of a good explosion?
   b. maintain a tight-lipped tolerance?
   c. express your feelings in a calm, loving manner?

2. You married for:
   a. love.
   c. children.
   c. status.

3. Your mate still hasn't finished installing your closet shelves. Do you:
   a. get in a professional?
   b. offer to help him?
   c. nag?

4. You've had your family. Do you sleep:
   a. in separate rooms?
   b. in twin beds in the same room?
   c. in each other's arms?

5. Years ago your mate had a flirtation. Now, do you feel:
   a. you've forgotten it?
   b. it can still give you a pang now and then?
   c. you can use it as a weapon in an argument?

6. Would you say that in general you speak more or less courteously to your mate than to other people?
   a. more.
   b. less.
   c. the same.

7. Your mate has an annoying habit—harmless, but it sends you up the wall. Do you:
   a. point it out on every occasion?
   b. try to learn to live with it? (after all, he's probably trying to live with one of yours)
   c. ask your mate whether you have an annoying habit that you could shed for him in exchange for his shedding this one for you?

8. Do you believe:
   a. you're very lucky to have married your mate?
   b. your mate should be grateful to you?
   c. you are both lucky to have found each other?

9. After several years of marriage, your mate is still very affectionate. Do you:
   a. tell him not to be so silly?
   b. tolerate him with a smile?
   c. return your mate's affection with enthusiasm?

10. Your best friend warns you that your mate may be wandering. How do you react?
    a. Yell at him, "How dare you treat me like this!"
    b. Get your mate to express his feelings of anger, hurt, and dissatisfaction with your relationship.
    c. Say smugly, "So long as I love him, I've nothing to worry about."

11. You know your mate hates watching television on his own, but there's a boring program on. Do you:
    a. snuggle up to him because there are times that you want him to do something that he dislikes to do?
    b. go to bed?
    c. stay, but work on something that you like to do while the show is going on?

12. Have you let your appearance go since you married?
    a. "Yes, but I've got a good excuse."
    b. "No. Looking nice is very important."
    c. "I must admit, sometimes I'm a sloppy dresser."

13. Without warning, your mate turns up with a guest. Do you:
    a. make the guest feel welcome because you also enjoy bringing guests home on the spur of the moment?
    b. make the guest feel welcome, but suggest to your mate afterward in a loving way that both of you should always phone the other before bringing a guest home?
    c. tell your mate to take the guest elsewhere?

14. For your tenth wedding anniversary your mate buys you a sexy piece of clothing. Do you:

a. get annoyed at the waste of money?

b. ask if you can exchange it?

c. feel terribly flattered?

15. When did you last tell your mate that you loved him?

a. the last time he told you?

b. you can't remember?

c. within the last twenty-four hours?

SCORING

POINTS:

1.	a–1; b–0; c–2	9.	a–0; b–1; c–2
2.	a–2; b–1; c–0	10.	a–0; b–2; c–1
3.	a–1; b–2; c–0	11.	a–2; b–0; c–2
4.	a–0; b–1; c–2	12.	a–0; b–2; c–2
5.	a–2; b–1; c–0	13.	a–1; b–2; c–0
6.	a–2; b–0; c–1	14.	a–0; b–1; c–2
7.	a–0; b–1; c–2	15.	a–1; b–0; c–2
8.	a–1; b–0; c–2		

HOW DO YOU RATE?

21–30. Should you lose your mate's love, it will be through no fault of your own. You are instinctively warmhearted and generous in almost any situation, and you have it in you to make a true marriage.

Now give the quiz to your mate. If his score is as high as yours, your relationship will undoubtedly grow more satisfying with the years.

11–20. You'd like to be kinder but it's an uphill struggle. Things can get on top of you, and you lose track of why you married. If your mate's score on this quiz falls into this category, too, then both of you are involved in a relationship wherein the two of you are getting pushed to the bottom of the pile by things that seem more urgent at the time.

0–10. What did you have in mind when you married? A marriage or a battleground?

YOU
AND YOUR
MOODS

How Happy Are You?

Nobody can expect to be happy all the time, and we are happier on some days than on others. But what we are concerned with here is happiness in its truest sense: the ability to gain real satisfaction from life.

The purpose of this test is to gauge how well you do this. Answer "Yes" or "No" to the questions before turning to the scoring key at the end.

1. Do you think that most people like you?
2. Do you find it easy to like most people?
3. Do you enjoy seeing others enjoying themselves and getting on in the world?
4. Do you like being among people, sharing interest and activity, going out socially?
5. Is it reasonably easy for you to get to know people and make friends?
6. Can you hold a conversation without becoming tense?
7. Do you sometimes become so interested that you forget about the other people there, and become completely unself-conscious?
8. Do you quite enjoy being the center of attention, having people looking at you, pointing you out, and listening to what you say?
9. Conversely, would you enjoy yourself just as much if the spotlight were turned on somebody else and you were ignored?
10. Do you often invite people to your home?

11. Are you pleased when a friend is praised in your presence?
12. Can you be friendly and sociable with the opposite sex without any feeling of awkwardness and strain?
13. Are you happily married? If you are unmarried, are you facing up to this honestly so that you are conscious of no serious frustration?
14. Have you at least one really absorbing interest?
15. Can you take criticism and instructions in a good spirit?
16. Does a failure or a difficult job spur you on to further effort?
17. Do you think that your job is useful and worthwhile?
18. Is it the job you wanted to do? If not, are you sufficiently interested in it to want to do it well?
19. Can you enjoy a joke against yourself?
20. Do you regard yourself as quite attractive and personable?

SCORING

Count 5 points for every "Yes." You may be able to score full marks, but a score of 70 or over may be regarded as good. Under 60 is not satisfactory.

This test covers the main aspects of being a genuinely happy person, someone capable of gaining real satisfaction from life. By going to work on any "No" answer you can use it to help you put right a tendency, or tendencies, that could make you unhappy.

Take, for example, the first question. If you think that most people dislike you, you will be on your guard with them, quick to see slights. If you react like this, there is something wrong with your attitude. Why have you come to believe that people do not like you?

Try to understand yourself. Counter the feeling by making the most of yourself. Become the kind of person you like—sympathetic, interested, understanding, generous.

Are You Moody?

We all have our moods. Without the depressions and elations of life, we would be uncreative, dull human beings. The word "moody" suggests a sullen, unhappy introspection. Some of us seem to be more affected by emotional depressions than others. This test will help you understand yourself and your moods.

1. Study the drawing below and give the reaction nearest your own.

    a.   It makes me sad _____

    b.   I don't understand what it is all about _____

    c.   It is funny _____

2. When the sky is overcast I feel unhappy.

            Yes _____   No _____

3. I often wonder if there is a hidden meaning in conversations or letters.

            Yes _____   No _____

4. I try to find excuses to avoid going to a funeral.

            Yes _____   No _____

5. I tend to stare down rather than to look up.

            Yes _____   No _____

6. I often ask myself: "What's wrong with me?"

Yes _____   No _____

7. I prefer mood music rather than rock.

Yes _____   No _____

8. If I had a choice, my living quarters would be dominated by warm colors such as yellow, red, brown, or gold.

Yes _____   No _____

9. News items that report murders, sex crimes, drug addiction, and violence hold a fascination for me.

Yes _____   No _____

10. When something hurts me psychologically, I would rather bear the pain silently than to tell those close to me.

Yes _____   No _____

11. It is difficult for me to forget heated arguments.

Yes_____   No _____

12. When events do not go my way I swallow down my discontent.

Yes _____   No _____

SCORING

1. Under psychological testing conditions, those who were of a moody nature reacted with sadness (a–10 points) to the drawing. Those who were more optimistic and less prone to unhappy emotions, selected b (3 points) as an answer. Those who were amused selected c (0 point).

2. Yes–10; No–0   8. Yes–0; No–10
3. Yes–10; No–0   9. Yes–10; No–0
4. Yes–10; No–0   10. Yes–10; No–0
5. Yes–10; No–0   11. Yes–10; No–0
6. Yes–10; No–0   12. Yes–10; No–0
7. Yes–10; No–0

YOUR SCORE:

90–120:   Testees in this bracket are moody people who dwell within their own thoughts and tend to find their introspections of an unhappy nature. It is not unusual for them to put the blame on others.

50–83:   This, according to studies, is an average range and one that is scored by those who believe that life is real and life is honest. They look upon each day with a kind of solemnity and evaluation.

0–43:   This bracket is indicative of those who live life to the hilt without taking stock of where they are going.

Are You Ruled by Your Emotions?

Your emotions to a very large extent determine the type of person you are—warm and loving or cold and reserved, imaginative or practical, conscientious or casual. To know your emotions is to know yourself and how to find happiness in life—whether to reach out for the stars or to seek contentment in simple things. You can discover your emotional strengths and weaknesses by answering the following questions. Divided into three sections—A, B, and C—they are simple and straightforward. But they are psychologically devised—if you answer them honestly—to tell whether you are ruled by your heart or your head and what you should do about it.

SECTION A

1.   Do you:
    a.   enjoy being with a big crowd of people?
    b.   prefer to be on your own?
    c.   find that sometimes it's one, sometimes the other?

2.   Do you find talking to strangers:
    a.   interesting and enjoyable?
    b.   rather frightening?
    c.   something in between the two?

3.   If a close friend of the opposite sex impulsively embraced you and kissed you in public, would you feel:
    a.   thrilled and delighted?

b.   a bit embarrassed?

c.   something in between?

4.   When something goes wrong for you do you see the funny side of things:

a.   nearly always?

b.   sometimes?

c.   never or hardly ever?

5.   Do you regard sex as:

a.   something to be enjoyed as often as possible?

b.   something to be avoided?

c.   something in between?

6.   You regard marriage as:

a.   old-fashioned and out of date?

b.   a social custom with which it is necessary to conform?

c.   an honorable and worthwhile institution?

SECTION B

1.   Which do you enjoy talking about most:

a.   books, films, plays, opera, ballet?

b.   your job and/or domestic affairs?

c.   or don't you enjoy talking?

2.   Do you regard gambling as:

a.   good fun?

b.   a social evil?

c.   something you can take or leave?

3.   When going to and fro between your home and work or your home and the shops do you:

a.   always go the same way?

b.   sometimes vary it?

c.   often vary it?

4.   Do you daydream:

a.   rather a lot?

b.   sometimes?

c.   never?

5.   Do you get headaches:

a.   fairly frequently?

b.   sometimes?

c. never or hardly ever?

6. In your home do you:
   a. have a place for everything and keep everything in its own place?
   b. never know where anything is?
   c. find that it's a bit of both?

SECTION C
1. In making decisions do you:
   a. make them quickly of your own accord?
   b. seek the advice of others?
   c. find that sometimes it's one, sometimes the other?

2. In conversation do you usually:
   a. do most of the talking?
   b. prefer to listen?
   c. come in somewhere between the two?

3. If you were watching a pornographic stage show would you be:
   a. amused?
   b. shocked?
   c. a bit of both?

4. A complete stranger stops you, tells you she has lost her purse, and asks you to lend her her fare home. She promises to send it back the next day. Assuming you could afford the loan, would you:
   a. lend her the money?
   b. refuse?
   c. or are you not sure?

5. A man has been with his firm for a long time. He is getting old and making mistakes that are costing the firm money. Would you:
   a. discharge him?
   b. say nothing because you are sorry for him?
   c. offer him the alternative of leaving or accepting a less responsible, lower-paid position?

6. You come home unexpectedly and find your wife or husband in the act of kissing the next-door neighbor. Would you:
   a. be so angry you feel like hitting them?
   b. pretend you have seen nothing and say nothing?
   c. react somewhere between these two extremes?

SCORING

HOW TO SCORE:

SECTION A	SECTION B	SECTION C
1. a–3; b–1; c–2	1. a–3; b–2; c–1	1. a–3; b–1; c–2
2. a–3; b–1; c–2	2. a–3; b–1; c–2	2. a–3; b–1; c–2
3. a–3; b–1; c–2	3. a–1; b–2; c–3	3. a–3; b–1; c–2
4. a–3; b–2; c–1	4. a–3; b–2; c–1	4. a–1; b–3; c–2
5. a–3; b–1; c–2	5. a–1; b–2; c–3	5. a–3; b–1; c–2
6. a–3; b–2; c–1	6. a–1; b–3; c–2	6. a–3; b–1; c–2

HOW YOU RATE:

SECTION A

15–18:   You are emotionally warm, outgoing, and uninhibited. You like people and have a cheerful disposition, which makes them like you. You have an easygoing, perhaps rather permissive outlook on life and are ruled largely by your emotions when it comes to love and sex. This can bring you both pleasure and happiness but it can also bring danger.

10–14:   You are well balanced between emotion and reason in the areas concerned. You are neither a pessimist nor an optimist, extrovert nor introvert, neither oversexed nor undersexed, but nicely in the middle. You have the ability to distinguish between good and bad in people, to put your love and trust in the right people, to enjoy life without making a fool of yourself.

6–9:   Emotionally you are rather shy and reserved. You have an old-fashioned sense of honor and morals, which is nothing to be ashamed of. But you are perhaps inclined to be a bit too staid and something of a pessimist. For you, your own company is sufficient. You don't need other people around you, don't like many people, nor make friends easily. This can be a mistake. Try to be a bit more outgoing and look more on the bright side.

SECTION B

15–18:   You are quick-witted and full of bright ideas, imaginative, and probably artistic in some way. You are the sort who will reach for the stars—and may fall short. But you are less likely to fall short if you know your emotional weaknesses and try to let reason do something about them. Your main weakness is that for all your brightness you are emotionally unpredictable. You will sometimes act impulsively and take unnecessary risks and will relax when you should be forging ahead.

10–14: This area of your emotions is nicely balanced between caution and recklessness, the imaginative and the practical. You will perhaps not reach as high as the stars but will get what you want. You are intelligent without being too sharp-witted, and your general attitude is neither too casual nor too controlled.

6–9: You are cautious, self-controlled, conscientious, and essentially practical. It is better for you not to reach for the stars but to live within your own capabilities. Your emotions can also make you tense, sometimes edgy, and sometimes a bit dull, and these are the areas in which you should employ more reason. Try to relax more and widen your interests.

SECTION C

15–18: You are completely self-confident to the point of dominance and perhaps even toughness. You think you know what you want from life and will let nothing stand in your way. You are shrewd to the point of suspicion, as well as sophisticated in your outlook and ideas and perhaps rather quick-tempered.

10–14: You are nicely balanced, neither oversuspicious nor too trusting, neither too tenderhearted nor too tough. You can display anger if sufficiently provoked but are by no means quick-tempered. You are not overassertive but neither are you the kind to let others walk over you. You are nobody's fool.

6–9: You're unsure of yourself, emotionally tenderhearted, mild-mannered, unworldly, and slow to rouse, with a completely trusting nature. You will find abundant pleasure in the simple things of life. But be careful that others do not take advantage of you.

Do You Blow Your Stack Easily?

Do you blow your stack easily? Do little things get you irritated? Are you often angry with other people?

If your answer is "Yes" to any of these questions, you may be suffering from a severe lack of tolerance—which could affect your job, your marriage, and your happiness. This special test reveals your TQ, or Tolerance Quotient, to help you find out how tolerant you are.

In each of the following questions, pick the one answer that relates closest to your feelings:

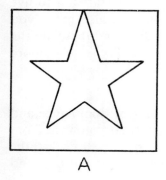 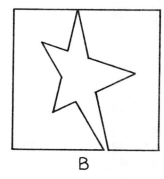 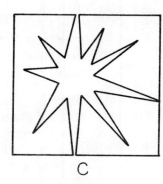

A   B   C

1. Above are three drawings of a star. Which most closely resembles the star you would visualize in a dream: a, b, or c?

2. You have been offered your choice of a house pet. Would you rather have:
    a. a dog?
    b. a cat?
    c. a parakeet?

3. A casual friend is fifteen minutes late for a luncheon date and your time is limited. Do you
    a. make no mention of it when he finally arrives?
    b. ask if his watch is out of order when he does show up?
    c. leave and go someplace else to eat by yourself?

4. Your candidate lost the last election. When the subject of national problems comes up, do you
    a. refrain from telling people how you voted?
    b. remind others that you were smart enough to vote for the loser?
    c. predict the country's downfall because of political mismanagement?

5. The waitress has neglected to bring the cream for your coffee despite two reminders. Do you
   a. drink your coffee black?
   b. reach over to an adjoining table and borrow the cream pitcher?
   c. demand that the coffee be taken off your check?

6. A friend who is always having financial problems is pregnant with her fifth child. Do you
   a. congratulate her?
   b. offer condolences?
   c. warn her she can ill afford the additional responsibility?

7. Your car won't start for the fourth morning in a row even though you've had the repairman check it each time. Do you
   a. call a cab to get to work, resolving to try a new service station?
   b. call the serviceman and tell him you are getting impatient?
   c. threaten to sue the repairman?

8. Your youngest child has "surprised" you while you were away by baking a chocolate cake that is lumpy and tastes odd. Do you
   a. eat a tiny piece and compliment her?
   b. suggest that no baking be done unless you are standing by?
   c. point out that you can't afford to have food supplies wasted?

9. A friend is showing off her home, and you note that her new custom-made drapes are unevenly hemmed. Do you
   a. praise her tasteful furnishings?
   b. suggest that she take a closer look at the drapes?
   c. point out she's been "taken" and ought to insist the drapes be remade?

10. You've parked on a crowded street and return to find a car has parked so close in front of you that you're wedged in. Do you
    a. do some more shopping in hopes the driver will show up shortly?
    b. struggle out of the space?
    c. demand that police tow the offending car away?

SCORING

Score yourself 3 points for each a. answer, 2 points for each b., and 1 point for each c. Add up the points.

ANALYSIS:

26-30: You have such a high Tolerance Quotient (TQ) that it's possible you underreact and people see you as a pushover. Very high TQ persons often suffer from an inferiority compelx.

21-25: You are an easygoing person with a high enough TQ to be a joy to have around since you are willing to "live and let live." You are wise enough not to allow minor irritations to cause you to lose emotional control.

16-20: You have a low-average TQ and occasionally overreact to events or other people's defects. With just a little effort you could learn self-discipline.

10-15: Your low TQ is the reason that you have so many problems in life. You are too quick to find fault and are likely to be thought a chronic complainer. While you might pride yourself on your "honesty," you are often overly critical.

YOU AND YOUR MIND

Are You a Creative Person?

"Imagination," wrote Pascal, "disposes of everything; it creates beauty, justice, and happiness, which are everything in this world." Not all of us were born with creative ability, and many of us have never used the creative talents we have. Professors Richard S. Scutchfield and Harrison Gough of the University of California devised a questionnaire and found that creative persons answered quite differently from less creative individuals. Using some of their questions as a basis, plus those from other studies, how would you answer the following questions?

1. Within limitations, I sometimes break certain rules of social etiquette and do things I am not supposed to do.

   TRUE _____   FALSE _____

2. I do not enjoy reading stories that use strange words, promote unfamiliar ideas, or tell of unknown places.

   TRUE _____   FALSE _____

3. For most questions, there is an answer that is based on fact.

   TRUE _____   FALSE _____

4. Teen-agers are not mature enough to leave home for any prolonged period of time.

   TRUE _____   FALSE _____

5. More people should take life more seriously than they do.

TRUE _____   FALSE _____

6. When people are nice to me, I wonder about their motives.

TRUE _____   FALSE _____

7. I enjoy experimenting, even if the results are unsatisfactory.

TRUE _____   FALSE _____

8. I think it is important to dress in accord with current trends.

TRUE _____   FALSE _____

9. I value my own self-respect more than I do the respect of others.

TRUE _____   FALSE _____

10. I think there is "a time and a place" for everything.

TRUE _____   FALSE _____

SCORING

Answers most often given by creative people:
1–TRUE; 2–FALSE; 3–FALSE; 4–FALSE; 5–FALSE; 6–FALSE; 7–TRUE; 8–FALSE; 9–TRUE; 10–FALSE

If you have answered with about 80 per cent in accord with the creative people, you have the indications of being a creative person. "The world of reality has its limits; the world of imagination is boundless." (Jean Jacques Rousseau)

Are You a Superbrain?

Race, creed, sex, and status don't matter. To join this colorful group, all you need is a genius IQ.

Carolina Varga Dinicu is a belly dancer.

Isaac Asimov is a well-known writer.

Theodore Bikel and William Windom are actors.

Leslie Charteris is the author of ''The Saint'' mystery stories.

R. Buckminster Fuller is an author and architectural engineer of world renown.

And what could the members of that diverse group possibly have in common? Answer: They're all exceptionally intelligent, and all belong to Mensa, one of the world's most interesting societies. The sole requirement for membership is an IQ score that puts you in the top 2 per cent of the population.

Could you qualify as a member? Statistically, one person in fifty can pass the Mensa test. And the society wants to *find those people*—before they succumb to acute boredom, chronic television, and other dread diseases. How do you find out if you're the one in fifty? Hint: If you start out by looking for forty-nine dummies, you're on the wrong track. We have a better idea: Try your hand at this test, constructed by Mensa. It won't tell you what your IQ is, but it will indicate roughly whether you come close to the Mensa ball park. Do the test as quickly as you can without sacrificing accuracy, and time yourself; you get points for speed.

A MINI-TEST FOR SUPERBRAINS

1. What is the next term in this series?
    7, 12, 27, 72, 127.

2. Complete the analogy by writing one word in the spaces, ending with the letter printed.
    Thermometer is to temperature as clock is to TIME E

3. Which one does not belong?

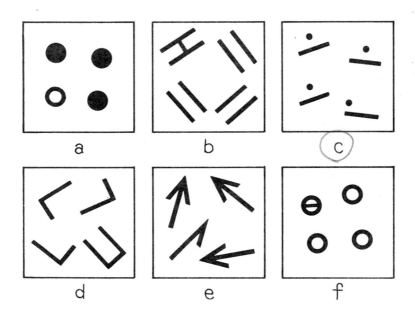

4. Underline the two words in parentheses that have the same relation as the first two words.

   Sitter is to chair as (cup, saucer, leg, plate, dish).

5. Underline the two words in parentheses that have the same relation as the first two words.

   Mother is to girl as (father, male, boy, son, daughter).

6. In the square below there is a rule of arithmetic that applies across and down the square so that two of the numbers in a line produce the third number in each line. Write the missing number.

2	7	9
5	4	9
7	11	?

18

7. Complete the series in the top line with a, b, c, or d below.

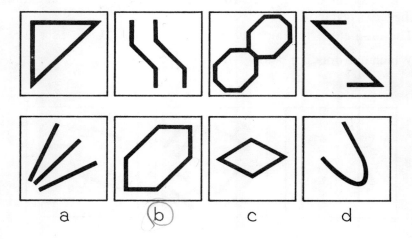

   a   b   c   d

8. In the following equation, the number missing from the left side is equal to the number missing from the right side. Write in the missing number.

$$\frac{1}{(9)} = \frac{(9)}{81}$$

9. Underline the words below that do not belong with the others:
   syrup, milk, water, beer, wine, honey.

10. Underline the two words that are nearly opposite in meaning:
    punish, annoy, spank, ignore, chastise, pacify.

11. If 7 belly dancers lose 20 pounds altogether in 8 hours of dancing, how many more belly dancers would be needed to lose a total of 20 pounds in only 4 hours of dancing, providing the new dancers shed weight only half as fast as the original 7?

    a. 7;
    b. 21;
    c. 27;
    d. 14;
    e. 12.

12. Some Mensa members are geniuses. All geniuses have some human virtues as redeeming qualities. Therefore:
    a. Mensa members all have some virtue.
    b. All geniuses are quality Mensa members.
    c. Some Mensa members have redeeming qualities.

13. Jones is younger than Smith. Robinson is older than Jones. Therefore:
    a. Smith is older than Robinson.
    b. Robinson is older than Smith.
    c. Jones is the youngest.

14. "Don't trade horses in midstream" means:
    a. You might fall off and get wet.
    b. Don't attempt something until you're fully prepared.
    c. Decide what you're going to do before you do it.
    d. Don't change plans when something is half completed.

15. What number, multiplied by 4, is equal to three fourths of 112?

16. What letter is next in the series below?
    B, E, I, N, ____.

17. Underline the two words in parentheses that have the same relation as the first two words.
    Needle is to thread as (cotton, sew, dress, leader, follower).

18.   Which one does not belong?
      a.   checkers;
      b.   chess;
      c.   gin rummy;
      d.   backgammon;
      e.   Chinese checkers.

19.   Select the two figures in the following series that represent mirror (or reflection) images of each other.

      a   b   c   d   e

20.

      a   b   c   d   e

SCORING

IQ TEST ANSWERS:

1.	207	11.	d
2.	time	12.	c
3.	c	13.	c
4.	cup, saucer	14.	d
5.	father, boy	15.	21
6.	18	16.	t
7.	b	17.	leader, follower
8.	9	18.	c
9.	syrup, honey	19.	a, e
10.	annoy, pacify	20.	d, e

SCORING SCALE:

Give yourself 1 point for each correct answer. You also receive an additional 4 points if you completed the test in less than 10 minutes; 3 points if you completed it in less than 15 minutes; 2 points if you completed it in less than 20 minutes; or 1 point if you completed it in less than 25 minutes.

IF YOU SCORED:

20–24 points:	You are probably highly intelligent, and an excellent candidate for membership in Mensa.
15–19 points:	The chances are you rank among the top of the population in intelligence—certainly a candidate for Mensa.
10–14 points:	A most honorable score, and one that indicates you should try the at-home Mensa IQ test.
Less than 10 points:	You are probably not Mensa material, but you're in good company with many successful businessmen, writers, artists, and other well-known figures who don't have exceptional IQs either.

Are You Still Learning?

Many people regard learning as a childish activity confined to schooldays, and come to a full stop once they achieve success in a job. Yet there have been great men who have not hesitated to start learning, say, a new language in their old age. Is your mind still open and receptive?

Try this test on yourself. Answer "Yes" or "No" to the questions. Then turn to the scoring key at the end.

1. Do you honestly believe that you still have a lot to learn?
2. Are people and their reactions often surprises to you?
3. Do you often feel dissatisfied with the way you deal with people and tell yourself that you must try to do better next time?
4. Do you find it fairly easy to adapt yourself to new people and different environments?
5. Is it reasonably easy for you to associate names with faces, or faces with names?

6. Are you an intelligent listener—do you acquire knowledge from listening to people, and to the radio, and do you assimilate it well enough to profit by it yourself as well as to pass it on to your friends?

7. Would you notice on your daily round a new kind of flower in a park or florist's window, an unusual breed of dog, a strange uniform, or an additional road sign or public announcement?

8. Is your attitude one of interest and inquiry when you see or hear anything new or different?

9. Are you in the habit of making a mental note of anything you do not understand in order to find out about it later?

10. Are you able to recognize when you need advice or assistance?

11. Are you quick to see when you have made a mistake?

12. But do you rarely make the same mistake twice?

13. Are you always ready to try out a new idea at work, play, inside your home?

14. Are you co-operative rather than skeptical or hostile when people want some change or reorganization?

15. Do you enjoy travel, educational, documentary films, and radio and television features?

16. Do you borrow nonfiction books from a library or buy nonfiction books for yourself?

17. Do you give your active support to as many cultural activities as possible—things like art and other exhibitions, concerts, ballet, the theater?

18. Can you honestly say that you are more capable and knowledgeable than you were, say, five years ago?

19. Have you acquired and developed at least one more hobby or interest in the past five years?

20. Are you much more concerned with the present and the future than with your past life?

SCORING

Count 5 points for every "Yes." A score of 70 or over is good; 60–70 is satisfactory; 50–60 is fair. Under 50 is not satisfactory.

To keep on learning makes life always vivid and interesting. Here are three ways to do it: Keep yourself alert by watching your health and avoiding getting overweight. Cultivate worthwhile hobbies and interests to stimulate the mind and keep it active. Remember that a desire for self-improvement will make you more interesting to your friends and the people you meet.

How Imaginative Are You?

It is hard for us to imagine, in this modern age, that there are still primitive tribes of people on earth who have not imagined the use of the wheel, which we take for granted. This test will help you evaluate your own powers of imagination. There is a warning, however. Unless your answers are completely honest, you may be disappointed with your score.

1. Take as long as you like to study the inkblot below. Count the number of things in the blot that your imagination can find, such as a face, a butterfly, etc. You may turn the inkblot around and view it from any side or angle to discover other forms.

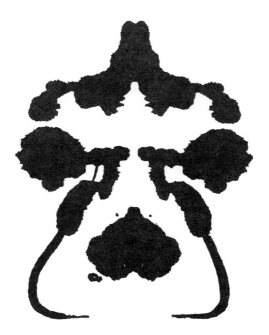

2. When you are about to fall asleep do you often find yourself reviewing the day's activities?

   Yes _____ Sometimes _____ Never _____

3. When you awaken from a night's sleep, do you find yourself suspended between a dream and reality for some time?

   Yes _____ Sometimes _____ Never _____

4. Have you ever tried to write a novel, a short story, or poetry?

   Yes _____ No _____

5. When surrounded by a group of stangers, as on a train or in a restaurant, do you find it interesting to imagine the lives of those around you?

   Yes _____   Sometimes _____   Never _____

6. Are forms and color especially important to you?

   Yes _____   No _____

7. When you read a novel or a short story, do you simultaneously envision the people and places in detail?

   Yes _____   Sometimes _____   Never _____

8. Do you think that if you were to overcome certain personality problems your life would be more successful?

   Yes _____   No _____

9. Do you find yourself upset for no reason?

   Yes _____   Sometimes _____   Never _____

10. Do you enjoy reading stories that involve the supernatural or science fiction?

   Yes _____   Sometimes _____   Never _____

SCORING

1. Score a point for each form your imagination found in the inkblot (5 points is the average score).
2. Yes–0; Sometimes–1; Never–5
3. Yes–5; Sometimes–3; Never–0
4. Yes–5; No–0
5. Yes–5; Sometimes–3; Never–0
6. Yes–5; No–0
7. Yes–5; Sometimes–2; Never–0
8. Yes–5; No–0
9. Yes–0; Sometimes–5; Never–0
10. Yes–5; Sometimes–5; Never–0

40–50 or more: People who rate this score have keen, imaginative minds. This very fact, however, may lead them to live in a "dream world" and to escape from everyday realities.

25-39:   This is a healthy, normal score, blending practicality with imagination.

0-24:   This is a poor measurement for imagination. The enjoyment and productivity of your imagination can be increased by consciously trying.

Are You a Quick Wit?

In this fast-moving world you have to be quick-witted. It's to the fleetest of mind that progress goes.

So, have you got your wits about you? Are you alert, able to make the right decision quickly?

In this quiz, the questions, different though they might appear, are all designed to test your speed of thought and action.

Ten minutes only are allowed to complete the quiz. At the end, answers and explanations are given, together with the number of marks you may award yourself.

Are you a real quick wit? Well, we'll see!

1. You're in a railway compartment when a fellow passenger has a heart attack. Do you:
    a. Pull the communication cord at once?
    b. Let the train continue and go to find the conductor?
    c. Allow the train to go on, but go along the corridor asking if there's a doctor?

2. You enter a room to find a young child out on the window ledge in a precarious position. Do you:
    a. Call softly to the child?
    b. Rush forward and try to grab the child?
    c. Try to creep up on the child quietly?

3. Which of these words is different from the others? Four can be prefixed by one word; the other cannot.)
    window; beans; pavement; polish; poodle.

4. What would you sooner have as a *long-term* investment, assuming that you merely stacked them away in a drawer:
   a. 1,000 dollars in cash?
   b. 1,000 dollars in diamonds?
   c. 1,000 dollars in gold?

5. You're on a bicycle when you see four bank robbers jump into a car. You notice their vehicle has a puncture and that there would be a fair chance of catching them on your bike. Do you:
   a. Chase after them at once?
   b. Stop a car and ask the driver to give chase?
   c. Just take the number and phone it to the police?

6. Which is the missing animal:

   don + (door opener) = (animal).

7. You are shipwrecked on a desert island. Which of these things would you sooner have with you at the time:
   a. A shotgun, ammunition, and spade?
   b. A three-year supply of canned food?
   c. A small boat?

8. You're near an electric railway when you see a man lying across the live line; there is a telephone booth nearby. Do you:
   a. Try to shift him?
   b. Telephone the police, then go back to the spot?
   c. Try to telephone the railway?

SCORING

Now look below for the answers you should have picked and for the verdict on your quick-wittedness!

ANSWERS:
Give yourself just three points for every one you've gotten right.

1. c. is the right answer. If you pulled the alarm cord, you would stop the train; there might be medical help available at the next station. The best thing is to go along the train looking for medical help; eventually you would come to the conductor anyway.

2. a. is right this time. Either of the other two alternatives would undoubtedly startle the child, and this could make the child fall.

3. "Pavement" is different from the four other words, which can be prefixed by the word "french"; "pavement" cannot.

4. 1,000 dollars in diamonds—b. Diamonds seem to keep their value much better than the other two alternatives.

5. c. is right. What would you do even if you caught up with them on your bicycle or in another car? You would be outnumbered, and the robbers would most likely escape just the same. Better to let the police know, and they can get their cars looking for the number quickly.

6. don + (key) = donkey.

7. a. seems right. With a shotgun, ammunition, and spade you could probably survive longer than the three years that the food would last you. Taking the boat is a complete shot in the dark; you're better off on the island.

8. b. is right. If you tried to shift him you would probably only electrocute yourself as well. The big thing is to stop any train running over him; and if you phone the police they would see to this (by warning the railway) and also to getting medical help there quickly. If you tried phoning the railway you might have trouble finding the right person and you would not be covering the medical side. By phoning the police and then going back to look out for oncoming trains you would take the best course available to you.

VERDICT:

If you've scored between *18 and 24,* you're very quick-witted indeed. You've learned that being quick-witted does not always entail jumping quickly into action on the first thought that comes into your head. You've learned that, in the long run, it is better to spend a little time on thought before taking action. You're a sharp one in any circumstances.

Between 9 and 15: You're quite quick-witted at times, but you're inclined to jump too quickly into action; your reaction is good but sometimes you take longer to get results simply because you haven't allowed a little time for thought.

Under 6: Sorry, a lot of sharpening-up needed here. You don't use your wits enough.

YOU
AND YOUR
BODY

Are You a "Junk Food" Junkie?

More people are going out to eat in "fast food" restaurants than ever before. As a result, "junk food" has become a staple in the American diet. This culinary shift from well-balanced, home-cooked meals to "junk food" has caused many people to suffer from nutritional deficiencies, overweight, and poor physical health. How much "junk food" do you eat? Are you a "junk food" junkie? Take this simple test and find out.

Check how often you consume the following "junk foods":

		Frequently	Some-times	Rarely	Never
1.	candy			✓	X
2.	hot dogs	X		✓	
3.	hamburgers	X	✓		
5.	french fries	X		✓	
6.	pizza		X✓		
7.	soda pop	✓		X	
8.	tacos				X✓
9.	ice cream	X✓			
10.	cookies		✓	X	
11.	fried chicken	X✓			

12.   potato chips

13.   pretzels

14.   submarines (heros)

15.   pie

SCORING

Give yourself four points for each "Frequently" answer, three points for each "Sometimes" answer, two points for each "Rarely" answer, and one point for each "Never" answer.

If you scored 15–29 points, you are a very sensible eater. Continue to avoid harmful "junk foods" and you will prevent numerous health problems.

If you scored 30–39 points, you are an occasional indulger in "junk foods." Be careful not to increase your intake of "junk foods" or you will place your health in jeopardy. Try your best to eliminate the "junk foods" you now eat or drink.

If you scored 40–49 points, you are a borderline "junk food" addict. Immediately re-evaluate your diet and begin substituting healthier, more nutritional foods for the "junk food" you now consume. Health problems are on the horizon if you do not act decisively to alter your current eating habits.

If you scored 50–60 points, you are a "junk food" junkie. You must change your pattern of eating or suffer the serious consequences to your health. If you cannot break the "junk food" habit on your own, consult your physician. He will provide you with a diet that can help to convert you from a "junk food" junkie into a sensible eater.

How Body-conscious Are You?

Some people are preoccupied with the way they look. Being so sensitive about their appearance, they often withdraw from social interaction while hiding their bodies beneath concealing garments.

Are you body-conscious? Take this simple test and find out.

Answer each question "Yes" or "No."

1. Do you tend to look in mirrors or reflecting windows when you pass them by?
2. Do you feel conspicuous wearing a bathing suit in public?
3. When wearing an outfit in public that exposes your stomach, do you prefer to keep your belly button covered?
4. When you smile at someone, do you try not to show your teeth?
5. When you have a blemish on your face, do you attempt to cover it up with creams, gels, salves, Band-aids, or the like?
6. Do you often dress in a manner that conceals your true weight?
7. Do you exercise or diet for the primary purpose of looking better?
8. Do you spend a lot of time fixing yourself up before going to work in the morning or before going out for an ordinary weekend evening?
9. Do you make sure the drapes are tightly drawn when undressing at night with the light on?
10. When you walk by a member of the opposite sex who is staring at you, do you suddenly feel extraconscious of your appearance?
11. Do you look in the mirror to see if you're getting wrinkles?

SCORING

Score a point for each "Yes" answer.

A score of 9 or over reveals that you are uptight. You worry too much about your appearance. You've got your work cut out for you. Accept yourself for what you are and focus your attention on living well rather than looking good.

If you scored between 5 and 8, you are a borderline case. Be careful! Your preoccupation with your physical image may well interfere with your enjoyment of life. Think less of how others may view you. It is not your physical form that you want to be respected for; it is the internal beauty that charms others and captivates their hearts.

A score of 2–4 indicates you have a healthy outlook toward your body. Your relatively minor concern with your appearance is a positive characteristic. It suggests that you are considerate of others and make an effort to contribute to the beauty of their environment.

If you scored 0 or 1, you are the type of person who feels totally at ease with his or her body. Although definitely not body-conscious, you run the risk of exhibiting too little concern for your appearance.

Are You Eating Right
for Health and Happiness?

What you eat often determines your emotional and psychological state, declares top nutritionist Dr. E. Cheraskin. "People who are nervous, irritable, and emotionally unstable—or suffer from memory loss, concentration difficulties, and problems with social and marital relationships—often experience such symptoms as a direct result of improper diet.

"Most Americans eat very badly," he noted. "Meal skipping is on the rise, with 8 to 15 per cent of most age groups bypassing lunch.

"Every fourth person skips breakfast, the most important meal of the day.

"But unless you get the fifty or more essential nutrients you need for emotional well-being, any psychological upsets you experience on a day-to-day basis are apt to be triggered by this lack."

To find out if you're eating properly for happiness and health, Dr. Cheraskin has devised this twenty-two-question quiz:

1. Is your appetite frequently poor?
2. Do you usually skip one meal or more a day?
3. Do you frequently eat sweet foods or drink sweet beverages between meals?
4. Do you often feel shaky or weak if you don't eat on time?
5. Do you usually have one or two drinks of an alcoholic beverage (such as whiskey, beer, or wine) daily?
6. Do you usually drink coffee or tea more than three times a day?
7. Do you usually eat one or more desserts each day?
8. Do you regularly use sugar in your coffee or tea?
9. Do you consume soft drinks almost daily?
10. Do you frequently eat starchy foods, like bread, macaroni, biscuits, breakfast cereals, and corn bread?
11. Do you eat sweets daily, like sugar, syrup, jellies, and candy?
12. Do you eat bakery products, such as cakes and pies, every day?
13. Do you daily eat ice cream, ice milk, or canned or frozen fruits?
14. Do you usually add salt to your food at the table?
15. Do you usually eat meat less than twice a day?
16. Do you eat less than three or four eggs a week?
17. Do you almost totally omit seafoods from your diet?
18. Do you usually avoid milk, cheese, and butter?
19. Do you avoid raw vegetables like lettuce, tomatoes, and carrots?

20. Do you usually eat green or yellow vegetables less than twice a day?
21. Do you avoid citrus fruits or juices daily?
22. Do you usually avoid other types of fresh raw fruits or juices?

SCORING

To find out how you stand, give yourself a point for each "Yes" answer, then see below.

"Your score will lie somewhere between 0 and 22," said Dr. Cheraskin. "The closer to 1 you score, the better your diet. On the other hand, as your score climbs, the more you're prone to mental problems.

"A score of 5 or less indicates your diet is providing most of the nutrients you need to remain calm, stable, and emotionally competent. You need to do very little to improve your eating habits.

"If you scored between 5 and 11, however, you may be somewhat careless in your choice of diet and should make an extra effort to provide the nutrients you might lack.

"People who score 12 or more are following a diet that leaves much to be desired. Chances are you're eating too many sugars and starches, too few proteins. The inadequacies of your diet are apt to be compounded by your habit of skipping meals entirely."

How Is Your Body Control?

Are you letting those muscles grow flabby through disuse? Does your stomach protrude? Your shoulders sag? Test yourself.

DIRECTIONS
Lie on the floor, point your toes, with palms flat on floor, as in figure 1. Slowly raise your legs to each position shown in figures 2–6. Head and arms *must* remain on the floor.

SCORING

Position 2 only	= not satisfactory
Position 3	= mediocre
Position 4	= satisfactory
Position 5	= good
Position 6	= excellent

Will a Diet Work for You?

Will a diet work for you?

"It may," says Dr. Neil Solomon, international nutritional health expert who practices medicine in Baltimore, Maryland. "But not everyone is emotionally ready to go on a diet."

Author of *Dr. Solomon's Easy, No Risk Diet,* he says dieting without a reasonable hope for success can be frustrating and physically hazardous.

To help you determine whether a diet will work for you, Dr. Solomon devised the following test. Answer each question "Yes" or "No."

1. Is there someone else in your family eager to lose weight, so that dieting will be a shared activity?
2. Do you generally fall asleep easily and sleep through the night without difficulty?
3. Are you determined to stop smoking as well as to lose weight?
4. Are you in a better financial condition with a brighter future than you were a few years ago?
5. If you had to skip a meal each day, would you prefer to skip breakfast?
6. Were you an obedient child who rarely talked back to your parents?
7. Do you have at least three unfinished projects around the house?
8. Is your physical well-being the main reason you want to diet?
9. Are your sexual relationships happy and satisfying?
10. Does the diet you are contemplating promise rapid weight loss with very little effort on your part?
11. Do you get depressed easily if things don't go your way?
12. Have you ever been on a reducing diet before?

SCORING

To find your score, give yourself 2 points for each "Yes" and a point for each "No" on questions 1, 2, 4, 8, and 9. Now give yourself 2 points for each "No" and a point for each "Yes" on questions 3, 5, 6, 7, 10, 11, and 12. Add your points.

If you scored 18–24 points, Dr. Solomon feels you're a good diet candidate because you're well motivated to complete projects you start.

If you scored 14–17 points, Dr. Solomon suggests you re-examine your desire to go on a diet. He feels it may be important for you to find some way to reward yourself other than food before you tackle dieting.

A score of 10–13 points indicates that it would be wise for you to seek psychiatric help before attempting a diet, Dr. Solomon said.

Is Your Lifestyle
Good for Your Health?

Your health and longevity depend a great deal on the lifestyle you live, say experts at Blue Cross and Blue Shield. "Everything you do from day to day is part of your lifestyle," said Dr. Richard C. Shaw, vice president and medical director of the Chicago-based Blue Cross and Blue Shield plan.

"And your lifestyle affects your physical fitness. Carelessness in any area of your lifestyle can lead to some serious health problems. And that's why it's important to know whether your lifestyle is contributing to health or sickness."

Answer each question, calculate your score—then read the score analysis at the end of the quiz to see if you need to make changes in your lifestyle.

1. How often do you exercise?
   a. four or more times weekly.
   b. three times weekly.
   c. weekly.
   d. seldom.

2. How often do you choose stairs over elevators and escalators?
   a. almost always.
   b. frequently.
   c. occasionally.
   d. seldom.

3. How many hours do you watch TV daily?
   a. none to one.
   b. one to two.
   c. two to four.
   d. four or more.

4. Are you overweight?
   a. no.
   b. yes, one to four pounds.
   c. yes, five to nineteen pounds.
   d. yes, twenty pounds or more.

5. How many alcoholic drinks—beer, wine, and liquor—do you average per week?
   a. none.
   b. one to seven.
   c. eight to fifteen.
   d. sixteen or more.

6. How many cigarettes do you smoke per day?
    a. none.
    b. less than five.
    c. five to ten.
    d. ten or more.

7. Do you smoke marijuana or use any illegal drugs?
    a. no.
    b. rarely.
    c. occasionally.
    d. frequently.

8. Do you drink alcoholic beverages within six hours after you have taken tranquilizers, barbiturates, antihistamines, or illegal drugs?
    a. no.
    b. rarely.
    c. occasionally.
    d. frequently.

9. Do you use drugs such as Darvon and Valium more often than recommended by a physician?
    a. no.
    b. rarely.
    c. occasionally.
    d. frequently.

10. How often are you depressed?
    a. almost never.
    b. seldom.
    c. occasionally.
    d. frequently.

11. Does anxiety or tension interfere with your daily activities?
    a. almost never.
    b. seldom.
    c. occasionally.
    d. frequently.

12. Do you get enough satisfying sleep?
    a. always.
    b. usually.
    c. occasionally.
    d. seldom.

13. (Women only) Do you practice breast self-examination?
    a. monthly.
    b. four times a year.
    c. rarely.
    d. never.

14. Do you drive faster than the speed limit?
    a. no.
    b. yes, but only five miles per hour.
    c. yes, five to fifteen miles per hour.
    d. yes, more than fifteen miles per hour.

15. Do you wear a seat belt in a car?
    a. always.
    b. usually.
    c. seldom.
    d. never.

16. Do you drive under the influence of alcohol, drugs, or medication?
    a. never.
    b. seldom.
    c. occasionally.
    d. frequently.

SCORING

Give yourself a point for each a. answer, two points for each b. answer, three points for each c. answer, and four points for each d. answer.

ANALYSIS:

If you scored 16–25, you have an excellent lifestyle based on sensible habits and a good awareness of personal health.

If you scored 26–35, you have a very good lifestlye, and with a little improvement you can move into the excellent category.

A score of 35–45 means you have a good grasp of general health principles, but need a bit more determination and commitment to achieve a healthier lifestyle.

If you scored 46–55, you're taking unnecessary risks with your health and you should set improving your lifestyle as a goal.

A score of 56 or more indicates that you either have little personal knowledge of good health habits or you choose to ignore them. You're in the danger zone and should start making improvements in your lifestyle today.

Are You an Alcoholic?

To answer this question, ask yourself the following questions and answer them as honestly as you can.

	YES	NO
1. Do you lose time from work due to drinking?		X
2. Is drinking making your home life unhappy?	X	
3. Do you drink because you're shy with other people?		X
4. Is drinking affecting your reputation?		X
5. Have you ever felt remorse after drinking?	X	
6. Have you gotten into financial difficulties as a result of drinking?		X
7. Do you turn to lower companions and an inferior environment when drinking?		X
8. Does your drinking make you careless of your family's welfare?	X	
9. Has your ambition decreased since drinking?	X	
10. Do you crave a drink at a definite time daily?		X
11. Do you want a drink the next morning?		X
12. Does drinking cause you to have difficulty in sleeping?		X

	YES	NO
13. Has your efficiency decreased since drinking?	X̶	
14. Is drinking jeopardizing your job or business?		X̶
15. Do you drink to escape from worries or trouble?		X̶
16. Do you drink alone?		X̶
17. Have you ever had a complete loss of memory as a result of drinking?		X̶
18. Has your physician ever treated you for drinking?		X̶
19. Do you drink to build up your self-confidence?		X̶
20. Have you ever been to a hospital or institution on account of drinking?		X̶

SCORING

If you answered "Yes" to any *one* of the questions, there is a definite warning that *you may be an alcoholic.*

If you answered "Yes" to any *two,* the chances are that *you are an alcoholic.*

If you answered "Yes" to *three or more, you are definitely an alcoholic.*

(The above test questions are used by The Johns Hopkins University Hospital, Baltimore, Maryland, in deciding whether or not a patient is alcoholic.)

YOU AND YOUR RELATIONSHIP WITH MEN

What Kind of Man Do You Attract?

Every woman knows exactly the sort of man she finds the most attractive. But are you aware of the kind of man who feels drawn, irresistibly, toward you? Is he the fiery, aggressive extrovert . . . the cool, stylish gentleman . . . the moody, sensitive nonconformist . . . or the generous, down-to-earth protector? This quiz has been specially compiled to help you find out.

1. You like most to spend an evening at:
   a. an excellent, intimate restaurant.
   b. a fashionable discotheque.
   c. a beautiful house where you can talk and listen to music.
   d. a lively and exciting party where there are lots of friends.

2. You prefer a man to:
   a. dominate you firmly.
   b. treat you exactly as an equal.
   c. adore you while still retaining his dignity.
   d. indulge you.

3. If you really want to attract a man, you decide to wear:
   a. a sophisticated and expensive creation from a top designer.
   b. a clinging satin dress.

    c. a revealing blouse and short skirt.

    d. something that you have made yourself.

4. What do you most like a man to wear?

    a. a tailored suit.

    b. a velvet jacket with fashionable, hip-hugging flared trousers.

    c. tight jeans and a denim jacket.

    d. none of these.

5. You prefer a man to:

    a. wine, dine, and flatter you.

    b. keep himself slightly cool and distant.

    c. be attentive and adoring one day, merely friendly the next.

    d. simply be fun.

6. Your party escort is slighted by one of the guests, and insults him. The other guests are horrified. You are:

    a. terribly embarrassed.

    b. furious with your escort.

    c. pleased that your escort stands up for himself.

    d. completely bored with the whole incident.

7. When your man flirts with another girl, what do you do?

    a. flirt with another man.

    b. join the two of them, hoping to get rid of the girl.

    c. feel insulted.

    d. feel amused.

8. When it comes to social conventions, how do you like a man to react?

    a. always rebel strongly against them.

    b. ignore them completely if they don't happen to suit him.

    c. adhere to them strictly without worrying about it.

    d. adhere to them with deliberate style.

9. When you go out in the evening, you prefer your man to:

    a. plan the whole evening meticulously ahead of time.

    b. let the evening develop spontaneously.

    c. take you wherever you say you want to go.

    d. any of the above, according to his mood at the time.

10. You are having a coffee on your own after shopping. An atrractive man sits down opposite and starts to talk to you. How do you react?

a. you respond to his conversation.
b. you cut him.
c. you let him carry on talking to see what he's like.
d. you get up and go.

SCORING

1. a–3; b–4; c–2; d–1
2. a–4; b–2; c–3; d–1
3. a–3; b–4; c–1; d–2
4. a–3; b–4; c–2; d–1
5. a–4; b–3; c–2; d–1

6. a–1; b–3; c–4; d–2
7. a–4; b–1; c–2; d–3
8. a–2; b–4; c–1; d–3
9. a–3; b–2; c–1; d–4
10. a–4; b–3; c–2; d–1

31–40: You attract the man who seems totally determined to get what he wants. He's tough, ambitious, and aggressive, a born extrovert. Underneath, however, he is often insecure. You attract him for two reasons: You can stand up to him, and so win his admiration and respect; you, too, are flamboyant and exude glamor, which makes him proud.

23–30: You are a natural magnet to the man who prizes style and does everything with polish. He is a man of taste with flair in his dress and dryness in his humor. He likes to do the right thing at the right time, but adds to it that little something that is his own. You attract him because you have the style and self-possession he values so highly.

15–22: You are probably the only kind of woman capable of understanding this kind of man. He is sensitive, gentle, temperamental, unconventional, and sensuous, and his moods are highly changeable. You attract him because you seem different from other women, have depth that they do not have.

14 or under: There's no nonsense about the type you attract: down-to-earth, stable, balanced. He makes an excellent husband and good father, and you're the sort of woman who brings out his strong protective instincts. Though shy with those whom he does not know, he is warm and loving toward people who win his trust.

How Feminine Are You?

Here's a fascinating quiz to help you size up your femininity rating.

1. Other considerations apart, do you favor clothes that are:
   a. warm and comfortable?
   b. provocative?
   c. in the fashion?

2. A woman's hair used to be described as her "crowning glory." Is this:
   a. much exaggerated?
   b. basically true?
   c. true only of some women?

3. Is makeup for you:
   a. as essential as dressing?
   b. rather a bore at times?
   c. merely a means to a deceptive end?

4. Do you believe that having a good figure (or at least appearing to have one!) is:
   a. every woman's major claim to be looked at?
   b. greatly overrated in many cases?
   c. nice in itself?

5. Outside of the U.S.A. and France, only about one woman in five uses perfume regularly. Are you in this fragrant minority?
   a. yes.
   b. definitely not.
   c. probably not—that "regularly" makes it difficult to say "yes."

6. What do you normally do when you see a baby at close quarters?
   a. coo.
   b. gush.
   c. usually neither.

7. Which of these three things are you *best* described as?
   a. talkative.
   b. aggressive.
   c. sympathetic.

8. Which of these three attributes would you *most like to be* regarded as?
   a. kindly.

    b. modest.

    c. good company.

9. It's said that there is a natural streak of hardness or toughness in all women. How much would you admit to having:

    a. very little indeed?

    b. a bit?

    c. quite enough?

10. When introduced to a man for the first time, is your attention fixed on his:

    a. smile?

    b. general appearance?

    c. eyes?

11. If you had the time, which of these three pursuits would you most like to take up?

    a. lampshade making.

    b. woodwork.

    c. leathercraft.

12. When you see a man wearing an apron in a kitchen, do you have feelings, however mild, of:

    a. amusement?

    b. pleasure?

    c. pity?

13. What is your home to you?

    a. everything.

    b. somewhere to live.

    c. something to run and care for.

14. Do you like being touched?

    a. not very much.

    b. yes.

    c. sometimes.

15. Which would you rather receive from a man?

    a. flowers.

    b. a love letter.

    c. advice.

16. Have you ever wished you were a man?

    a. no, never.

    b. once or twice.

    c. several times.

17. Which do you think is most important in a woman's life?

    a. her marriage.

    b. her children.

    c. her career.

18. Do you prefer men who are:

    a. a bit timid?

    b. demanding?

    c. strong and gentle?

19. Do you believe:

    a. women are better off today than ever before?

    b. women are in danger of losing something of their essential womanliness?

    c. women still have a very long way to go?

20. To be answered with the utmost honesty: Where are you happiest?

    a. caring for children.

    b. following your own interests.

    c. in a man's arms.

SCORING

NOW FOR THE SCORES:

1.	a–2; b–5; c–4	11.	a–4; b–1; c–3
2.	a–1; b–4; c–3	12.	a–3; b–1; c–5
3.	a–5; b–0; c–3	13.	a–5; b–0; c–3
4.	a–5; b–2; c–4	14.	a–1; b–5; c–3
5.	a–5; b–0; c–2	15.	a–4; b–5; c–0
6.	a–5; b–4; c–1	16.	a–5; b–2; c–1
7.	a–3; b–1; c–4	17.	a–4; b–5; c–1
8.	a–5; b–4; c–3	18.	a–1; b–4; c–5
9.	a–4; b–2; c–1	19.	a–3; b–5; c–2
10.	a–3; b–2; c–5	20.	a–5; b–2; c–5

NOW FOR THE VERDICTS:

If you scored 90–96, you are utterly and completely feminine—and as such must be a delight to every sane man within miles!

70–89:   You are as completely feminine as most mortal women can expect to be. Rejoice in the fact, and make use of it if need be, but, please, don't flaunt it too much—not only for the sakes of your less happily endowed sisters, but also for male peace of mind!

45–79:   You are not perhaps as completely feminine as you might think, which is undoubtedly a fact of your life that you'll be happier if you reckon with. But at the same time, you are still primarily a woman, with most if not all of a woman's graces and abilities. It's learning to live with your limitations that's the difficult thing for you.

Below 45:   Your essential femininity is well below normal, which, if you are a basically happy person, you must have recognized long ago. The important thing with you is to realize that none of us is entirely 100 per cent female (or male), and for that fact alone we must always make allowances.

Would You Make an Ideal Mistress?

You don't really want to be anyone's mistress, of course. Not for real. All the same, there have surely been times, between typing the boss's letters, or in the middle of the washing up, when you have daydreamed of being a rich man's plaything . . . draped in diamonds, cuddled in mink, looking ravishing as you loll on a tigerskin rug, sipping (even bathing in) champagne, drifting around his apartment in see-through undies.

Could you be a twentieth-century Cora Pearl, the English girl who became the rage of Paris? Or a latter-day Lola Montez, whose love cost the King of Bavaria his throne?

You don't have to have looks. Some of history's best-known mistresses have been less than pretty. A good figure is more important than a pretty face. The ability to radiate sex is more important than either.

You must also be provocative, tantalizing, shrewd, clever . . . and as hard as nails. Love—for the ideal mistress—has to be a business, not an indulgence.

The ideal mistress knows that she isn't a wife and doesn't try to become one. She is the erotic alternative. No mistress, in the real mink-and-diamonds class, would make the mistake, as one young lady did recently, of moving into the same house as her lover's wife. That's asking for trouble.

Could you make some man an ideal mistress?

1. Which quality do you find most attractive in a man?
   a. his looks.
   b. his virility.
   c. his ability to make money.

2. If you did take a lover, would it be:
   a. someone to whom you were really attracted?
   b. someone who could give you a good time?
   c. or would you much rather be married?

3. Diamonds, it is said, are a girl's best friend. Would you prefer your lover to give you:
   a. diamonds?
   b. a house of your own?
   c. his undying love?

4. In trying to captivate a man, which would you try to emphasize most?
   a. your face.
   b. your body.
   c. your braininess.
   d. your personality.

5. As a mistress, which of the following would you regard as an essential part of your wardrobe?
   a. some exotic French perfume.
   b. sheer black stockings.
   c. a nice warm bathrobe.

6. Your lover comes to call. Would you receive him:
   a. in the nude?
   b. in a diaphanous negligee?
   c. in a slinky trouser suit?

7. Presumably the two of you would talk . . . at first, at least. Which two of the following subjects would you encourage him to talk about?
   a. himself.
   b. you.

   c. books and films.

   d. sex.

   e. money.

   f. current affairs.

8. If he started telling you a joke you had heard before, would you:

   a. stop him?

   b. finish it for him?

   c. pretend it was new?

9. If he started talking about his troubles at work, would you:

   a. send him home to his wife?

   b. yawn with boredom?

   c. listen sympathetically?

10. Most men, it is said, remain little boys all their lives. Do you think this is:

   a. true?

   b. perhaps partly true?

   c. nonsense?

11. Do you think sex is:

   a. more pleasurable for men than for women?

   b. enjoyable for both?

   c. rather overrated?

12. Cooking. Do you:

   a. detest it?

   b. like to do some now and then?

   c. enjoy it?

13. Which of these colors would you pick for your most alluring nightie?

   a. yellow.

   b. red.

   c. black.

   d. white.

   e. green.

   f. blue.

14. Your boss asks you to work late, but the leer on his face suggests that he has more than work in mind. Would you:

   a. try anything once?

   b. ask for a raise?

    c. refuse and start looking for another job?

15. A magazine wants to take pictures of you in the nude. Would you:
    a. refuse indignantly?
    b. ask how much they'll pay?
    c. be delighted?

16. If money were no object, would you prefer to dress:
    a. flamboyantly?
    b. elegantly?
    c. casually?

17. If you think people are talking about you to your disadvantage, does it:
    a. worry you a lot?
    b. worry you a little?
    c. leave you quite unperturbed?

18. If your lover suddenly announced he was going to divorce his wife and marry you, would you:
    a. jump for joy?
    b. feel sorry for the wife?
    c. start looking around for another lover?

19. Your lover's wife comes hammering at the door. Would you:
    a. dress as attractively as possible before letting her in?
    b. let her in just as you are?
    c. pretend you are not at home?

20. Your lover tells you he has found someone else and that this is the parting of the ways. Would you:
    a. fly into a rage?
    b. burst into tears?
    c. yawn languidly?

SCORING

HERE'S HOW YOU SCORE:

1. a–1; b–2; c–5 (you can't be an ideal mistress without money)
2. a–3; b–5; c–1
3. a–3; b–5; c–1 (property is a girl's best friend these days)
4. a–1; b–5; c–0; d–3 (he doesn't care about your brains)
5. a–3; b–5; c–1

6.   a–3; b–5; c–1 (leave something to the imagination)
7.   a–3; b–5; c–1; d–3; e–5; f–1
8.   a–1; b–5; c–3
9.   a–5; b–1; c–3 (let his wife listen to his troubles)
10. a–5; b–3; c–1 (the ideal mistress knows her lover is a child at heart)
11. a–5; b–3; c–1
12. a–5; b–3; c–1
13. a–3; b–5; c–5; d–1; e–3; f–1 (red reveals your own passionate nature; black is erotic, to tempt him)
14. a–3; b–5; c–1
15. a–1; b–5; c–3 (money matters most)
16. a–5; b–3; c–1
17. a–1; b–3; c–5 (ideal mistresses don't worry what people think)
18. a–1; b–3; c–5 (nor do they want to marry)
19. a–5; b–3; c–1 (show her what she's up against)
20. a–3; b–1; c–5 (there's always another—and bigger—fish in the sea)

IF YOU SCORED...

78–or over: You should have lived in King Charles' golden days . . . or in Paris at the time of the second Empire. You would have had lovers lining up at your door, toasting you in champagne, showering you with diamonds. You're not only sexy, but also sharp and clever with it. You'd make an ideal mistress, all right—and make your lovers pay dearly for the privilege.

49–77: You, too, could be an ideal mistress, but only to a man you really loved or to whom you were strongly attracted. You're bursting with sex . . . and full of heart as well. The trouble is, you'd also feel sorry for his wife, worry what people were saying about you, and probably end up with enough guilt complexes to stuff a psychiatrist's couch.

48 or under: On the face of it, you're not cut out to be anyone's mistress. All you ask of life is a husband, a home, children, and peace of mind. You'd rather wear comfortable flat shoes than sexy high heels, rather go to bed in a long, warm nightie than a baby-doll outfit. You're one for a quiet, placid, contented life. But still waters, they say, sometimes run deep. So we could be wrong.

Is Your Man a Male Chauvinist Pig?

Women's liberation has gone a long way to reshaping women's attitudes to their role in society. But has the new thinking rubbed off on your man? Or is he still an old-fashioned male chauvinist pig? Try this quiz . . . it may help you discover who really wears the pants in your family.

1. When you go on a vacation, you usually go where:
    a. he wants?
    b. you decide?
    c. it is best for the entire family?

2. If you were to have a baby, he would:
    a. learn about delivery and early child care?
    b. leave it all to you?
    c. call for family help?

3. If you were to go with him to a convention, he would:
    a. suggest you go shopping?
    b. tell you to stay in the room?
    c. leave your time to your discretion?

4. He:
    a. likes your friends?
    b. prefers only his own acquaintances?
    c. enjoys his and your friends?

5. In household routine, he:
    a. is eager to help?
    b. lets you do it all?
    c. is there in a pinch if you need him?

6. He:
    a. asks you to help select his clothing?
    b. doesn't care a bit what you think?
    c. asks you to do his shopping?

7. In elections, he:
    a. expects you to vote as he does?
    b. encourages you to vote according to your convictions?
    c. discourages you to vote at all?

8. When it comes to your wardrobe you:
    a. please yourself?

b.   wear what he likes?

c.   buy what your friends like?

9.   When you have an appointment with him and are late, he usually:

a.   gives you hell?

b.   says nothing and broods?

c.   says he's happy you arrived safely?

10.   When you meet after a period of being apart he:

a.   is interested in knowing about your activities?

b.   wants to talk about himself?

c.   turns on the TV?

11.   Assume that each of you cut your finger in the same place. Which one of you would complain more?

a.   he?

b.   you?

c.   both the same?

12.   He considers women's lib:

a.   a reason to be more courteous to women?

b.   a reason to let them open their own doors?

c.   a passing, silly topic?

13.   He:

a.   lets you handle your own money?

b.   thinks he should handle it?

c.   feels you each should handle your own?

14.   In your lovelife you:

a.   must fulfill his sexual needs?

b.   are the object of his care?

c.   try to please each other?

15.   He feels animals:

a.   are best as objects of a hunt?

b.   are meant to be members of the family?

c.   should be left to roam wild?

16.   He:

a.   likes to have you run your fingers through his hair?

b.   objects to being fondled unless it's an overture to lovemaking?

c.   wants to initiate all physical contacts?

17.   If you want an extravagant item, you can get him to agree by:
      a. preparing his favorite meal?
      b. telling him how you can budget in order to afford it?
      c. raising a storm?

18.   If you were to buy him a sports coat, you would look for:
      a. a firm-bodied tweed?
      b. a soft cashmere with a silk lining?
      c. a well-cut, unpatterned blue serge?

19.   He:
      a. always opens doors for you?
      b. opens doors only if people are watching?
      c. opens his own doors and lets you open yours?

20.   Do you think the man in your life would like
      to see you as depicted in this cartoon?
      a. no.
      b. only in privacy.
      c. would thrive on my showing myself to others.

SCORING

1.	a–6; b–2; c–4	11.	a–6; b–2; c–4
2.	a–2; b–6; c–4	12.	a–2; b–6; c–4
3.	a–2; b–6; c–2	13.	a–2; b–6; c–4
4.	a–2; b–6; c–2	14.	a–6; b–2; c–4
5.	a–2; b–6; c–4	15.	a–6; b–2; c–4
6.	a–2; b–6; c–2	16.	a–2; b–4; c–6
7.	a–6; b–2; c–6	17.	a–2; b–4; c–6
8.	a–2; b–6; c–4	18.	a–4; b–2; c–6
9.	a–6; b–4; c–2	19.	a–2; b–4; c–6
10.	a–2; b–6; c–6	20.	a–6; b–4; c–2

100–120: He is a dominant personality. He wants things his way and you'd better heel-to. It isn't all that bad, however, because he is the great provider, rustic, and under it all there is a heart of gold. In his opinion, women, like children, are meant to be seen and not heard.

80–98: He is a noble creature. He has a robust opinion of himself, but he also has an inkling of what womankind is all about. If you behave like a lady, he will respond by being a gentleman.

58–78: Lucky for you. This is a fun score. You can be yourself and be comfortable with him. You both have moods, yet respect the feelings of each other.

40–56: This is a purr-fect situation for any woman who wants a cozy male. He is willing to be loved, adored, and petted. He is also willing to have the female take care of him.

Can You Hold the Man You Love?

He may love you deeply at this very moment, but you must remember that love is blind. Unless you watch your step he may suddenly see you through different eyes.

Try answering the following questions truthfully and you will probably learn something to your advantage.

Check a. or b. according to choice, and then check your score at the end.

1. a. Do you openly criticize his dress in public?
   b. Or do you tell him that he would look very nice in garments of a different hue when you are alone together?

2. a. Do you entertain visions of changing his habits in lots of ways?
   b. Or do you feel that he is just about perfect the way he is?

3. a. If he should be late for a date, do you accept his apologies with a smile?
   b. Or are you apt to scold him?

4. a. When dining out with him, do you always make a point of choosing inexpensive dishes?
   b. Or do you let yourself go, as they say?

5. a. Supposing he bought you a gift that was entirely unsuitable. Would you thank him prettily?
   b. Or would you indulge your true thoughts?

6. a. When at a party, do you try to attract the attention of the other men present?
   b. Or do you concentrate almost entirely on your escort?

7. a. Assuming that you invited him home for a meal, would you try to find out what his favorite dishes were?
   b. Or would you expect him to like whatever you thought fit to put before him?

8. a. If and when he voices an opinion, do you always state your point of view strongly and emphatically, even if it means contradicting him?
   b. Or do you try to see his point of view first?

9. a. Assuming that you are not interested in football, or whatever his favorite game may be, would you accompany him to a game just to please him?
   b. Or would you tell him you would prefer to go to the movies, etc.?

10. a. Do you expect him to bring you flowers or chocolates every time you have a date?
    b. Or do you tell him that they are not absolutely necessary as long as he is with you?

SCORING

ANSWERS:

Score 5 points for each correct answer: 1–b; 2–b; 3–a; 4–a; 5–a; 6–b; 7–a; 8–b; 9–a; 10–b. Maximum total score is 50.

If you have genuinely scored 40–50 points you should have no difficulty at all in holding him.

A total of 25–35 points means that you are being a trifle selfish at times.

A total of 20 points or under indicates that you stand an excellent chance of losing him in the near future.

Do You Like or Dislike Men?

Here's a little quiz that will help you ladies figure out whether you like or dislike men. Answer each question "Yes" or "No." When you've finished, give yourself a point for each "Yes" answer, then check the scoring key to see how you really feel about men.

1. Most men consider women inferior.

    Yes _____   No _____

2. I often find myself gossiping about men in a put-down manner.

    Yes _____   No _____

3. I wish I weren't dependent on men for sex.

    Yes _____   No _____

4. When my sex relationship goes wrong, I generally blame the man.

    Yes _____   No _____

5. I often pretend to have orgasms.

    Yes _____   No _____

6. If I had to spend six months on a desert island with a stranger, I'd choose a woman.

    Yes _____   No _____

7. I've had more unhappy than happy experiences with men.

    Yes _____   No _____

8. I have a strong fear of being raped.

    Yes _____   No _____

9. Men in my life are supercritical of me.

    Yes _____   No _____

10. Men in my life have caused me a great deal of stress.

    Yes _____   No _____

11. Most men are interested in a woman for sex only.

    Yes _____   No _____

12. The average woman is taken advantage of by men.

    Yes _____   No _____

13. My mother ran our family.

    Yes _____   No _____

14. I would feel guilty if I taught a class of men how to seduce a woman.

    Yes _____   No _____

15. My father didn't really love me.

    Yes _____   No _____

16. I get along best with men by careful planning and manipulation.

    Yes _____   No _____

17. Men prevent women from getting ahead in the business world.

    Yes _____   No _____

18. I hope women's liberation finally puts men in their place.

    Yes _____   No _____

19. My father really wanted a boy.

    Yes _____   No _____

20. Boys have more fun than girls.

    Yes _____   No _____

SCORING

If you scored 18–20, you dislike men and view them as a race apart.

15–17 means you're suspicious and wary of men.

13–14 shows you feel men are mostly interested in your physical attractions.

10–12 means you tolerate men as necessary evils.

7–9 shows you see men as real people and think there are a lot of good men.

3–6 means that you consider men among your best friends.

0–2 reveals that you love men and wouldn't be without one for anything.

Are You Afraid of Being Romantic?

Romance makes the world go around, and if you happen to be romantically inclined, you'll love this quiz. Many people say that the romance has gone out of life, but this isn't strictly true, as most people are romantic when they feel love and warmth toward their partner.

We know that the signs of the zodiac denote that some star signs are more romantic than others. However, generally speaking, we can all feel, at some stage in our lives, that we want to express ourselves romantically, thus creating an air of love and security.

This easy-to-take and incidentally painless quiz will tell you just how tender and loving you can be. Alternatively, when you mark your scorecard you might discover that you're really a cold and heartless mortal who needs a little bigger helping of tenderness in order to achieve a satisfactory and romantic life.

Answer each question "Yes" or "No."

1. Are you ever inclined to send him a solitary rose with a note that says: "I love you?"

        Yes _____   No _____

2. When he kisses you, do you stroke the back of his hair?

        Yes _____   No _____

3. When you're not seeing him, do you ever leave little notes in his pocket telling him how much you miss him?

Yes _____   No _____

4. Do you call him ''darling'' very often?

Yes _____   No _____

5. Have you ever called him on the phone just to say that you adore him?

Yes _____   No _____

6. You've had a row. Would you phone first to make it up?

Yes _____   No _____

7. After three months you finish with your boyfriend. Do you keep his letters?

Yes _____   No _____

8. Have you ever held his hand while he's driving?

Yes _____   No _____

9. When you kiss and cuddle do you whisper sweet nothings in his ear?

Yes _____   No _____

10. You discover that he has a hangup on garlic, but you loathe the smell. Are you prepared to put up with his garlic breath?

Yes _____   No _____

11. Do you ever feel afraid of displaying your feelings toward him?

Yes _____   No _____

12. Have you ever told him how much you love him?

Yes _____   No _____

13. Are you ever tempted to do silly things like sending him a lock of your hair?

Yes _____   No _____

14. Do you think that your boyfriend (or husband) could be more romantic?

Yes _____   No _____

15. Do you consider that you're in love?

Yes _____   No _____

16. Does your heart flutter when he touches you?

Yes _____   No _____

17. Have you felt this way before?

Yes _____   No _____

18. Do you consider yourself faithful to one man?

Yes _____   No _____

19. Is one boyfriend enough for you?

Yes _____   No _____

20. When he's romantic toward you, do you feel embarrassment?

Yes _____   No _____

SCORING

1. Yes; 2. Yes; 3. Yes; 4. Yes; 5. Yes; 6. Yes; 7. Yes; 8. Yes; 9. Yes; 10. Yes; 11. No; 12. Yes; 13. Yes; 14. No; 15. Yes; 16. Yes; 17. No; 18. Yes; 19. Yes; 20. No.

If your scorecard does look like this, then you are basically a romantic person who enjoys being in love and who knows how to capture a man's heart.

However, if you have more "Nos" than Yeses," well, you should think strongly about your relationship and ask yourself whether or not you are putting enough into it.

Are You the Woman He Dreams About?

Answer the following questions truthfully and learn whether you possess the qualities he admires most. Check a. or b. according to choice, and then check your score at the end.

1. a. Are you invariably late for a date?
    b. Or do you do your utmost to get there on time?

2. a. Do you feel that your wishes should always come first?
    b. Or do you try to meet your boyfriend halfway in that respect?

3. a. Are you prepared to make allowances for his shortcomings?
    b. Or do you point out his failings at every given opportunity?

4. a. Do you encourage him to spend more than he can afford?
    b. Or do you use your discretion in that respect?

5. a. Supposing you had arranged to accompany him to some rather dull affair and you subsequently received an invitation to a lively party, would you turn the party down?
    b. Or would you make some excuse to your boyfriend and go to the party instead?

6. a. Do you try to boss him?
    b. Or do you let him make the decisions in most cases?

7. a. Do you always take great pains with your appearance before going out on a date?
    b. Or do you tend to be a trifle slapdash in that respect?

8. a. Assuming that you are pretty adept at ice skating, or something of that nature, and he cannot master the sport, are you patient with him?
    b. Or do you tend to criticize his efforts?

9. a. Do you flirt with other men in his presence?
    b. Or do you frown upon that kind of behavior?

10. a. Do you pry into his affairs?
    b. Or do you feel that it's better that he should tell you things of his own accord?

SCORING

ANSWERS:
(Score 5 points for each correct answer.)

1–b; 2–b; c–a; 4–b; 5–a; 6–b; 7–a; 8–a; 9–b; 10–b. Maximum total score is 50.

If you have genuinely scored 40–50 points, then you have nothing to worry about.

A total of 25–35 points means that you tend to be a trifle self-centered.

A total of 20 points or under would indicate that you are going the wrong way about keeping a man!

Can You Handle Men?

In every woman's existence, men play a very large role. Her happiness, her success, as often as not depend on one or more members of the so-called stronger sex. Unfortunately, what makes women's life so precarious sometimes is the fact that men are remarkably peculiar creatures. Recently a well-known Frenchwoman compared a man to an elephant with a wasp in his ear. Handle him right, and he will move mountains to please you; but go about it the wrong way, and he will balk at a molehill.

Worst of all, most women are afflicted with the odd delusion that they know absolutely for certain how to handle *their* own men, whatever else may be true about their fellow sisters—and discover much too late that they were wrong from start to finish.

Answer the following questions honestly, and you will learn whether you are a genuine man-tamer—or are in immediate danger of having your dreams and hopes crushed beneath an aroused elephant's feet.

Mark a. or b. according to choice, and then check your score at the end.

1. a. Do you go out of your way to compliment the man you are interested in on his wit, his appearance, his prowess at games, etc.?
   b. Or do you think that this sort of vanity is purely a feminine trait, and that men want to hear the truth and nothing but the truth about themselves, no matter how unpleasant it may be?

2. a. When he takes you out to a party, do you deliberately set out to charm other men present—perhaps to make him a little jealous?
   b. Or do you devote yourself primarily to him?

3. a. Assuming you are working with men around you, do you seek their advice now and then—whether you need it or not?
   b. Or do you think it's much better not to bother them at all?

4. a. Do you take an intelligent interest in his job, his hobbies, and so on?
   b. Or are you so concerned with your affairs that you have no time for anything else?

5. a. Assuming you happen to disagree with his opinions on, say, politics or religion, do you immediately and forcibly press your point?
   b. Or are you prepared to listen to him first, and—so to speak—suspend your judgment until he has presented his case?

6. a. Are you quite ready to fall in with his moods?
   b. Or do you think he should adjust himself to yours?

7. a. Supposing he'd commit some social *faux pas* in public. Would you laugh at him?

    b. Or would you try to cover up his embarrassment as best as you could?

8. a. Do you consider men to be thoroughly level-headed creatures who at work will judge women strictly on their merits?

    b. Or do you believe that they may be swayed by a pretty smile?

9. a. Do you think that at heart most men are either hostile to or contemptuous of women and hence should be always treated as actual or potential enemies?

    b. Or do you feel that most men are genuinely fond of women, and that although they sometimes may do foolish things, the harm is more likely to be due to ignorance or carelessness rather than a deliberate intent to hurt?

10. a. Can you say you honestly understand, and appreciate, why men now and again prefer to spend their time in a wholly masculine company with no women around?

    a. Or do you think it's simply a ridiculous affectation with which you have no sympathy?

SCORING

Score a point for each correct answer.

1–a; 2–b; 3–a; 4–a; 5–b; 6–a; 7–b; 8–b; 9–b; 10–a. Maximum total score is 10 points.

If you have genuinely scored 8–10 points, then no man is a match for you. Your slightest wish is his command—and very happy is he in his bondage! You go through life armed with a magic wand, and all men are there to serve you.

A total of 5–7 points means that as a man-tamer you do not wholly qualify. As most other women, you make your mistakes when it comes to handling men, but by and large you get along with them well enough. The danger is that you may fail just when you'd need to succeed most. There is, of course, no reason why you should not improve the delicate art of manhandling. To you, virtuosity would come easily.

A total of 4 points or under would indicate that you really have not the slightest idea how to deal with the other half of humanity. Possibly you pride yourself on your independence in this respect. If that is so, you'd do well remembering that "pride goeth before a fall."

Moreover, you must be leading a lonely life—it would seem an altogether high price to pay for self-reliance. Naturally, it is your life, and nobody has the right to tell you how to spend it. All the same, why not give the men around you the chance to help and be your friends? They really can't be the bad lot you apparently suspect them of being.

Will You Make a Good Wife?

Marriage counselors, psychologists, doctors, and members of the clergy were consulted on the qualities they have found to be most important assets to a good wife.

1. Have you dated a number of different people?

    Yes _____   No _____

2. Do you think physical love is the most important part of marriage?

    Yes _____   No _____

3. Does illness, either your own or of others, frighten you?

    Yes _____   No _____

4. Do you plan to center your family life around your children?

    Yes _____   No _____

5. On a date do you often feel your escort is showing too much attention to someone else?

    Yes _____   No _____

6. Do you have sufficient education, talent, or ability to be able to support yourself comfortably without marriage?

    Yes _____   No _____

7. Do you dress for dinner with your family as neatly, though not necessarily as elaborately, as you do for a date?

    Yes _____   No _____

8.   Do you have some hobbies that you enjoy?

         Yes _____   No _____

9.   Can you name two girlfriends with whom you share confidences?

         Yes _____   No _____

10.   Have you developed a time sense—the ability to keep to a schedule without being reminded?

         Yes _____   No _____

11.   When you make a blunder, can you laugh at yourself?

         Yes _____   No _____

12.   Does criticism hurt you deeply?

         Yes _____   No _____

13.   Do you generally like and enjoy the friends of the men you go out with?

         Yes _____   No _____

14.   Would you rather go dancing than be with a few friends at home?

         Yes _____   No _____

15.   Can you recall pleasant experiences as a child when you made mud pies or waded in mud?

         Yes _____   No _____

16.   Do you dress according to the latest styles and fads?

         Yes _____   No _____

17.   Do you think marriage is a fifty-fifty arrangement?

         Yes _____   No _____

18.   On a date are you considerate of your escort's pocketbook?

         Yes _____   No _____

19.   Do other people's problems bore you?

         Yes _____   No _____

20.   Is it difficult for you to apologize?

         Yes _____   No _____

SCORING

ANWERS:

1. Yes. You wouldn't buy a dress without looking around first.
2. No. Physical love wears off. Respect lasts.
3. No. You will have everything from measles to operations to face.
4. No. Your husband must be the first consideration.
5. No. If you have said "Yes," you are likely to be a jealous wife.
6. Yes. You must be able to take care of yourself for your own inner security as well as in case of an emergency.
7. Yes. Neatness and good grooming must be a habit, not an occasion.
8. Yes. Marriage presents many occasions when you must be self-contained and happy with your own activities.
9. Yes. A well-adjusted wife must have close women friends as well as those among the opposite sex.
10. Yes. Without the ability to schedule yourself, you'll have a difficult time running an organized household.
11. Yes. A sense of humor is very often the oil on troubled waters.
12. No. In meeting the many problems of marriage, there are bound to be times of suggestion and criticism.
13. Yes. You had better like them. Your husband's friends will be around.
14. No. If you don't prefer an evening at home, what will you do when most of them will be spent there?
15. Yes. If you said "No," you may have trouble with all the messy, unpleasant chores of housework.
16. No. If you said "Yes," your husband will soon be broke buying clothes.
17. No. You must plan to give all you have to your marriage.
18. Yes. If you aren't considerate on a date, it is unlikely you will be when you are married.
19. No. Marriage is based on listening sympathetically rather than talking.
20. No. The ability to say, "I'm sorry" can save a lot of heartache and anger.

16–20 correct: Your qualifications are excellent. You are mature, thoughtful of others, and possess a great deal of common sense and sensitivity toward others.

11–15 correct: You will be a very good wife although there are still some childish characteristics you will have to overcome. Be sure you never marry on a short acquaintanceship.

1–10 correct: Marriage for you now would be a mistake. You need some time to grow up and to think of others instead of yourself. Better think through your answers and make some personality changes.

YOU
AND YOUR
SEX LIFE

Do You Have Sex Appeal?

Don't laugh off the idea. Whether a person is fifteen or forty, nineteen or ninety, there is that certain urge to be desirable. Yet sex appeal is a complex thing made up of various subtle, complex elements. Physical beauty alone is not the answer. Soap bars help, a jaunty suit is an asset, eye shadow is enticing—but there is more to being sexy than meets the eye.

You and you alone can develop the attitude of mind that will lure others to you. This quiz will help you. Put yourself in the following situations and select the reaction nearest your own.

1. You are introduced to a new person. You:
   a. look into his (or her) eyes.
   b. hang your head.
   c. look at his (or her) clothing.

2. Your date (or mate) plans some event that turns out to be a failure. Perhaps you have a flat tire or the food at the restaurant was miserable. You say:
   a. "You dummy, you can't do anything right."
   b. "It was fun to muddle through that one together."
   c. "Nice try, chum. Let's do better next time."

3. You are with your date (or mate) at a social affair. You:
   a. are indifferent to your partner and turn on your charms for others.

    b. focus most of your attention on the person you are with.

    c. crawl into a protective, unobtrusive shell.

4. As you evaluate your approach to people in the area of sexual relationships, you:

    a. believe the strong come-on works best.

    b. feel you are best suited to be hard to get.

    c. like people on a human level whether it is sexual or not.

5. You step on your bathroom scales and find you are far heavier than you should be for your age, height, and bone structure. You:

    a. assure yourself that everyone loves a roly-poly person.

    b. immediately go on a diet.

    c. seek professional advice from a qualified doctor and follow instructions.

6. You are with your date (or mate) and find yourself with several children whom you don't know. You:

    a. are irritated because they are around.

    b. enjoy playing and talking with them.

    c. take an objective observer's attitude.

7. When it comes to purely clinical facts about the physical aspects of sex, you:

    a. are well informed from reliable sources such as doctors, teachers, medical books, etc.

    b. have learned all you know about sex from your parents and/or people your own age.

    c. are uninformed and react primarily on a purely instinctive basis.

8. In an honest evaluation of your emotional make up, you conclude that you:

    a. often have a lousy disposition.

    b. are generally in a good mood.

    c. try to show those around you that you are never especially happy or sad, elated or depressed—in short, an unemotional person.

9. You have the urge to be close physically to your partner. You:

    a. take the initiative with sudden bold moves.

    b. hide your feelings and needs.

    c. are tender and caressing in the hope he (or she) will feel as you do.

10. Here are two classic statements about sexual relationships: "There are no frigid women, only clumsy men," and "There are no impotent men, only insensitive women." You:

a. agree

b. disagree

c. are challenged by one or both of the statements.

11. In your daily life you:

a. are as neat and clean as possible when you are in contact with your companion.

b. take the attitude, "You'll have to take me, dirty as I am."

c. quickly splash on perfume, colognes, and use a strong mouthwash in an attempt to cover any unpleasant body odors.

12. When you are talking with someone you really like, you:

a. tend to lean toward that person.

b. usually lean backward from him (or her).

c. are rather rigid in your posture when listening or speaking.

13. When you talk about your parents and your early formative years you:

a. usually have warm, loving statements to make.

b. try to make your partner feel sorry for you.

c. kick your past "under the rug" and refuse to talk about it.

14. When it comes to gift-giving you:

a. think it is a waste of money even on major occasions such as birthdays, anniversaries, Christmas, etc.

b. enjoy making little surprise presents for no reason at all.

c. like to overwhelm your partner with lavish gifts even if sometimes you can't afford them.

15. In your contacts with your date (or mate), you:

a. find it satisfying to say, "I love you."

b. can't quite get the words out.

c. use the word "love" to many people and for many things, such as "I love your new car," "I love our new neighbors," etc.

16. When with your date (or mate), you:

a. make it a point to talk about your past successful conquests in the arena of romance.

b. never mention your past romances unless asked and then answer honestly.

c. refuse to talk about your previous involvements, wishes, disappointments, successes.

17. In order to be appealing you:

a. often feign illness or the need to be comforted as a come-on for affection.

b. try to be bright and shining even if you feel terrible.

c. are frank with your partner about the way you feel.

18. When you are with others, you:

a. behave in a manner so your partner will be proud of you.

b. belittle your partner to prove your superiority and his (or her) need of you.

c. stress the abilities and positive qualities of your partner.

19. In your dealings with people in general you consciously or subconsciously:

a. desire the approval of the opposite sex.

b. work for the approval of your sex.

c. hope you are liked and admired by both sexes.

20. The young couple in the picture shown are obviously attracted to each other. How many qualities do they each have and have together that indicate they both have sex appeal? Don't read below the picture until you've answered.

You should be able to find at least six or even more qualities that indicate mutual attraction and sex appeal, such as looking at each other, holding hands, sharing a cup together, well-groomed hair, dressed properly for the setting, and finding a romantic place to talk. Give yourself a point for every idea you had. They do not necessarily have to be those mentioned above.

SCORING

1.	a–6; b–2; c–4	11.	a–6; b–2; c–4
2.	a–2; b–6; c–4	12.	a–6; b–2; c–4
3.	a–4; b–6; c–2	13.	a–6; b–4; c–2
4.	a–2; b–2; c–6	14.	a–2; b–6; c–4
5.	a–2; b–4; c–6	15.	a–6; b–2; c–4
6.	a–2; b–6; c–4	16.	a–2; b–6; c–2
7.	a–6; b–4; c–2	17.	a–2; b–4; c–6
8.	a–2; b–6; c–4	18.	a–6; b–2; c–4
9.	a–4; b–2; c–6	19.	῾a–4; b–4; c–6
10.	a–6; b–2; c–4	20.	You fill in your own score.

WHAT YOUR SCORE MEANS

100–120:   If you rate in this range, you not only know about sex appeal, but also live it. There is that certain glint in your eye, that certain smile, the tone of your voice that make people love you. Sex appeal has nothing to do with age. With the great asset you have, there is also a price. Some people may be jealous of you. When you sense this, turn on your charms and share your talents with them.

80–98:   You have a high rating, but sometimes you get so involved with daily routine that you forget the wonder of being able to give and to receive. You may forget the warm feeling of just holding hands without a word being said. But all in all you have what it takes!

58–78:   You have a few steps to accomplish before you have true sex appeal. But don't worry, you can develop the charm if you want. The real secret is to make the others around you really happy . . . even to the point of pampering them at times. Remember: If *you* want to be loved, to be sexy, you have to reach out with affection. It takes "two to tango," two to admire each other, and a sincere interest in the goodness of life.

46–56:   Obviously you're not the greatest sex symbol around. Think through the reasons you *feel* you're not. Somewhere on the road of life you developed an inferiority complex larger than a

Halloween pumpkin head. There are many people in the world who want *you* to develop that certain charm called sex appeal. They are waiting for you to look into their eyes, to hear you say, "I love you." When you can do this with sincerity, you've got sex appeal all wrapped up.

Are You an Uninhibited Lover?

Some people feel totally free when making love. Others feel somewhat restrained. Are you the type of lover who is apprehensive when it comes to sex, or are you the sort of carefree individual who "lets it all hang out"? Take this test to find out!

1. Would you rather make love with the lights on?
   a. Yes.
   b. No.

2. Would you make love at a drive-in movie?
   a. Yes.
   b. No.

3. Do you have no self-consciousness when standing naked in front of your lover?
   a. Yes.
   b. No.

4. Would you feel free to give your lover a passionate kiss in public?
   a. Yes.
   b. No.

5. Do you feel free to initiate foreplay with your lover?
   a. Yes.
   b. No.

6. If you and your lover were out at night on what seemed to be a deserted beach, would you willingly go skinny-dipping?
   a. Yes.
   b. No.

7. Do you enjoy making love in places other than bed?
    a. Yes.
    b. No.

8. Do you feel comfortable telling your lover what pleases you most?
    a. Yes.
    b. No.

9. Do you like to experiment by making love in different ways?
    a. Yes.
    b. No.

10. You and your lover are lying in a bed that creaks with the slightest movement. Your kids are watching TV in the adjoining room. Would you and your lover still have sex?
    a. Yes.
    b. No.

SCORING

Give yourself a point for each "Yes" answer.

If you scored 10, you are a provocative and uninhibited lover. Nothing stands in your way of sexual fulfillment.

A score of 8–9 suggests you are the "explorer" type of lover who views sex as an exciting adventure. Although at times a bit shy, you look forward to each sexual encounter with great anticipation.

A score of 5–7 indicates that your inhibitions are interfering with the pleasure to be derived from your sexual experiences. Make an effort to loosen up. You'll get a lot more out of your love life.

A score of 4 or less reveals that your inhibitions have put the damper on your love life. Sex is not a mechanical process. If you let yourself go, it can be quite a ball!

Sex Quiz

The ultimate orgasm is rarely if ever reached by the modern "civilized" person. Carefully we have been taught to deny ourselves the animal pleasure of feeling the strength of the full orgasm. Hopefully someday we will be able to regain some of our primitive ability to enjoy our bodies.

Where do you stand in the orgasm department, both knowledge-and experiencewise? Answer the following questions "Always," "Usually," "Sometimes," or "Never." See the end of the test for scoring, answers, and some fascinating facts and fallacies.

1. Do you reach an orgasm when you have sexual intercourse?
    Always_____ Usually_____ Sometimes_____ Never_____

2. Is it difficult for you to reach an orgasm?
    Always_____ Usually_____ Sometimes_____ Never_____

3. Do you fantasize during your orgasm?
    Always_____ Usually_____ Sometimes_____ Never_____

4. Do you experience a feeling of well-being, relaxation, satiation, and complete satisfaction after orgasm?
    Always_____ Usually_____ Sometimes_____ Never_____

5. Do you experience a falling sensation during orgasm?
    Always_____ Usually_____ Sometimes_____ Never_____

6. Do you make uninhibited verbal sounds during orgasm?
    Always_____ Usually_____ Sometimes_____ Never_____

7. Do you strive to attain an orgasm at exactly the same time your partner does?
    Always_____ Usually_____ Sometimes_____ Never_____

8. Do you move freely during orgasm?
    Always_____ Usually_____ Sometimes_____ Never_____

9. Do you hold your breath when having an orgasm?
    Always_____ Usually_____ Sometimes_____ Never_____

10. Do you think it is a good idea for a man to hold an erection more than twenty minutes before climaxing?
    Always_____ Usually_____ Sometimes_____ Never_____

11. Do the physical surroundings greatly influence your orgasm?
    Always_____ Usually_____ Sometimes_____ Never_____

12. Is the intensity of your orgasm affected by who your partner is?

Always_____   Usually_____   Sometimes_____   Never_____

13. Are you able to reach an orgasm within five minutes after insertion?

Always_____   Usually_____   Sometimes_____   Never_____

14. Do you reach your orgasms through other than genital stimulation, for example, by breast play, kissing?

Always_____   Usually_____   Sometimes_____   Never_____

15. Do you think it is desirable to be able to reach orgasm without any direct physical contact—for example, listening to music, watching movies?

Always_____   Usually_____   Sometimes_____   Never_____

16. Can you reach an orgasm with someone you don't particularly love?

Always_____   Usually_____   Sometimes_____   Never_____

17. Do you reach an orgasm when you masturbate?

Always_____   Usually_____   Sometimes_____   Never_____

18. When you masturbate, are your orgasms as pleasurable as intercourse?

Always_____   Usually_____   Sometimes_____   Never_____

19. Do you feel like lighting up a cigarette or having a drink of alcohol within five minutes after you have completed intercourse?

Always_____   Usually_____   Sometimes_____   Never_____

20. When you feel an orgasm approaching can you stop it or delay it if you desire?

Always_____   Usually_____   Sometimes_____   Never_____

21. Do you sense pain in the genital area during orgasm?

Always_____   Usually_____   Sometimes_____   Never_____

22. Do you enjoy having an orgasm by oral means?

Always_____   Usually_____   Sometimes_____   Never_____

23. Is it at all important to you that your partner reach an orgasm?

Always_____   Usually_____   Sometimes_____   Never_____

24. While having intercourse do you fantasize some sexual act, encounter, or being with another person to help you reach an orgasm?

Always_____   Usually_____   Sometimes_____   Never_____

25. Would you describe your orgasms as high points in your life?

Always_____   Usually_____   Sometimes_____   Never_____

SCORING

1. If you don't reach orgasm during lovemaking you are highly armored against sexual feelings. Early parental attitudes toward children's sex curiosity, hostility toward the opposite sex, and a lack of self-liking often cause absence of sexual feelings and inability to reach orgasm.
    Always—4;   Usually—3,   Sometimes—2;   Never—1

2. If you do reach orgasm but it is difficult or takes a long time, you are also blocking genital reactions, but less so.
    Always—1;   Usually—2;   Sometimes—3;   Never—4

3. If you fantasize that you are making love with your appealing secretary, or envision an attractive, virile movie star, you may be helping yourself achieve an orgasm, but your mind has entered into the picture where only feelings should reign, thereby depriving you of the fullest possible orgasm.
    Always—1;   Usually—2;   Sometimes—3;   Never—3

4. If you do not feel completely relaxed, refreshed, or ready to fall into a deep, natural sleep after having had an orgasm that should feel like electricity going through your body from your toes to your head, you have not reached a complete orgasm, and you are missing the best part of sex.
    Always—4;   Usually—3;   Sometimes—2;   Never—1

5. As you experience the complete orgasm there should be a skyrocket feeling, a zooming through the surf on an enormous wave, a climbing to the stars, a roller-coaster effect with falling, sinking, swinging, a loss-of-control feeling. This is all packed into the true orgasm—but to get there you have to give up your control; if you don't you miss out on half the glorious fun.
    Always—4;   Usually—3;   Sometimes—2;   Never—1

6. Moans of joy, screams of ecstasy, sighs, yells of delight—it makes no difference, as long as whatever does come out of your mouth, comes out naturally and freely.
    Always—4;   Usually—3;   Sometimes—2;   Never—1

7. The old wives' tale that simultaneous orgasm is the ideal to be strived for can be disastrous to you and your partner. If you allow yourself to be overly concerned with this when you are climaxing, you deprive yourself of pleasure and place a heavy burden on your

partner. Begin sensually enjoying lovemaking throughout your body and leave your mind out of bed.

Always—1;   Usually—2;   Sometimes—4;   Never—3

8. Movement during orgasm indicates how loose your body is. Basically, the uptight or frozen person finds it difficult to move during orgasm, which in turn makes for a jerky or very spastic climax of a smooth, flowing, peak-pulsating experience.

Always—4;   Usually—3;   Sometimes—2;   Never—1

9. Holding your breath just prior to or during orgasm cuts off feelings from the genital area. Try taking deep breaths into the diaphragm and stomach as you enjoy making love. This deep breathing will intensify sensual sensations throughout your body, particularly in your genitals.

Always—1;   Usually—2;   Sometimes—3;   Never—4

10. Holding an erection is considered by many men as a sign of virility, but held for a long period of time it is more likely a sign of impotence. Holding an erection "to please" can deprive the male of full satisfaction. Climax as your body dictates, and both partners will soon find the pleasure greater and the pressure less.

Always—1;   Usually—2;   Sometimes—3;   Never—4

11. Soft lights, silky sheets, and a quiet room are all conducive to your attaining an orgasm. However, if you are unable to reach orgasm because the setting isn't just right, you are letting external things affect you too much for your own good time. The highly complex sex system is triggered off by a million little things, so don't limit yourself to just a few environmental imperatives.

Always—1;   Usually—2;   Sometimes—3;   Never—4

12. Do you become aware of the smell, the look, the feel, the sound, and the aura of your partner? Are you attuned to the magical, sexually arousing techniques of your lover? If you are not affected by your partner's uniqueness while making love you are completely cut off from your emotional feelings and are existing in a living death. It is certainly possible to reach a climax with almost any partner on a purely physical stimulation level, but be aware of the fact that this type of orgasm is only secondary and lacks the fulfillment of a deep and satisfying orgasm with someone you are involved with on an emotional basis.

Always—4;   Usually—3;   Sometimes—2;   Never—1

13. Normally functioning lovers can reach orgasm within five minutes providing they are uninhibited, free, and unarmored. The orgasm reflex does not know how to tell time; it only knows how to tell feelings. The brain getting in on the act is what prevents the orgasm reflex from operating in a natural manner. The orgasm can burst forth in five minutes, one minute, or an hour. The tyranny of associating the clock with the sex act deprives many of their right to the best possible feelings.

    Always—4; Usually—3 Sometimes—2; Never—1

14. As a general rule, any orgasm achieved from other than penis-vagina contact is of a secondary nature. In the male a residue of sperm is left in the prostate, and in the female a feeling of discontent, no matter how slight, rests within the emotional reservoir.

    Always—1; Usually—2; Sometimes—4; Never—3

15. It is possible to reach orgasm through other than direct physical stimulation—for instance, listening to some particularly stirring music, watching a violent sports event such as a car race (in ancient Rome women were known to climax during the gladiatorial tournaments), or being shot around on a roller coaster. Again, however, this is another secondary release.

    Always—1; Usually—2; Sometimes—4; Never—3

16. As long as the person you are making love with does not physically turn you off, you can have an orgasm. A really full orgasm, however, necessitates complete rapport with the partner, a total unity of body and emotion.

    Always—2; Usually—3; Sometimes—4; Never—1

17. If you are able to reach an orgasm when you masturbate, and are not guilt-ridden, then you are among those who are sexually adjusted. Masturbation is a natural function of the human body. Until you are capable of enjoying your own sensuality and your own body, you can't enjoy another person's body.

    Always—4; Usually—3 Sometimes—2; Never—1

18. Masturbation orgasms are normally not the same as orgasms achieved during intercourse. If they are, you have been fixated at a level known as the masturbation level. You need to work on getting more fulfillment out of your sex life—with a member of the opposite sex.

    Always—1; Usually—2; Sometimes—3; Never—4

19. The ultimate orgasm ought to leave you so relaxed and ready to melt away that there is no energy left available or desire for a cigarette or a drink. If you find yourself constantly wanting these inhibitors of good feeling it is time for you to question whether you are open to getting the most pleasurable sex experience out of your relationships.

Always—1;   Usually—2;   Sometimes—3;   Never—4

20. The more your ability to delay your orgasm by the use of your will power and brain, the less you are giving in and letting go. Our bodies are built to give us a never-ending source of pleasure. Only by shifting the brain into gear do we stop these feelings.

Always—1;   Usually—2;   Sometimes—3;   Never—4

21. Pain in the genitals shows that the area is armored against good feeling. In the male the prostate gland has hardened to such a degree that pushing the semen out is painful and the orgasm comes in a jerky, spasmodic manner. In the female the pelvis and vagina have become so constricted against pleasurable feelings that the forceful orgasm causes pain rather than enjoyable sensations.

Always—1;   Usually—2;   Sometimes—3;   Never—4

22. To enjoy having orgasms by means other than intercourse is excellent, as it indicates you have the flexibility to allow yourself a variety of forms of stimulation, thus increasing sensual pleasuree. However, orally induced orgasms are of a secondary nature and should not be the only means by which orgasm can be reached.

Always—4;   Usually—3;   Sometimes—2;   Never—1

23. Unless you are a confirmed sadist or are fixated at the level of masturbation and look at coitus as merely an opportunity to work off some unneeded energy, you ought to be able to derive tremendous joy and fulfillment from arousing your partner and helping him (or her) achieve a satisfactory orgasm.

Always—3;   Usually—4;   Sometimes—2;   Never—1

24. If you are making love with a person for whom you have a strong orgasmic feeling, the need to fantasize is at a zero point. To fantasize about a larger penis, a prettier girl, or a gentler or stronger lover is to fill in the blank spots in the relationship.

Always—1;   Usually—2   Sometimes—3;   Never—4

25. The peak spots in your life ought to be varied: work, play, creativity, learning, and at the top of one of the mountains of joy should be sex. In fact, physical sexual joy ought to be on the top peak in your life. If you find other activities assuming an equal or more advanced position,

stand still and scrutinize whether or not you are using these activities as secondary releases. If people are not gratified in bed they will usually take that frustration and put it into hostile goadings of their family and acquaintances. Or they will take that energy and put it into things that are time-consuming: cooking, sports, meetings, conventions, anything that will allow them to drain off their sexual energy.

Always—4; Usually—3; Sometimes—2; Never—1

WHAT YOUR SCORE MEANS TO YOU

Score 25–46: You have managed to seal your emotions in a sterile container, your body. If you have an orgasm at all, it is a shock to your system, which is devoted to depriving your body of all sensual stimulation. Start, right now, to partake of the joys of life through your body feelings.

Score 47–65: The battle between your cultural training and your animal drive is destroying most of your sexual feelings. Your body wants the pleasure of expanding and enjoying good feelings and your consciousness is constantly armoring against sensations.

Score 66–84: You are starting to realize the potential of the true orgasm—a free-flowing, outward, all-embracing loss of conscious will power, a euphoric condition. Remember: The mind searches for intellectual data, while the body is on a constant hunt for joyous feelings. There is a time for each. Continue to be happy with your loss-of-control orgasms.

Score 85–100: You are a member of the elite society who have received the medal of orgasmic honor. The expansive, outward, full-feeling orgasms you obviously are achieving can only lead you to a successful, richly rewarding life. If you are able to liberate those with whom you come in contact, all the better!

Will Your Sex Drive Pass Sixty-five?

Will you have a sex life after sixty-five?

You can. Lots of people do. But it all depends on the way you live right now.

Here is a quiz to help you determine how joyous your sex life will be in the later years. For each question, select the one answer that best applies to you.

1. How would you rate your sex life at present?
   a. very satisfactory
   b. satisfactory
   c. unsatisfactory

2. How's your health today?
   a. excellent
   b. fair
   c. poor

3. What amounts of drugs or medicines do you take?
   a. very little
   b. little
   c. probably too much

4. How much are you using alcoholic beverages?
   a. very little
   b. little
   c. probably too much

5. Are you stimulated by being around very attractive members of the opposite sex, regardless of their age?
   a. definitely
   b. sometimes
   c. not usually

6. How hard do you try to stay in good physical condition?
   a. a lot
   b. a moderate amount
   c. very little

7. Do you overeat?
   a. not at all
   b. sometimes
   c. often

8. Does your health permit you to engage in regular sexual activity?
   a. decidedly
   b. probably
   c. probably not

9. Do you have as much interest in sex as you did five years ago?
   a. decidedly
   b. probably
   c. probably not

10. How would you rate your sex drive today?
    a. very interested
    b. moderately interested
    c. not interested

11. In sexual activity, are you tense?
    a. not in the least
    b. a little
    c. very

12. Do you think that members of the opposite sex who are your age or older find you attractive?
    a. probably
    b. maybe
    c. probably not

13. Do you think you're more stimulating company in a mixed group than in one made up of your own sex only?
    a. undoubtedly
    b. probably
    c. makes no difference

14. If your spouse were to pass away, would you look for another mate after a period of time?
    a. very likely
    b. possibly
    c. probably not

SCORING

Now score yourself. Give yourself two points for each a. answer, one for each b., and none for each c.

And here's what your score means:

20–28:   You're extremely likely to have an active sex life well past sixty-five. What's more, you'll enjoy it to the fullest.

15–19:   You should have at least a moderately active sex life after sixty-five, and you'll derive real enjoyment from it.

14–18:   You need to take better care of yourself and to work harder at getting along with the opposite sex. If you do, your capacity for sex in the later years will be at least moderately satisfactory.

13 or below: Start making changes in your life now if you want to enjoy sex when you're over sixty-five. This means working to improve your health and physical condition, your initiative and interest in sex—immediately.

What is Your Sexual I.Q.?

How much do you know about human sexuality? You may be surprised to discover that you don't know as much as you think you do.

We now know that many of our sexual beliefs, values, and attitudes are based on false information. They produce sex behavior that results in unhappiness, broken marriages, and a great deal of unnecessary anxiety.

In recent years, sex-education programs have sought to dispel our ignorance and increase our enjoyment of sex.

How well informed are you about human sexuality? Take this test and find out.

**ALL ANSWERS TO THIS TEST
ARE TO BE GIVEN AS "TRUE OR FALSE."
IF ANY PART OF THE STATEMENT IS FALSE,
THE ENTIRE STATEMENT
IS TO BE CONSIDERED FALSE.**

	TRUE	**FALSE**
1. Intense sexual attraction and activity can exist in a long-term relationship between a couple whether they love each other or not.	_____	_____
2. Sex relations are expressions of a physical need. Therefore, they do not necessarily express love.	_____	_____
3. The degree of premarital sexual satisfaction is one of the best predictors of how satisfactory sex relations will be after marriage.	_____	_____
4. Happily married couples have sex relations whenever the husband wants sex relations.	_____	_____
5. Happily married couples make sex relations last as long as it is pleasing to both, not just till the man is satisfied.	_____	_____
6. Men are generally ready for orgasm sooner than women.	_____	_____
7. Men, on the average, do not respond any more intensely or quickly to sexual stimulation than do women.	_____	_____

	TRUE	FALSE

8. If men respond to physical urges for sex more quickly than women, they learn to do this. They are not born needing sex more often than women.   _____ _____

9. Failure to achieve sexual satisfaction is more disturbing emotionally to a man than to a woman.   _____ _____

10. Enlargement of the clitoris is observed in some sexually excited women. This means such women have greater sex drive and capacity for orgasm than women who don't show this response.   _____ _____

11. Many women can achieve orgasm only by manual stimulation of their clitoris. Such women have less desire or capacity for sex than women who can achieve orgasm through intercourse.   _____ _____

12. Active, satisfactory sex relations between married couples after sixty is mostly achieved because their sex relations have been mutually satisfactory in the years before sixty.   _____ _____

13. Marriage counselors generally recommend that the man be more aggressive than the woman in preintercourse sex play.   _____ _____

14. In sexual excitement a woman's breasts, lips of her vagina, and the vagina itself all become either firm or noticeably larger.   _____ _____

15. Any coital position pleasing to both partners is equally effective for satisfaction in intercourse.   _____ _____

16. Sex play before intercourse is desirable largely to ready the woman for satisfaction. The man is ready immediately.   _____ _____

17. Some women can have more than one orgasm during intercourse. Such women are usually irritable and unsatisfied if they have only one orgasm.   _____ _____

	TRUE	FALSE

18. The best way for a woman to be adequately stimulated during intercourse is to explain her sexual likes and dislikes to her partner beforehand. _____ _____

19. The hymen or other areas of female genitalia are likely to be affected or damaged by active physical exercise such as horseback riding. _____ _____

20. An intact hymen is certain evidence that a woman never had intercourse. _____ _____

21. There is no sure way for someone else to decide whether a woman has ever had intercourse. _____ _____

22. For a woman who starts sexual intercourse with an intact hymen, intercourse may continue to be quite painful for some time after her first sexual experience. _____ _____

23. When a woman exhibits vaginal spasm that results in closing her vagina and preventing intercourse, she is indicating an involuntary learned idea that sex relations are painful and dangerous. _____ _____

24. When there is a marked difference in the size of the male and the female organs, this almost always causes unsatisfactory sex relations. _____ _____

25. Marital failure and divorce are often caused by a fundamental difference in the capacity of the wife and the husband to want and enjoy sex relations. _____ _____

26. The usual aftereffect of orgasm in normal sex relations is fatigue and weakness, rather than pleasurable relaxation. _____ _____

27. When a woman suffers continued pain in sexual intercourse with no discoverable medical cause, the usual reason is her guilt or fear about sex. _____ _____

	TRUE	FALSE

28. Most commonly, when a woman is unresponsive in intercourse, either she fears pregnancy or she has been taught it is immoral to exhibit desire.

29. If sex relations become less frequent in a marriage where they were once excellent, the probable cause lies in nonsexual conflicts.

30. Common male impotency problems—failure to maintain erection, premature ejaculation, or failure to achieve orgasm—are mostly due to nonsexual emotional problems.

31. The wish to be together immediately after sexual needs are satisfied is a good indicator of a successful sexual adjustment.

32. Enjoyable sex relations during the first few weeks of marriage may be quite unreliable in predicting how good sex will be later in the marriage.

33. Newly married men often reach orgasm much too soon to satisfy their wives. These men can learn to time themselves better with experience or suitable instruction.

34. When a man continues to reach orgasm too soon regardless of experience or teaching, professional help is indicated and is often successful in outcome.

35. Previous homosexual experiences may or may not affect adult sexual performance and adjustment.

36. It is very unlikely that a homosexual will change his basic sexual experiences by getting married.

37. A wet dream is a periodic discharge of male sex fluids similar to menstruation.

38. The usual cause for a wet dream in males is the tension produced by erotic thoughts before going to sleep, rather than sexual dreams.

	TRUE	FALSE

39. Women, as well as men, have dreams that relieve sex tensions. _____ _____

40. According to most physicians, modern methods of birth control rarely harm the health or fertility of either sex. _____ _____

41. In general, medically approved methods of birth control are highly effective. _____ _____

42. Use of birth-control methods affects the pleasure of intercourse for either partner according to their emotional attitudes toward birth control in general. _____ _____

43. Condoms (rubber sheaths), contraceptive pills, vaginal diaphragms with contraceptive cream, and IUDs (intrauterine devices) are all effective methods of birth control. _____ _____

44. The "safe period" or rhythm method is an effective method of birth control. _____ _____

45. Withdrawal by the male before orgasm, intercourse without male orgasm, or douching immediately after sex relations are effective methods of birth control. _____ _____

46. The IUD (intrauterine device) is an effective birth-control method that requires no preparation just before sex relations by either husband or wife. _____ _____

47. Usually surgical sterilization for birth control performed on either man or woman produces no change in sexual desires or pleasure in either sex. _____ _____

48. Male circumcision increases the ability of the man to enjoy sex relations. _____ _____

49. Menstruation is best defined as a clearing of the womb to prepare again for possible pregnancy. _____ _____

50. Intercourse during menstruation is dangerous to a woman's health. _____ _____

	TRUE	FALSE

51. During menstruation a woman's resistance to infection or disease is significantly lowered. _____ _____

52. It is impossible to become pregnant from intercourse during menstruation. _____ _____

53. Menstruation normally becomes more regular and less difficult after marriage. _____ _____

54. The fluid that normally flows from the penis before orgasm can contain sperm and therefore produce pregnancy. _____ _____

55. It is possible for a woman to become pregnant from having intercourse just once. _____ _____

56. A man must reach orgasm in order for him to cause a woman to conceive. _____ _____

57. A woman is most likely to become pregnant about two weeks before menstruation begins. _____ _____

58. It is not possible for a woman to become pregnant again after the birth of a baby, until she has menstruated at least once. _____ _____

59. Unresponsiveness during sexual intercourse on the woman's part has no effect on the possibility of her becoming pregnant. _____ _____

60. Certain pregnancy tests can give accurate results about twelve days after intercourse has occurred. _____ _____

61. When to resume intercourse after pregnancy is relative to the woman's health and should be decided on the doctor's advice. _____ _____

62. When a woman is having a baby, her cervix and vagina are torn as the baby passes through them. _____ _____

63. A woman's vagina is slightly larger in diameter after she has had a baby. _____ _____

64. Large sex organs in a male indicate great desire and capacity for sexual intercourse. _____ _____

		TRUE	**FALSE**

65. There are no known chemicals, whether internally or externally used, that will increase sexual desire in either men or women.   _____   _____

66. The larger a woman's breasts are the greater her sex responsiveness and desire.   _____   _____

67. There are no known foods that will increase sexual desire.   _____   _____

68. Masturbation, either in adolescence or adulthood, has no physical effect on sexual desire, capacity, or ability.   _____   _____

69. The degree to which masturbation affects intelligence and emotional control depends on how frequently one masturbates.   _____   _____

70. The only measurable physical effect of masturbation on the human body is a temporary reduction in sexual tension.   _____   _____

71. Men or women with either gonorrhea or syphilis want and can have sexual relations to about the same degree as they did before they were infected.   _____   _____

72. When a discharge from gonorrhea disappears without medical treatment, the person is uncured and dangerous to others.   _____   _____

73. Almost every case of either syphilis and gonorrhea can be cured.   _____   _____

74. Sex relations during menopause do not significantly change a woman's physical or emotional health.   _____   _____

75. A woman may safely discontinue birth control any time after menopause has started.   _____   _____

76. During and after menopause a woman's desire and capacity for orgasm remain about the same as before menopause.   _____   _____

77. Many women who are unable to have orgasm are able to conduct active, long-term, enjoyable sex relations.   _____   _____

	TRUE	FALSE

78. There is no convincing evidence of a connection between sexual dissatisfaction and heavy smoking.   _____ _____

79. It is possible for a young man to be impotent with girls his own age and to be aroused by much older women.   _____ _____

80. Measuring the time of conception from her first period, the younger the mother, the better chance she has of delivering a child without birth defects.   _____ _____

81. Pornography arouses men more than women because it is designed for men by other men. Women probably can be equally aroused by a woman's pornography, designed for women by women.   _____ _____

2. Sexual satisfaction in women is positively related to the amount of formal education she has had.   _____ _____

83. There is a higher risk of disease or birth defect in children born from the mating of two people who are related to each other (first cousins, etc.).   _____ _____

84. Blood tests can only prove negative paternity, in that they can determine a man is surely not the father of the child, but cannot prove he is the father.   _____ _____

85. An undescended testicle does not affect a man's potency or his ability to father children.   _____ _____

86. Men's nipples can be as sensitive to erotic stimulation as women's.   _____ _____

87. Contraceptive pills tend to increase the size of a woman's breasts.   _____ _____

88. Surveys indicate that sexual thought of some kind occurs in males between twelve and twenty-five about once every other minute.   _____ _____

	TRUE	FALSE

89. A penis larger than a woman's vagina can cause pain for a woman during sexual intercourse. _____ _____

90. Retarded children do have sexual drives and require careful sexual education. _____ _____

91. There is a definite rhythm increase and decrease to sexual desire in women. This is related to her mentrual cycle. _____ _____

92. The sex of a child at conception is related to the conditions and timing of intercourse. _____ _____

93. The fact that many married women can be regularly aroused sexually by men other than their husbands does not indicate they are unhappy with their marital sex life. _____ _____

94. If a male has not reached puberty by fifteen, he is probably a medical problem. _____ _____

95. All normal boys masturbate to some degree. _____ _____

Included below, where the author felt it was necessary, are amplifying remarks to the answers given.

ANSWERS TO QUESTIONS

1. True. This question is designed to emphasize the idea that sexual need and affection or love are separate and independent feelings. Any person can experience either feeling without the other one being present.

2. True. The same point is illustrated here as in No. 1.

3. True. It is probable that a better predictor of adequate sexuality in marriage would be all behavior in courtship rather than sex behavior exclusively. It is also important to notice that marriage can cause profound psychological transformations in attitude. Therefore, sex behavior for a few weeks after marriage may become noticeably more inhibited and/or less frequent, even if there has been active sex behavior before marriage.

4. False. Obviously good sex relations involve the free mutual expression of desire for sex, and equally important, the freedom of refusal, by either partner without producing anger or vindictiveness in the other partner. They do not center simply on the husband's desires.

5. True.

6. True. There has been much discussion and argument over this question. It is designed to let you know that the female orgasm is different physiologically from the male orgasm. The woman usually requires considerable preparation in sexual foreplay to become ready for orgasm. Her orgasm consists of large muscle contractions producing release of tension. Any normal male who has not recently had an orgasm has sperm and fluid available in his testes ready for ejaculation.

7. True. This question is designed to refute the commonly held idea that men are far more driven toward sex satisfaction than women, and are consequently always more easily aroused. Actually, women exhibit the same variation in their capacity to be aroused as men. It ranges from high to low.

8. True. The sense of this question is the same as in No. 7.

9. False. Men do not differ greatly from women in their needs for orgasm. This question has the same intent as No. 7 and No. 8. Men have differing strength of desires for orgasm, from high to low. The degree of their emotional disturbance when not achieving orgasm will relate to the strength of their needs. Women vary in their response in the same way. These are largely learned responses for both sexes.

10. False.

11. False.

12. True.

13. True. The general sense of this question relates to the greater need in most women for some preparation toward arousal through foreplay than men. If a man understands the degree of her need he will spend sufficient time with the woman to get her aroused before actual intercourse occurs. There are, of course, occasions where women with high drives have, as sex partners, men having low drives. In such cases less foreplay for the woman is necessary. Indeed, the man may need it more. Also, there are the psychological exceptions of men who demand or need the woman to be the aggressor in the foreplay. If this is understood by both parties, it is also completely healthy.

14. True.

15. True. Sex counselors do not feel that any position of sexual intercourse is either more desirable, more normal, or more moral than any other. The only determining factor for its use is the free agreement by both partners to use it and the pleasure achieved by both partners when using it.

16. False.   This question has to do with bringing attention to the false idea that men are universally more strongly driven for sex than women and are constantly ready for it. There is a sizable group of men who need considerable investment in time and effort from their female sex partners in order to achieve an erection. This often happens after the woman is already fully aroused. She then has the choice of waiting for him, or having a climax before him. This answer does not contradict No. 6; sperm and fluid that accumulate in the testes do not guarantee that a man will achieve an erection. Most sexual arousal has to do with a receptive state of the mind being present, not instinct or automatic physical response.

17. False.   It is not correct to state that all women who can have more than one orgasm *must* have more than one in order to achieve satisfaction. Most women who are multi-orgasmic can achieve major satisfaction after the first orgasm. They simply continue to achieve more satisfaction with secondary orgasms.

18. True. Of course, partners frequently learn the sexual likes and dislikes of their mates simply through repeated sex experience. Nonetheless, the best kind of sex relationship is one where a desire or dislike can be freely and easily pointed out by either partner to the other before sexual behavior occurs.

19. False.

20. False.   Sometimes the hymen is destroyed in intercourse; sometimes it is not.

21. True.   Obviously if No. 20 is false, then No. 21 must be true. The widely held conception that the presence of a hymen is sure proof of virginity is false.

22. True.

23. True. This question illustrates the views of modern marriage counselors that sexual reactions are habitual and learned to a much greater degree than they are automatic reflexes.

24. False.   It is very rarely true, for instance, that an unusually large or small penis necessarily prevents sexual satisfaction. Attitudes of acceptance or rejection of sexual organs, including the opposite male belief in the desirability of small-diameter vaginas, are learned and have no relation to the physical facts.

25. False.   Marital failure in bed is most frequently caused by marital failure out of bed. Many hostile feelings are caused by nonsexual arguments and are carried into sex relationships. If there is a solid supporting relationship between the married couple they are almost always able to devise some satisfactory way to have sexual relations, even if they argue. But if they are frustrated and embittered, they rarely are compatible sexually.

26. False.   There is no necessity for the relaxed and slightly tired feeling that comes after satisfying sex relationships to be an unpleasant one. When postintercourse fatigue and weakness occur with perceptible intensity and duration in either of the sex partners it almost always means that one person was having intercourse unwillingly, or in a tense, guilt-laden way.

27. True.

28. True.

29. True.

30. True.

31. True.   This question was included to illustrate the desirability for what sex counselors call "afterglow." This feeling should be present after satisfactory sex relationships. Both partners should feel close, warm, and comfortable. This is the natural result of healthy sexual communication. If the sexual act is casual, mechanical, or occurs under stress, one or both partners tend to reject the other immediately after intercourse, even when mutual orgasm occurs. They then try to get away from each other as fast as possible.

32. True.   This question indicates how sensitive sex relationships are to the development of nonsexual problems in marriage. Rarely do these problems appear immediately in a marriage. They usually appear when the novelty wears off and the two people discover each other's peculiarities and are forced to adjust to them. They develop ongoing differences of opinion that frequently show up in a lessening of sexual satisfaction.

33. True.   This question tries to emphasize that sexual counseling is highly effective in a wide variety of sexual problems that many people believe are unsolvable. Often nontreatment results in permanent damage to the relationship.

34. True.   The sense of this question is the same.

35. True.   Homosexual experiences in a young adult's life do not mean he inevitably will become a homosexual as he grows older. Many adolescents and pre-adolescents of both sexes experiment with homosexual experiences and then go on to heterosexual adult lives.

36. True.   Many homosexuals marry persons of the opposite sex. They often have children. They may continue their homosexual activities secretly. Sometimes they repress the feelings, but the desire remains latent. It is fairly common to observe a homosexual leaving his mate after having been married a number of years, to take up a life of full, open homosexuality.

37. False.   A wet dream is a normal discharge of semen often occurring while a male is having a dream about sex. It is not periodic and not in any way related to menstruation.

38. True.   The presleep erotic thoughts produce the sexual tension and help produce the supporting dream as well.

39. True.

40. True.

41. True.

42. True.   This question points out that no birth-control device for either male or female need interfere with the pleasure of the sex act if the device is properly used.

43. True.

44. False.   Also to be included in the category of unreliable or unsafe techniques of birth control are: withdrawal by the male before orgasm, douching immediately after sex relationships, and sex relations without male orgasm.

45. False.

46. True.

47. True.   If a reduced drive for sex appears in either the male or female after sterilization, it has to do with psychological tensions, not from the physical effect of the operation itself.

48. False.   Circumcision has no measurable effect on the ability of a man to enjoy sex relations.

49. True.

50. False.   Intercourse during menstruation is exclusively a matter involving the taste or pleasure of both partners. It does not affect physical health.

51. False.   This question is designed to combat the idea that menstruation is either an illness in itself or it produces substantial decrease in the body's resistance to infectious or other related diseases.

52. False.   It is possible for a woman to become pregnant anytime in her menstrual cycle, including the period of menstrual flow.

53. False.   No significant changes necessarily occur in a menstrual cycle after a woman marries.

54. True.

55. True.

56. False.   Because No. 54 is true, No. 56 *must* be false. The only condition necessary to produce pregnancy is the introduction of live sperm cells into the vagina and finally reaching and fertilizing the ovum.

57. True.

58. False.   While it is not likely, it is definitely possible for a woman to become pregnant after the birth of the baby but before her first subsequent menstrual period.

59. True.   This question is designed to bring out that degree of passion that is displayed by a woman during sexual intercourse has absolutely no relationship to the possibility of her becoming pregnant. She can be either very excited or wholly uninterested during intercourse. If the sperm reach the egg she can become pregnant in both instances with equal likelihood.

60. True.

61. True.   There is no absolutely certain formula to determine when intercourse is supposed to recommence for a woman after the birth of her baby. Each woman differs somewhat in this respect.

62. False.   The cervix and vagina relax and stretch. They are not torn by the baby's passage.

63. True.

64. False.   The size of a male's genital organs has no relationship to his desire or capacity for sexual intercourse.

65. True.   This question is designed to let you know that all the yet existing folktales about various sexual stimulants are false. None have actually been discovered that do the job. Claims made for any chemical as to its capacity to increase sexual arousal have never been proved.

66. False.   There is no relationship between the size of a woman's breasts and her capacity for responsiveness or desire for sex.

67. True.   This is true in the same way that No. 65 is true. All the legends that state that some type of food will increase sexual desire are false.

68. True.   This item is included to indicate that all sexual problems connected with masturbation have to do with emotional attitudes generated by guilts or fears a child learns to *associate* with masturbation, not with the act itself.

69. False.   Masturbation has no physical effect on adult intellectual ability. Almost all men masturbate sometime during their lives, usually during their adolescence, and so do a majority of women.

70. True.

71. True.   This question is included to point out that venereal disease is not only dangerous in the sense of being highly communicable, but also its presence in the human body does not necessarily reduce sexual desire or activity. An infected person, not knowing or not caring he is infected, can go on with an active sex life and infect or reinfect others.

72. True.   One of the most dangerous characteristics of gonorrhea is that it can remain infectious in the body without visible physical symptoms.

73. True.

74. True.

75. False.   A woman may *only* safely discontinue birth control after her menstruation periods have totally stopped.

76. True.

77. True.   This question indicates women rely very heavily for their sexual satisfaction upon comfortable attitudes between themselves and the man. A woman usually has to feel that sex relationships communicate genuine interest and affection, not just expression of sexual need.

78. True.

79. True.   This condition arises when a young man becomes extremely guilty about his sexual desire, particularly if he has been frequently warned that he will get girls pregnant if he is promiscuous. He then comes to regard six relationships with older women as safer than with young women.

80. False.   The idea that the younger the mother the healthier and more ready for children she is, only becomes true after she has had time to mature physically from the time she begins her menstrual period. If a girl becomes pregnant very soon after she first begins her period she is more likely to produce malformed or mentally retarded children than the more mature mother.

81. True.   This question is included to amplify the view that sexual desire in women is just as strongly arousable as it is in men. However, men have controlled the sexual freedom of women through all of recorded history. Consequently many myths and misconceptions have arisen— all with the sense that women have weaker sex drives than men. They are all false. Men and women vary in the same way—some have weak, some strong sex drives.

82. True.   All the studies done on women coming from the same culture have indicated this to be so. There are many theories about why this occurs, or why, at least, this is so consistently reported. No current explanation is satisfactory, but whatever the reason, that's what we observe.

83. True.   This is only true because there are people who are carriers of various abnormal physical and mental attributes in genes that are called "recessive." Thus abnormal characteristics will not usually appear in the offspring unlesss both the male and female parents carry them. These characteristics will have very much less chance of appearing in couples mating from two widely separated families. The recessive genes are less likely to be present than if the parents are related. If there are no abnormal genes present, incestuous mating will not produce deformed children with any greater frequency than nonincestuous mating.

84. True.

85. True.   Both testicles must be undescended before his abulity to sire children is impaired.

86. True.

87. True.

88.   True.

89.   True.   This is only true if a male with a large penis thrusts too strongly into a woman's vagina. He may touch the tip of her cervix, thus causing pain. If he is gentle in his thrusting, no pain need occur—mere size need not of itself be the cause of pain because the woman's vagina is sufficiently resilient to accommodate almost any size penis if she is relaxed and accepting.

90.   True.

91.   True.

92.   True.

93.   True   This simply illustrates the fact that most normally sexed males and females have continuous sex desires. These need not necessarily center on one's legal or loved sex partner. They can focus on practically any other sexually stimulating person who may be encountered. If either mate considers sexual fidelity to be a keystone of the relationship, then each can solve the problem by choosing to represse or ignore these desires. It is rarely possible to avoid having sexual desires toward randomly appearing people.

94.   True.

95.   True.

SCORING

Score a point for each correct answer.

A score of 80–95 indicates that you are very well informed indeed. Dr. Robert K. Alsofrom, creator of this test, reveals that he has yet to run across a perfect score.

A score of 70–79 places you in the "average" category.

A score of 60–69 puts you in the "below average" category.

A score below 60 indicates a relative ignorance about human sexuality.

How Turned On Are You From A to Z?

To find out how "turned on" you are, look at each activity listed from A to Z. Examine the answers below. Next to each activity (a, b, c, etc.) write the number of the answer that applies most strongly to your feelings about the subject.

There are no right or wrong answers, but you must answer each question. Think of it only with regard to yourself. If you personally had a chance to participate would you feel:

1. I am sickened and repulsed by the thought.
2. I am definitely not interested.
3. I might enjoy it if I tried it.
4. I like to do this once in a while.
5. I enjoy doing this every time I get a chance.
6. I never tire of doing this.

"TURN ON" THINGS

a. Group Nudity _____
b. Erotic Literature _____
c. Talking About Yourself _____
d. Fantasizing _____
e. Sex with Men _____
f. Sex with Women _____
g. Sex with Both _____
h. Sex with Much Older Partners _____
i. Masturbating _____
j. Power _____
k. Work _____
l. Eating _____
m. Exhibitionism _____
n. Pampering Yourself _____
o. Pregnancy _____
p. Sex Orgies _____
q. Try Anything Once _____
r. Flirting _____
s. Rock Music _____
t. Classical Music _____
u. Bowel Movements _____

v.   Oral Sex _____
w.   Sex with Much Younger Partners _____
x.   Body Odors _____
y.   Anal Intercourse _____
z.   Interracial Sex _____

SCORING

YOUR SCORE: _____

Score 26–52:   You need artificial respiration! You are definitely "turned off" and "tuned out." You might as well be dead because you are scared to death of living. You have managed to arm yourself against the troubles of life, and, in so doing, you have contrived to arm yourself against the joys of life as well. You are so far gone that it is dubious that you could help yourself out of your rut. Run, don't walk, to your nearest "headshrinker."

Score 53–85:   You are afraid of getting "turned on" unless someone takes you by the hand and rapes you into it. You realize that you are missing something but you lack the guts to go out and make it happen. Think of something you have thought of trying but for one reason or another have been putting off. THEN GO OUT AND DO IT!! The first step is always the hardest. Stop putting stumbling blocks on your path to happiness.

Score 86–105:   Congratulations! You have exposed yourself to the world and found your happiness quota forever on the upswing. You know better than anyone else that there are certain areas of exploration and fun that you haven't tried. Continue having a good time and pass your magic formula to friends and psychiatry.

Score 106–131:   Wow! You are really on high boil! People around you cannot help but feel and see the glow of a truly turned-on person. There is nothing you won't give a try, and if it's wild enough you'll love it. Your only problem is you become bored easily and must constantly be on the lookout for something new and titillating. There are times when you'll need to slow down a little. Don't worry. You won't miss out on anything! You just need to spend more time really deeply enjoying all the things you have guts enough to try.

Score 132–156:   You are either a new, unheard-of kind of animal, a master in self-deception, or a bold-faced liar! If most of your answers fall in the "I never tire of doing this" category, you must be exhausted by now and ready for a long rest cure. Are your answers based on the real you or the fantasized you? Try taking the test and your answers to a friend whose judgment you trust, and ask him or her to score you. If you are not surprised at the difference between your score and the score your friend thinks you should have—then congratulations—you are a new species upon the earth!

YOU AND YOUR MARRIAGE

Does Marriage Wither or Bloom?

An old Chinese proverb says: "if you want a good time for a long time—get married. If you want a good time for a lifetime—grow a garden."

Putting the garden into your marriage involves cultivating your partner into a blossoming person. Without such care, your marriage may wither and become one of the many that fail.

Take this quiz to find out if you are nourishing a sturdy marriage or turning yours into a wasteland. Circle the answer closest to your own attitude. Answer each question.

PART I
Your marriage
is a living thing
and it must be cultivated
to blossom.

1. Do you strive to arrange your life so that you and your mate will spend time together when you are both well rested and untroubled?
   a. We do talk about it, but never seem to find time.
   b. I always set aside time for my mate and I cherish these moments.
   c. Circumstances, money, children . . . all these things keep us from each other. We haven't had time alone together in years.

2. How do you handle bossism in your family?

   a. We've figured out each other's best talents and we divide up our lives that way fifty-fifty.

   b. I have strong opinions, but I give in when I find my mate just won't accept them.

   c. We have an ironclad but silent agreement . . . each of us performs certain do not intrude upon the other's area.

3. Our lives have fallen into a certain pattern; if things are going well I:

   a. Take it for granted and follow a set routine.

   b. Praise him for the commonplace considerations and sometimes we discuss our common goals and where they will lead.

   c. Point out how hard I'm trying to make this marriage work.

PART II
**How well do you communicate
with your mate?**

4. When you are anxious to tell him something, do you:

   a. Come right out with it or say nothing at all?

   b. Prepare him by saying, "I have something to say that you'll be interested in . . . ?"

   c. Ask him what he thinks of the central idea, then express your own thoughts?

5. When you're concerned about an aspect of your sex life, do you:

   a. Keep the problem to yourself, hoping it will work out?

   b. Discuss it freely with your husband, asking for his advice or help?

   c. Confide the problem to a person whose opinion you regard as informed?

6. When your husband comes to you troubled and worried, do you:

   a. Tell him you've had similar problems and explain what you did to solve them?

   b. Try to make him feel better by saying that everything will be all right?

   c. Try to put yourself in his position and ask him to explain why he feels as he does?

PART III
Attached to each rose stem
are a few thorns. How do you handle
these problems?

7. Your husband comes home from work after a rough day, but you've had a tough day too, so:
   a. You tell him all the things the kids have done wrong, and you fill him in on your bad day.
   b. No matter what's on your mind, you're cheerful and interested, and save your problems until after he's eaten.
   c. You try to cope with all the inconsequential daily annoyances. If it's of major importance you wait until he's had dinner, his mind is free, and then you calmly discuss the problem.

8. At times you sense that your husband is lonely perhaps even bored when you're together. You are having feelings of isolation:
   a. There's nothing we can do about these feelings.
   b. After a few years you can expect a letdown in interest.
   c. You know boredom takes over when hopes are stifled or growth stops, so you come up with something new to try or you join him in one of his interests—like football.

9. Something seems to be dreadfully wrong with your marriage:
   a. You'll go on pretending that everything is fine and it will be.
   b. Your best friend knows all your fears and anxieties, but you can't bring yourself to tell your husband the problem.
   c. Painful as it is, you must come to grips with the problem as soon as it presents itself and discuss it with your mate, trying to get help from him.

10. One of the greatest problems in marriage is money. In your marriage:
    a. The money just seems to go without specific planning.
    b. Your husband handles the money and gives you an allowance.
    c. Generally you both decide how to spend the money and the allowance each should have.

PART IV
You have the opportunity
of participating in the growth
and shaping of another. How well
are you both leafing out?

11. Since my marriage I sometimes feel that I am not as interesting a person as I once was:
    a. But I'm sharing baby-sitting chores with another mother and we're both going back to school.
    b. But married life is centered around a husband and children; that's a woman's lot.
    c. But I've found some classes that interest us both and we're planning to attend together.

12. My husband wants to advance in his position and now he has the opportunity:
    a. Even though I feel a little insecure about making changes I know we both must grow and I'm encouraging him to move ahead.
    b. Whatever he wants to do is fine with me.
    c. We're happy as we are now . . . let's stay that way.

SCORING

Your marriage has a life span all its own. It's up to you to nourish and protect it, to ward off dangerous pests, to shape it, see that new buds blossom out, and above all to see that it gets plenty of sunshine.

Add up your score to see how your marriage is doing.

Questions 1–3   a x 2   =
                  b x 3   =
                  c x 1   =
Questions 4–10   a x 1   =
                  b x 2   =
                  c x 3   =
Questions 11–12   a x 3   =
                  b x 1   =
                  c x 2   =

If you scored 30 or more, read a. If you scored 20 or more, read b, if you scored 19 or less, read c.

a. A bouquet of roses to you from your rose garden. Your answers indicate a thriving marriage that portends a lifetime of blossoming. To you the marriage is a commitment to nourish your husband and to explore the possibilities your life together offers. The door of opportunity is open, allowing you both to share life and to grow together. Circumstances are not allowed to keep you apart, for you give of yourself. During arguments you yield to him if you feel that the misunderstanding is fraying the fabric of your relationship. Your approval and praise are the nutrients helping him and your marriage to bloom. You explore his view on a subject you wish to discuss. When he is troubled you listen and allow him to express his feelings, helping him to understand his position. You realize that home is a haven, the place to escape from stress, and you try to keep it that way. If boredom seeps through, you explore his hidden facets to discover what interests you both. When disasters threaten, you take action and do not wait until your marriage is weakened by the assault. You pursue interest that differ from his and remain an interesting person with individuality to offer him. You are enhanced by your marriage and so is he.

b. Some pest control is needed now for more lush growth. Your answers indicate that you have a good attitude toward your marriage but are allowing some creepy crawlies to blight the best parts. It's to your best interest to care for him and for him to care for you. But this caring requires time spent alone together. A set routine brings a slump into complacency, which may make any marriage droop. Vigorous interest is needed to banish this skulker. If pesty sex problems persist, it might be wise to discuss them with a professional (physician or psychologist) before turning them onto your mate. Boredom and loneliness may nibble at any marriage when new growth stops. Your rose garden will flourish again if you tell your grievances to your husband instead of your best friend. Finding interests completely separate from your husband's, which will give you both something to discuss, keeps him from looking over other varieties. Remember: Marriage blooms when each partner helps enhance it.

c. Let the sunshine in. Your answers indicate that your marriage isn't as much fun as it used to be. Some sunshine is needed along with those showers to perk up your rose garden. The hours of intense sharing seem to have passed, but that feeling of oneness can still be rekindled. Along with every problem comes the possibility of a solution, and now you must look at the promise your marriage yet holds. Snip off those dead leaves of recrimination. Prune away hurt feelings. Encourage vibrant new growth. You must also be able to add some interests so he'll notice your bloom. Speak to him with words of praise. Concentrate on his virtues and ignore his faults. Try to understand his needs and hopes and fears. Get to know him again. Develop yourself so that you're not a clinging vine.

Do You Still Surprise Your Husband?

1. Turning out a drawer one day you come across some memory-stirring mementos of the early days of your marriage, not courtship. Do you:
   a. smile ruefully and burn them?
   b. wonder whether it might not be best to throw them out?
   c. show them to your husband in a quiet moment as things you really treasure?

2. Do you keep up some sort of correspondence, however infrequent, with men friends of premarriage days, including both flames and not reallies?
   a. goodness, no.
   b. did for a time.
   c. yes.

3. Are there any men in your life now who, knowing you are married, nevertheless respect and admire you and obviously enjoy the acquaintanceship?
   a. only one.
   b. more than one.
   c. none that I know of.

4. When did you last burst spontaneously into song because you were feeling particularly happy about something?
   a. can't remember.
   b. yesterday.

c ⌄ during the past year.

5. Do you find it easy to take your husband's hand at moments when you know he needs affection, or cheering up, or encouragement in a dark mood?

   a. ⌐of course.

   b. sometimes.

   c. not as often as he would like.

6. Which does your husband find most astonishing:

   a. when other adult people come to ask your advice on their personal problems?

   b. when you feel the need to go to ask other people's advice on yours?

   c. that you have any problems that you must talk about?

7. One day, quite out of the blue, you take a completely new and absorbing hobby, something you've never done before, and make a real success of it. Is your husband:

   a. rather puzzled but not unenthusiastic?

   b. delighted?

   c. a bit cool about the whole thing, because he thought he knew all of the real you?

8. Your husband one day has a long chat with someone who knows you pretty well and who sees a good side of you that you know your husband is somewhat blind to. Is your partner:

   a. totally disbelieving?

   b. rather proud?

   c. put out because he thought he knew all of the real you?

9. When you and your husband decide to take a vacation abroad you announce that you're going to attend evening classes in the language of the country you're visiting. Is he:

   a. simply astounded?

   b. merely full of ridicule?

   c. genuinely encouraging?

10. Can you think of any circumstances in which you might seriously consider marrying again?

   a. no, none?

   b. possibly?

   c. not very likely?

SCORING

To score full marks as a husband-surpriser, and therefore a stimulating and enjoyable wife, these are the answers you should have given:

1–c;   2–c;   3–b;   4–b;   5–a;   6–a;   7–a;   8–b;   9–a;   10–b.

But if you scored 7 or over, you're doing pretty well as the kind of wife husbands secretly like to have, however much they may say otherwise!

If your score was between 5 and 7, you're about average.

If you achieved 5 or less you're not really the sort of wife who keeps a man constantly interested. So snap out of it while you've still a chance.

Do You Rate as a Mate?

Do you wonder if your mate still finds you sexually attractive? It's a subject your mate is unlikely to talk about freely, so if you're not sure, here's a quiz to help you find out. Jot down your a., b., or c. answers and check the result at the end of the quiz.

If both of you do the quiz separately, them compare results; you might have a very interesting discussion afterward:

1. Does your mate ever mention going away, just the two of you, for a weekend together?
    a. quite often.
    b. occasionally.
    c. rarely or never.

2. How does your mate pay you a compliment about your appearance?
    a. completely without any prodding.
    b. after you've hinted you'd like one.
    c. after you've bluntly said one is overdue.

3. When you get a compliment, how does it sound to you?
    a. very sincere.
    b. okay.
    c. pretty mechanical.

4. Does your mate ever surprise you with a hug or a kiss?

a. fairly often.
b. occasionally.
c. never.

5. Does your mate hold your hand, or make other signs of affection, when you're in public?
  a. fairly often.
  b. occasionally.
  c. rarely or never.

6. Your appearance aside, do you think your mate still finds you interesting as a person?
  a. definitely.
  b. probably.
  c. probably not.

7. What do you think your mate feels about your weight?
  a. it's just about right.
  b. you're moderately overweight (or underweight).
  c. you're much too overweight (or underweight).

8. What do you think your mate feels about the way you dress?
  a. just about right.
  b. needs moderate improvement.
  c. needs considerable improvement.

9. In recent months, has your mate seemed rather critical of other aspects of your appearance?
  a. no.
  b. perhaps occasionally.
  c. yes.

10. Do you think your mate finds you as neat, clean, and tidy as you should be?
  a. invariably.
  b. most of the time.
  c. only sometimes.

11. How do you think your mate feels about your looks vs. your age?
  a. you look younger.
  b. you look your actual age.
  c. you look older.

12. Do you think your mate sees you as an active person?
  a. definitely.

b. fairly active.

✓ (c.) not particularly active.

13. When your mate shows affection for you, is your response a warm one?

a. always.

(b.) most of the time.

✓ c. sometimes.

14. In other ways, do you let your mate know you still find him (or her) sexually attractive?

a. often.

✓ (b.) sometimes.

c. rarely or never.

SCORING

HOW TO SCORE:

Give yourself 2 points for each a. answer, 1 point for each b., and nothing for each c.

A score of 24–28: Your mate still finds you very sexually attractive indeed. Congratulations!

19–23: Shows you're doing pretty well, too, but you can make it even better by seeing what you can do about those b. and c. replies.

14–18: Means you're doing about average—keeping your appeal in some ways, slipping in others. Review those c. responses and try to improve them.

9–13: Means there are a number of problems that need working on—and you are to blame!

Less than 9: Real improvement is needed. Start immediately!

The four most important factors in remaining sexually attractive to your mate are: 1. maintaining your good health and physical attractiveness to the greatest extent possible; 2. working hard to be the kind of person your mate will find most appealing; 3. keeping up activities that will help you stay alive and interesting; 4. showing your mate you are receptive to love and affection, even at the most unexpected moments.

Are You Headed for Divorce?

Are you worried that you may be headed for divorce?

This test will help you find out if you're in a high-risk divorce category . . . and also help strengthen your marriage by pinpointing problem areas for you to correct.

"Husband and wife should take the test together," advises Dr. Selma Miller, president of the New York Association of Marriage and Family Counselors, who compiled the test.

"See if you and your spouse agree or disagree on each point and discuss it. If you come across problem areas, see where you can change your own behavior—don't always blame your spouse. If something is bothering you, the time to discuss it is now, not later in divorce court!"

You each should answer the following 18 questions "Never," "Rarely," "Sometimes," "Often," or "Always." Keep tab of your scores:

1. Do you have trouble expressing your feelings?
2. When you try to express yourself, do you feel that your mate doesn't understand you?
3. Have you stopped spending time with your mate just enjoying each other?
4. Do pleasurable experiences often turn into arguments?
5. Have you stopped looking forward to sex with your partner?
6. Are your sexual desires basically imcompatible?
7. Do you find that you have trouble communicating your sexual needs and desires to your mate?
8. Do you fight about the way family money should be spent?
9. Do you feel that your spouse spends more money on himself (or herself) and considers his (or her) needs before yours?
10. Do you disagree over how to bring up your children?
11. Do your children go to your spouse for permission after you have refused them what they want?
12. Do you lie to your spouse?
13. Do you feel your in-laws are threats to your marriage?
14. Do you find you have lost respect for your mate?
15. Does your spouse have specific habits that cause you unhappiness or discomfort, such as drinking, gambling, etc.?
16. Do your spouse's moods cause disruption in your household?
17. Do you have frequent, heated, ideological conflicts on subjects such as religion and politics?
18. Are you ashamed to introduce your mate to friends and colleagues?

SCORING

Score yourself 1 point for each "Never," 2 points for "Rarely," 3 points for "Sometimes," 4 points for "Often," and 5 points for "Always."

Add up your separate scores and rate yourself:

0–39:   "You two are compatible and probably very happy," said Dr. Miller. "Even so, a good marriage takes constant work to keep it that way. Keep talking things out."

40–69:   "While you're probably both happy together, there appear to be a number of areas that need some work," she said. "Without work, you could become a divorce risk."

70–90:   "You two should definitely sit down and discuss the problem you're having in marriage and work out a plan to solve them.

"If your scores turn out to be significantly different from each other's, this is the time and place to begin to discuss the areas in which you do not see eye to eye, and develop a better understanding of each other.

"You are only divorce-prone if you don't try to work out these difficulties."

How Compatible Are You with Your Mate?

Here's a quiz to try on yourself and your wife (or husband) or date. It's been approved by psychologists as a rough test by which you can rate your companionship as based on similarity or on complementarity. It can't tell you whether either is good or bad, successful or unsuccessful, and it isn't infallible—but it may clue you in on some of the factors you think about and discuss between yourselves.

1. If people suddenly stop laughing and talking as you come near, do you think they were talking and laughing about you?

    Yes _____   No _____

2. Would you start to worry if you were asked to go to the boss's office unexpectedly?

    Yes _____   No _____

3. Would you feel competent if asked to speak in public?

Yes _____   No _____

4. Do you believe the news you read in the paper or hear on TV?

Yes _____   No _____

5. When going on vacation, do you start in good time to get clothes cleaned, newspaper delivery stopped, and other preparations made?

Yes _____   No _____

6. Would you lose your temper if someone played a practical joke that made you look ridiculous?

Yes _____   No _____

7. Do you always want to share with someone when something pleasant happens?

Yes _____   No _____

8. If you were trapped in a stalled elevator, would you panic?

Yes _____   No _____

9. Do you like the fights best on television?

Yes _____   No _____

10. Do you think Christmas preparations and card-sending a nuisance?

Yes _____   No _____

11. Do you enjoy cocktail parties?

Yes _____   No _____

12. Could you take an active part in a group joke-telling session?

Yes _____   No _____

13. Do you expect people to like you?

Yes _____   No _____

14. Are you upset if an unexpected visitor spoils plans you have made?

Yes _____   No _____

15. If you don't know the answer to a question, do you admit it?

Yes _____   No _____

16. Are you a good story teller?

Yes _____   No _____

17. If you were going on vacation with a friend, would you leave the planning to him (or her)?

          Yes _____   No _____

18. Do you prefer conversation with friends to reading a book?

          Yes _____   No _____

19. Do you prefer a symphony concert to a game of bridge?

          Yes _____   No _____

20. Do you sometimes feel you haven't had the luck you deserved?

          Yes _____   No _____

21. When things go well for you, do you start to worry?

          Yes _____   No _____

22. Would you be happy living alone?

          Yes _____   No _____

23. If someone else got the credit for your achievement, would you brood over it?

          Yes _____   No _____

24. Do you change the TV program to one you like, even if someone else would prefer another program?

          Yes _____   No _____

25. Do you consider yourself a carefree, happy-go-lucky person?

          Yes _____   No _____

SCORING

ANSWERS:

First determine the number of questions that you and your partner answered in the same way. Then see how many you answered in the opposite direction. Multiply by four to get the percentage answered in each way.

If you have answered more than 50 per cent in the same way, it suggests that your relationship is based primarily on similarity. If over 50 per cent are answered in opposite directions, complementarity appears more important.

Now check each of your answers to 2, 3, 6, 8, 13, 14, 15, and 21. Give yourself a point for each "yes" answer 3, 13, and 15. Give a point for each "no" answer to 2, 6, 8, 14, and 21. This is your "Express

Adequacy/Stability'' score. A score of 8 suggests possible overconfidence; 4–7 is average to above-average; under 4 might suggest shyness or lack of self-confidence.

Next, give yourself a point for each of the following questions that you and your partner answered in the same way—7, 20, 21, 22, 23, and 25, plus a point for each question if you have not answered 12 and/or 16 alike. The higher your score, the higher should be your compatibility.

For many questions the strength of your agreement or disagreement can be very important. If you strongly disagree about 9, 10, 17, and 24, for example, your compatibility could be surprisingly lowered, and a need for further open heart-to-heart discussions is suggested.

How Well Do You and Your Mate Communicate?

How well do you and your mate communicate?

Here's a little quiz that will quickly reveal how well you relate to each other. Just answer the following twenty questions ''Yes'' or ''No,'' give yourself a point for each correct answer, then check the scoring key.

1. Do you know where your mate wants to be in ten years?

        Yes _____   No _____

2. Do you openly show affection for each other?

        Yes _____   No _____

3. When jealous of your mate, do you show it?

        Yes _____   No _____

4. Do you know how to dress to please your mate?

        Yes _____   No _____

5. Can you discuss religion and politics with your mate without starting an argument?

        Yes _____   No _____

6. Do you verbalize your sex desires?

        Yes _____   No _____

7. Are you able to criticize your mate openly?

    Yes _____   No _____

8. Do you often feel your mate doesn't understand you?

    Yes _____   No _____

9. Do you often feel you and your mate really don't know each other?

    Yes _____   No _____

10. When you fight, does the same one always have to give in to make peace?

    Yes _____   No _____

11. Are you and your mate completely open about money matters?

    Yes _____   No _____

12. Do you and your mate laugh at the same jokes?

    Yes _____   No _____

13. Are you afraid of your mate?

    Yes _____   No _____

14. Do you think your mate could write an accurate biography of you?

    Yes _____   No _____

15. Does your mate know your most hidden fantasy?

    Yes _____   No _____

16. Do you feel you have to hide many of your moods from your mate?

    Yes _____   No _____

17. Does your mate know your biggest fault?

    Yes _____   No _____

18. Do you often know what your mate is going to say before he (or she) says it?

    Yes _____   No _____

19. Are you both genuinely interested in each other's work?

    Yes _____   No _____

20. Can you accurately judge your partner's mood by observing his or her body language or facial expressions?

    Yes _____   No _____

SCORING

ANSWERS

1 Yes; 2 Yes; 3 Yes; 4 Yes; 5 Yes; 6 Yes; 7 Yes; 8 No; 9 No; 10 No; 11 Yes; 12 Yes; 13 No; 14 Yes; 15 Yes; 16 No; 17 Yes; 18 Yes; 19 Yes; 20 Yes

SCORING KEY:

If you scored 1–5, there's little communication between you and your mate, but you're getting something out of the relationship or you wouldn't be together.

If you scored 6–9, communication is lacking in your relationship but you're hoping things will improve.

If you scored 10–13, you know there are weak points in your relationship, but you are agreeable to patching them up.

If you scored 14–17, you've got a great thing going. You may not see eye to eye on everything, but the open communication makes the differences challenges.

If you scored 18–20, you've either just fallen in love or you have a fantastically high understanding of what makes a relationship endure.

Are You Still in Love with Your Spouse?

Are you still in love with your spouse?

If you're like millions of Americans, chances are it's been ages since you've given your feelings toward your mate some serious thought.

But now here's your chance to quiz yourself about those innermost feelings, with a twenty-five-question test designed by former Harvard psychiatrist Dr. William Appleton and top psychologist Dr. Layne Longfellow.

"I think every married person should ask himself or herself these questions," said Dr. Appleton, who's now in private practice. "Although love means something a little bit different to everyone, the points this test cover can really make you sit up and consciously think about the way your feelings have changed, lessened, or intensified."

Dr. Longfellow, international psychology lecturer and consultant in Berkeley, California, agreed. "Love cannot be measured exactly, but it's important and essential that we stop every once in a while and take stock of our feelings," he declared.

Answer the following twenty-five questions "True" or "False," taking the test by yourself. Your mate should do the same. Then the two of you should discuss the results, advised Dr. Longfellow.

1. I still like to surprise my spouse with little gifts.
2. I still try to find activities for us to do together that my partner would enjoy.
3. I still do some of my spouse's little chores for him (or her) so he (or she) will have more leisure time to enjoy.
4. I make as much of an effort to please my partner when we make love as I used to.
5. I still find it easy to become physically aroused by my spouse.
6. I look forward to making love with my partner.
7. I seldom want to pull away when my spouse touches me.
8. I almost always enjoy touching my spouse.
9. I am looking forward to the time when the children are grown and we can be alone again.
10. I still find my spouse as attractive as ever.
11. I feel proud when I recognize one of my spouse's qualities in our children.
12. I seldom feel resentful if my spouse asks me to do something.
13. I find it easier to forgive my spouse's shortcomings than I used to.
14. I still make an effort to like the people my spouse likes.
15. I could take a week-long trip alone with my spouse and not be bored.
16. I am still interested in my spouse's job and career.
17. My good relationship with my spouse is still more important to me than always emerging the winner in disputes, even though I know at times I am right.
18. I feel my spouse and I are best friends.
19. I feel good and never obligated when my spouse does something special for me.
20. I make every effort to compromise with my spouse on our differences in rearing our children.
21. I still perform household chores or repair and maintenance work with a minimum of resentment.

22. I show less irritation and make less complaints to my spouse than I used to.

23. I don't let the demands of my job prevent me from continuing to meet my spouse's needs.

24. I look my partner straight in the eye as often as I used to and still enjoy it when our eyes meet.

25. I am more accepting of visits by in-laws than I used to be.

SCORING

Score yourself. Add up the number of statements you have marked "True" and score yourself this way:

1–13 true. "This is a pretty good indicator that you need to give your feelings and relationship some serious thought," advised Dr. Longfellow. Added Dr. Appleton: "Ask yourself what you and your spouse can do to improve the situation."

14–17 true. "This is a sign that some improvement is needed in your marriage," said Dr. Longfellow, who was formerly with the Menninger Foundation.

18–25 true. "Chances are that you are still in love with your spouse and your relationship is in pretty good shape," he said.

If you scored low, but still have very positive feelings about your spouse in other areas, "you shouldn't worry too much," said Dr. Appleton, co-author of the book *How Not to Split Up.* "Not everyone fits into the same mold when it comes to love."

"But these questions serve as a pretty good guide for most people and could lead to some very valuable soul-searching."

"Use some discretion," cautioned Dr. Longfellow.

"If you discover that you've made a low score and suspect bringing it up with your spouse might be disruptive to the relationship, I advise against it.

"On the other hand, for many, discovering a low score and sitting down and talking about it might be just the thing that would start some changes in your attitudes."

How Easy Are You
to Live With?

Most people think, "I'm very easy to live with," unconsciously implying, "if only the other person can see things my way." The fact is that when people live together, they can't always see eye to eye. That's why disagreements occur. Most conflicts stem from one partner's feeling inadequate in any one of many areas: as a woman, as a man, as a wife, as a father, as a provider, or by comparison with a friend or a colleague. To feel inadequate makes one feel anxious, and a common way of alleviating anxiety is to raise one's own self-esteem by belittling someone else, usually in the area where that person is most vulnerable. In a marriage situation, a man may try to raise his own self-esteem by lowering the self-esteem of his wife. When this happens, the wife's only recourse is to strike back in an attempt to lower her husband's self-esteem and raise her own. The result is a vicious cycle of attack and counterattack. It certainly isn't easy to live with someone who feels inadequate. Are you easy to live with? Is your husband? Don't answer that until both of you take the test below by Naomi Leiter, M.D. The questions were devised for self-evaluation and must be answered honestly. Avoid the temptation to hedge by answering "Sometimes." Questions should be answered "Yes" or "No." Put down the first answer that comes to mind. If you are tempted to change it—don't. When you've answered all the questions, turn to the scoring key to discover how easy you are to live with—and why.

1. Do you like your partner?

        Yes _____   No _____

2. Do you ever blame your partner for your mistakes?

        Yes _____   No _____

3. Are you envious of your partner's success?

        Yes _____   No _____

4. Do you expect your partner to know when you need loving without telling him?

        Yes _____   No _____

5. Do you keep your suspicions to yourself?

        Yes _____   No _____

6. Do you make hidden sacrifices for your partner or your children?

        Yes _____   No _____

7. Are you jealous of your partner's relationship to anyone?

Yes _____   No _____

8. Do you become disorganized when your partner gets angry with you?

Yes _____   No _____

9. Do you attack or embarrass your partner in public?

_____   No _____

10. Do you continue to do things that your partner has complained about?

Yes _____   No _____

11. Do you insist on having your way?

Yes _____   No _____

12. Can you tolerate your partner's weaknesses?

Yes _____   No _____

13. When you are wrong, can you admit it?

Yes _____   No _____

14. Are you satisfied with your partner's position and earnings?

Yes _____   No _____

15. Do you still listen carefully to what your partner has to say?

Yes _____   No _____

16. Do you feel cheated when your partner doesn't want sex?

Yes _____   No _____

17. Are your allegiances to your parents stronger than you allegiances to your partner?

Yes _____   No _____

18. Are you able to ask for help when you need it?

Yes _____   No _____

19. Can you tolerate being alone—or your partner's need to be alone?

Yes _____   No _____

20. Do you enjoy the leisure time you spend with your partner?

Yes _____   No _____

SCORING

1. Correct Answer: Yes. It is easier for two people to live in harmony if they both like and respect each other. It is sad how many people stay together for years and years even when the answer to this question is obviously No.

2. Correct Answer: No. It is very difficult to get along with someone who cannot take the responsibility for his or her own actions. A sure way to antagonize anyone is to shift the blame onto them. Blaming others may temporarily increase one's own self-esteem, but it always leads to further discord and lowers the self-esteem of the other person.

3. Correct Answer: No. If you are a successful individual in your own right, then you are less likely to be envious of your partner's success and more understanding of his successes or failures. Envy always gets in the way of intimacy.

4. Correct Answer: No. Playing the game, "Guess what I need?" always ends in disaster. It is best to be open and direct. Always remember that the best way to get love is to give love.

5. Correct Answer: No. Suspicion tends to fester and cause trouble. If you are suspicious that your partner is keeping something to himself, the more you wonder without talking to him about it, the more chance there is for enmity. Openness should be the rule.

6. Correct Answer: No. Martyrs do well only in history books. In contemporary family life, they are out of place—and in general, they are very difficult to live with. The state of martyrdom often deserves, and gets, crucifixion.

7. Correct Answer: No. Jealousy is always a sign of insecurity. Since jealousy is the fear that someone else is closer to your partner than you are, you must try to banish the monster. You must develop a greater intimacy by talking to your partner in a completely honest way.

8. Correct Answer: No. If you are disorganized by your partner's anger, it is a sure sign that he's gotten you very anxious. (To be anxious is to be afraid of a nameless fear.) Try not to take personally everything a spouse says in anger. A spouse's anger is often based on his (or her) own insecurity and is usually used to blame you in an attempt to make him (or her) feel better. Don't take the bait.

9. Correct Answer: No. Public honesty, as popularized in *Who's Afraid of Virginia Woolf?* is a frank perversion of the concept of openness. Knowing your partner intimately is your special privilege and flaunting his sensitivities in public is a violation of that intimacy and a demonstration of your cruelty.

10. Correct Answer: No. A patient of mine who liked a three-minute egg rightfully saw his partner's chronic "bad timing" (five minutes) as hostile and an example of their marital discord.

11. Correct Answer: No. Living with another person obviously requires a certain amount of give and take. No one likes to give all the time—and the person who always takes has contempt for the person who always gives.

12. Correct Answer: Yes. Rejecting your partner for his (or her) weaknesses is often related to your own insecurity and sense of weakness. Supporting your spouse in his (or her) weak area is healthy. Some people are very good at sniffing out and exploiting another person's shortcomings. Men or women who have this knack are among the most difficult people to live with.

13. Correct Answer: Yes. It is more pleasant to live with someone who can admit a mistake, apologize, and learn from the error.

14. Correct Answer: Yes. Dissatisfaction with your partner's position and earnings often masks a basic emptiness that no amount of money and no title can dispel.

15. Correct Answer: Yes. "Talking to the wall" is one of the most frustrating human experiences. The job of listening carefully to what your partner says requires empathy, which begins by putting yourself in your partner's place.

16. Correct Answer: No. Being disappointed is not the same as feeling cheated. Being disappointed allows room for understanding of the other person's feelings. Two people's needs do not always correspond. In this day and age, when immediate gratification seems to be so highly valued (as a valid reaction to centuries of a double standard and rigid sexual taboos), we tend to forget that human sexuality is extremely sensitive to emotional states.

17. Correct Answer: No. Many continuing family arguments have as their basis the hidden fact that a partner's way of doing things is different from a parent's. Such arguments imply that it is wished that the partner were more like the parent. Disappointment and bickering will arise from an atmosphere in which parental allegiance outweighs allegiance to a spouse.

18. Correct Answer: Yes. Remember, it is just as hard to live with someone who never needs to be helped as it is to live with someone who always asks for it.

19. Correct Answer: Yes. Aloneness is not the same as loneliness. The capacity to be alone is a sign of maturity that goes hand in hand with the capacity to tolerate another person's need for periods of aloneness.

It presumes the ability to do something with one's time. (This, of course, is not isolation or withdrawal from society. That's something else entirely.)

20. Correct Answer: Yes. Two people can reduce the degree of difficulty in living together if they can share leisure time in mutually satisfying activities. If each day can include such activities, so much the better.

HOW DID YOU SCORE

10–5 Correct: You are not easy to live with. In fact, you are downright difficult to get along with.

6–14 Correct: There is an average degree of human difficulty in living with you, and there is still room for improvement on your part.

15–19 Correct: You are easy to live with. Your partner is fortunate.

20 Correct: Take the test over again, and if you still score 20 correct, I'd like very much to meet you!

P.S.: If you are difficult to live with, what are you going to do about it?

Do You Have a Good Marriage?

How well is your marriage working?

If you can't answer that question with confidence, here's a little quiz that'll help you out. It was developed by Dr. Ernest Dichter, a New York psychologist.

Just grab a pencil and answer each question "Yes" or "No." Confine your answers to your relationship during the past few months. When you finish, use the scoring key to determine your score. Then read the explanations to find out what your score means.

1. Have you and your mate done anything together that was exciting or exceptionally pleasant?

                Yes _____   No _____

2. Have you or your mate introduced each other to any new friends or acquaintances?

                Yes _____   No _____

3. Do you and your mate have any definite plans about what you're going to do with your lives during the next year or two?

Yes _____   No _____

4. Have you and your mate had an open discussion about your relationship, regardless of whether it's been better or worse?

Yes _____   No _____

5. Do you and your mate repeatedly discuss certain topics such as money or relatives?

Yes _____   No _____

6. Have you and your mate bought little gifts for each other?

Yes _____   No _____

7. Do you and your mate select clothes for each other or ask each other's opinion before buying?

Yes _____   No _____

8. Have you and your mate taken up a new hobby or started a self-improvement program together?

Yes _____   No _____

9. Do you and your mate enjoy pretty much the same lifestyle?

Yes _____   No _____

10. Do you tell your mate if something such as his (or her) hairdo or clothing displeases you?

Yes _____   No _____

11. Do you criticize your mate in front of others?

Yes _____   No _____

12. Do you praise your mate in front of others?

Yes _____   No _____

13. Do you let your mate sleep even though you are wide awake?

Yes _____   No _____

14. Do you and your mate discuss books, movies, and TV shows with each other?

Yes _____   No _____

15. Are you sympathetic and helpful when your mate is physically ill?

Yes _____   No _____

16. Do you urge your mate to tell you about his or her day?

Yes _____   No _____

17. Are you impatient when your mate has a minor ailment?

Yes _____   No _____

18. Do you do things you really don't enjoy in order to please your mate?

Yes _____   No _____

19. Are there any activities—tennis, fishing, golf, etc.—that you prefer not to share with your mate?

Yes _____   No _____

20. Do you and your mate sleep in separate bedrooms?

Yes _____   No _____

21. Do you and your mate share a double bed?

Yes _____   No _____

22. Do you and your mate watch the same TV programs most of the time?

Yes _____   No _____

23. Do you and your mate like the same books?

Yes _____   No _____

24. Do you and your mate always go on vacations together?

Yes _____   No _____

25. Do you and your mate share your money, income, and investments?

Yes _____   No _____

SCORING

NOW CHECK YOUR SCORE:

1.	Yes–1; No–0	6.	Yes–1; No–0	11.	Yes–0; No–1
2.	Yes–1; No–e	7.	Yes–1; No–0	12.	Yes–1; No–0
3.	Yes–1; No–0	8.	Yes–1; No–0	13.	Yes–1; No–0
4.	Yes–1; No–0	9.	Yes–1; No–0	14.	Yes–1; No–0
5.	Yes–0; No–1	10.	Yes–1; No–0	15.	Yes–1; No–0

16. Yes–1; No–0	20. Yes–0; No–1	24. Yes–1; No–0
17. Yes–0; No–1	21. Yes–1; No–0	25. Yes–1; No–0
18. Yes–1; No–0	22. Yes–1; No–0	
19. Yes–0; No–1	23. Yes–1; No–0	

If you scored 21–25 points, yours is a near-perfect marriage. If you scored 15–20 points, you have a good marriage and compare favorably with most other couples. A score of 10–14 shows there's some strain or difficulties in your marriage relationship. A score of 9 or less means your marriage could be in real trouble.

Should You Tell Your Husband Everything?

There are people who think after marriage that they should bare their souls to their husbands or wives. There are those too, who believe that "silence is golden" and "what you don't know won't hurt you." The truth lies somewhere in the middle, according to the marriage counselors, but where you hide the facts is of utmost importance. This list of questions is not complete by far, but may give you some hints.

FOR WOMEN ONLY:
Should you tell your husband:

1. If you think he is not progressing on his job as he should?

Yes _____   No _____

2. If you have a bank account outside your joint one?

Yes _____   No _____

3. If an old male acquaintance came to see you while he was away?

Yes _____   No _____

4. If you bought some extravagance in a weak moment that the budget couldn't stand?

Yes _____   No _____

5. If your doctor told you you need an operation or medical care you feel you cannot afford?

Yes _____   No _____

6. If you found some pictures of his ex-girlfriends in an old suitcase, trunk, etc.?

Yes _____   No _____

7. If your husband has lowered his standards of courtesy and manners since your marriage?

Yes _____   No _____

8. If your daughter tells you in confidence that she has "a crush" on the boy next door?

Yes _____   No _____

9. If your son's principal tells you your son has deliberately thrown a rock through a classroom window?

Yes _____   No _____

10. That you love him?

Yes _____   No _____

SCORING

ANSWERS FOR WOMEN ONLY:

1. No. Your job is to inspire, to help, not to undermine his confidence by belittling his progress.
2. Yes. Unless you are saving up for a special surprise, your account should be known to your husband.
3. Yes. If you don't tell him, the neighbors will.
4. Yes. If you tell him, he'll give you a lecture and then pat your head. If he finds out on his own, you may be well spanked.
5. Yes. "A stitch in time" may eliminate greater problems later.
6. No. Who wants a man who has not had other girlfriends? And out of these he selected you. The fact that he saved the pictures shows he's a wonderful sentimental romanticist! Put the pictures back and be happy.
7. Yes. But be careful how you handle it and be sure *you* are as careful in *your* standards as during the days before you were married.

8. No. You were given the confidence of your daughter. If you tell this, your husband may suspect you will confide any small thing in the family life.

9. Yes. This is a serious affair, calling for a family conference.

10. Yes. Snuggle up and whisper it. The famous *"I love you"* works miracles in a marriage!

Should You Tell Your Wife Everything?

"Silence is not always tact and it is tact that is golden, not silence." (Samuel Butler)

In marriage, it is not what you say, but how you say it. Not what you tell, but whether it is important or not to your relationship with your wife. Try these questions and check with the opinions of marriage counselors.

FOR MEN ONLY:
Should you tell your wife:

1. That you had several girlfriends before you met her?

    Yes _____   No _____

2. If you have been demoted in your job?

    Yes _____   No _____

3. If there are some things about the housekeeping, the discipline of the children, etc., that bother you?

    Yes _____   No _____

4. If your wife is gaining or losing too much weight?

    Yes _____   No _____

5. What your income is?

    Yes _____   No _____

6. If there is a girl on the job or in the office who is flirting with you?

    Yes _____   No _____

7. If you have persistent head pains, stomach problems, or other illnesses?

Yes _____   No _____

8. That you are still dreaming of faraway places, new successes, ungrasped ambitions?

Yes _____   No _____

9. When you get a ticket for a traffic violation?

Yes _____   No _____

10. That you love her?

Yes _____   No _____

SCORING

ANSWERS FOR MEN ONLY:

1. Yes. Let her know, but don't pine about them or compare their cheese souffle with hers. A carefully dropped hint may help you a bit, however.
2. Yes. Failure is hard to admit, but she will come to your rescue, and she needs to know in order to adapt her budget and way of life.
3. Yes. It is easier in the long run to see her tears than to have her wonder about your grouchiness. A little tact will even keep the tears from falling.
4. No. Try to discover the cause. If this doesn't work, take her along when you have *your* physical checkup and lure her to a doctor.
5. Yes. Your wife needs to know whether she can buy steak or frankfurters, a new suit or not. The budget is a matter for the understanding of the entire family.
6. No. If you are such a boy as to let this bother you, don't mention it. If you are a grown-up man, it's hardly worth talking about.
7. Yes. Don't be brave and strong. Say you do not feel well, and then do something constructive about it. See your doctor.
8. No. We are all privileged to have our own dream world. You are not obligated to tell your wife what you are dreaming about . . . unless you want to.
9. Yes. It will help your feeling of guilt (and then she will likely tell you something she has done wrong that she has been aching to spill out).
10. Yes. "Love consists in this, that two solitudes protect and touch and greet each other." (Rainer Maria Rilke)

Who Is the Boss?

Cartoonists delight in depicting henpecked males. Columns for the lovelorn contain the weeping words of neglected women. The battle of the sexes still rages. It helps if you recognize your own attitude toward the male and the female. With this knowledge, you will not buck the tide but accept the fact with good grace. This test will help you assess your reactions to man-woman relationships.

1. In the cartoon sequence below make a check over either the man or the woman in each drawing A and B.

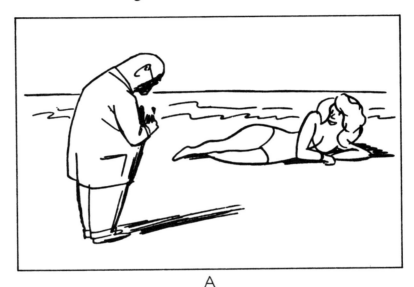

A

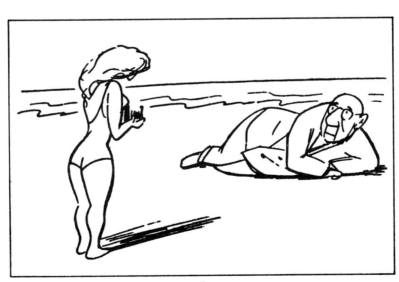

B

Keep in mind your mate or favorite date.

Make your selection for the following questions. If you are a man, answer He as "I do" and She as "She does." If you are a woman, answer She as "I do" and He as "He does."

2. Over a period of time, who waits more often?
   HE _____   SHE _____   ABOUT THE SAME _____

3. When dining out, who usually orders the more expensive meal?
   HE _____   SHE _____   ABOUT THE SAME _____

4. Who does most of the talking?
   HE _____   SHE _____   ABOUT THE SAME _____

5. Who runs the trivial little errands?
   HE _____   SHE _____   ABOUT THE SAME _____

6. When planning an evening out, whose wishes are usually followed?
   HE _____   SHE _____   ABOUT THE SAME _____

7. In times of crisis (from a cut finger to a flood), who is calmer?
   HE _____   SHE _____   ABOUT THE SAME _____

8. Who makes more suggestions about what the other should wear?
   HE _____   SHE _____   ABOUT THE SAME _____

9. When things are lost, left, or misplaced, who usually finds them?
   HE _____   SHE _____   ABOUT THE SAME _____

10. Who has the better memory?
    HE _____   SHE _____   ABOUT THE SAME _____

11. Who is more conservative about money matters?
    HE _____   SHE _____   ABOUT THE SAME _____

12. Whose friends are seen more often?
    HE _____   SHE _____   ABOUT THE SAME _____

13. Who is more fastidious about clothing?
    HE _____   SHE _____   ABOUT THE SAME _____

14. Who most often tries to break the order of bad habits?
    HE _____   SHE _____   ABOUT THE SAME _____

SCORING

If you have checked the member of your own sex in both A and B, give yourself 2 points.

If you have checked one male and one female in A and B give yourself 0.

For questions 2 through 14 give yourself 0 points for each "About the Same" answer.

If you are a male, count the number of answers you gave as She—a point each. If you are a female, count the number of answers you gave as He—a point each.

ANALYSIS:

10–5: This score would indicate that no one is the boss in your opinion. You do not feel any domination of one sex over the other. But don't pat yourself on the back for this score, because you may find yourself in a state of confusion as to who takes the leadership role.

6–10: This is an average score that balances the responsibility of a man and wife, a date and mate, or a working team.

11–15: There is no question about who is the boss. If you have scored this for your own sex, you may have to watch being too bossy and domineering. If you scored this for the opposite sex, just relax and follow the lead.

Are You Living with a Bored Husband?

Alas, too many women do not realize that when their husband's interests go out the window, he is likely soon to walk out the door. Wives are prone to disregard some of the danger signals and to shrug them off as a natural stage of marriage. Ladies, beware. Take this quiz and see if your matrimonial stage is sagging.

1. Does he refer to "your" children, "your" home, "your" friends instead of "ours"?

Yes _____   No _____

2. Is your husband perpetually too tired to help in the house or yard, to spend time with the children or neighbors?

Yes _____   No _____

3. Does he often look disgusted or express displeasure with the appearance of the house?

Yes _____   No _____

4. Does he groan or complain about every bill he has to pay?

Yes _____   No _____

5. Do your problems seem to irritate him?

Yes _____   No _____

6. Does he comment favorably about something relatively unimportant but new—address, a new recipe, a change in furniture arrangement?

Yes _____   No _____

7. Does he say "I know" or "No" before you finish a statement?

Yes _____   No _____

8. Does he seem eager to find reasons to go out alone and/or urge people indiscriminately to come to your house?

Yes _____   No _____

9. Is he often silent at home for days at a time?

Yes _____   No _____

10. Has he ceased to use some pet term of endearment?

Yes_____   No _____

SCORING

Count the number of "Yes" answers.

0–3 Yes answers: You stand on solid footing. If your husband is this alert and happy, keep him so. Marriage is no time to relax.

4–7 Yes answers: Madame, you are teetering on a ledge. You and only you, can analyze the problems. With some careful thought, you can eliminate the problems.

8–9 Yes answers: No doubt you are either unhappy or you don't care about your marriage. Perhaps you could talk this quiz out *unemotionally* and the two of you can get to the source of your untogetherness.

10 Yes answers: This is the most challenging score of all. Unless you and your husband are content to live in separate isolated emotional and mental cells, it is up to you to use every wile known and perfected by the female of the species. Don't show him this quiz. Take each point. Plot and plan to make the answers *No* one year from today. You could, however, get help from qualified people such as your doctor or members of the clergy. Keep friends and relatives out of this project.

How Well Do You Really Know Your Spouse?

It is often said that the most intimate relationship one can have is with one's spouse. Your husband or wife is supposed to be the one person with whom you can share everything—your dreams, desires, and innermost feelings. You more than anyone should know who your spouse *really* is.

Have you taken the time to learn about your marital partner? In this cute test we challenge you to find out if you know your spouse as well as you think you do.

1.   What is your spouse's favorite color?
2.   Does your spouse prefer taking a bath or a shower?
3.   Where would your spouse most like to go on a vacation?
4.   In what city was your spouse born?
5.   How tall is your spouse?
6.   What type of movie would your spouse rather see—a drama or a comedy?
7.   What trait does your spouse like most about you?
8.   What trait does your spouse like least about you?
9.   What is your spouse's favorite food?
10.   If your spouse could be in any occupation, what would it be?
11.   What is your spouse's favorite TV program?
12.   What is your mother-in-law's maiden name?
13.   What is your spouse's No. 1 pet peeve?
14.   Does your spouse tend to be politically conservative or liberal?

15. Who is your spouse's best friend?

16. What is your spouse's shoe size?

17. What is your spouse's greatest fear?

18. How much does your spouse weigh (within five pounds)?

19. What is your spouse's favorite pastime?

20. If your spouse could trade places with a famous celebrity, who would it be?

SCORING

NOW HAVE YOUR SPOUSE CHECK YOUR RESPONSES

Score a point for each correct answer.

If you scored 15 or over, you are to be congratulated. You are the rare individual who has shown the interest and taken time to truly learn about your spouse. When you allow yourself to know someone, you have opened the door to long-lasting friendship.

If you scored 8–14, you and your spouse know each other fairly well. You should, however, take the time to learn more about your mate. You may be surprised to find out how interesting he (or she) really is.

If you scored below 7, it is obvious that you do not show enough interest in your spouse. Better open up the lines of communication with your mate before you discover there is no one around to talk with.

YOU
AND YOUR
FAMILY

Are You a Good Parent?

What kind of parent are you? Too strict? Too lenient? An inspiration to your children? Or do you hold them back? This simple quiz can give you a good idea whether or not you need improvement.

Just answer each of these questions "Yes" or "No":

1. Are you proud of having your children "toilet trained" at an early age?

   Yes _____   No _____

2. Do you reward your children for "straight A's" on their report cards?

   Yes _____   No _____

3. Do you freely answer your children's questions about sex?

   Yes _____   No _____

4. Do you know what your children's nutritional needs are in regard to protein, vitamins, and minerals? Do you feed them accordingly?

   Yes _____   No _____

5. Do you touch, hug, and kiss your children, especially those over the age of seven?

Yes _____   No _____

6. Do you insist that your children keep their room really clean?

Yes _____   No _____

7. Can you comfortably admit to your children, "I'm wrong"?

Yes _____   No _____

8. Do you respect your children's privacy, phone calls, mail, etc.?

Yes _____   No _____

9. Are you constantly saying things like, "Well, when I was young, things were different," "Spare the rod and spoil the child," "Children should be seen and not heard?"

Yes _____   No _____

10. Do you share your successes and your problems with your children?

Yes _____   No _____

11. Do you use food as a means of punishing or rewarding your children?

Yes _____   No _____

12. Have you carefully planned your children's training, education, and religion?

Yes _____   No _____

13. If they made a "parent machine" that could bring up your children exactly as you know would be best for them, would you use it?

Yes _____   No _____

14. Do you criticize or punish your children in front of others?

Yes _____   No _____

15. Do you attend Scout meetings, PTA, school programs, sports events, etc., that might be boring to you?

Yes _____   No _____

SCORING

Score yourself a point for each answer as follows: 1 No; 2 No; 3 Yes; 4 Yes; 5 Yes; 6 No; 7 Yes; 8 Yes; 9 No; 10 Yes; 11 No; 12 No; 13 No; 14 No; 15 No.

1-2:   Parenthood is not for you. Your strict, regimented, dictatorial lifestyle is better suited to soldiers than to children.

3-5:   Below average. Ease up on your children—let them travel at their own speed.

6-8:   Average. Sometimes you like your children, sometimes you don't—and that's pretty normal.

9-11:   Above average. Bringing up your family is a joy to you.

12-13:   Rare parent. You are a springboard from which your children can devise their own dive into life. You have your own full life and they have theirs.

14-15:   Perfect parent. You offer your children the gift of freedom.

Do You Earn Your Family's Respect?

This test is based on a list of the most common grievances connected with loss of family respect. The list was compiled by Dr. Mary Margaret Walker, a licensed marriage counselor in California.

Dr. Walker says: "It is entirely possible to have respect for a person without love, but the reverse is not true. In my dealings with thousands of married couples, I've found there is no true love without respect." Respect is an important prerequisite of love.

Your answers to the following questions, based on Dr. Walker's observations and studies over twenty years, will help determine if you earn your family's respect.

1. Do you think that most important decisions should be made jointly by husband and wife?

     Yes _____   No _____

2. Do you agree with the old saying, "Children should be seen and not heard?"

Yes _____   No _____

3. Do you often refer to the virtues (or vices) of your own mother and father?

Yes _____   No _____

4. Do you cater to your pets to the discomfort of your family?

Yes _____   No _____

5. Do you think one member of the family should have the sole responsibilities for handling the finances?

Yes _____   No _____

6. Do you think your home is a place to "fall apart" in your personal grooming (husband unshaven, wife in hair curlers)?

Yes _____   No _____

7. Are you as polite to members of your family as you are on the job or in public?

Yes _____   No _____

8. Do you usually have an even temper at home?

Yes _____   No _____

9. Do you use sarcasm to control your spouse or your children?

Yes _____   No _____

10. Do you act your age?

Yes _____   No _____

11. Do you believe that everyone has a right to privacy—possessions which must not be used by others and everyone should have time to be alone?

Yes _____   No _____

12. Do you refrain from voicing disparaging remarks about people of other religions, races, or creeds?

Yes _____   No _____

13. Does your family usually know where you are?

Yes _____   No _____

14. Do you often exhibit genuine affection to the members of your family?

Yes _____   No _____

15. Are you willing to carry cheerfully your share of family duties (shopping, cleaning, picking up personal belongings, doing extra duties during an emergency)?

Yes _____   No _____

16. Are you habitually immoderate in certain things (drinking, smoking, eating, sexual activities)?

Yes _____   No _____

17. Do you make only those promises that you can and do keep?

Yes _____   No _____

18. When faced with a failure or a problematic situation, is it easier for you to lie or alibi than to tell the truth?

Yes _____   No _____

19. Do you use sex as a reward or a punishment with your mate?

Yes _____   No _____

20. After taking an over-all evaluation of yourself, do you find that you like yourself most of the time?

Yes _____   No _____

SCORING

ANSWERS

Check the answers below with your answers and give yourself a point for each correct answer. After you add up your points, see the paragraph relating to your total score.

1 Yes; 2 No; 3 No; 4 No; 5 No; 6 No; 7 Yes; 8 Yes; 9 No; 10 Yes; 11 Yes; 12 Yes; 13 Yes; 14 Yes; 15 Yes; 16 No; 17 Yes; 18 No; 19 No; 20 Yes.

YOUR SCORE:

15–20 correct: In general, your behavior and attitudes command respect. You operate democratically, especially if you answered correctly on questions 1, 2, and 5, and are aware of the rights of others.

8–14 correct: Probably you are a very nice person, but it is doubtful you really work at being respected. Many people accept

11. A neighbor informs you that your eight-year-old child was caught playing "doctor" with hers. You:
    a. discuss it with your child.
    b. tell your child that he or she is never to do that again.
    c. say nothing to your child, since it is normal for kids to play "doctor."

12. At a family outing to the zoo, your nine-year-old's curiosity is aroused when he or she sees animals mating. You:
    a. watch and make light comments.
    b. walk away and try to distract his or her attention.
    c. give simple, brief answers to any questions.

13. You find your eleven-year-old reading an adult sex magazine. You:
    a. are embarrassed.
    b. think it is cute.
    c. feel outraged and stunned.

14. At what age should you begin to tell your children about birth control?
    a. preadolescence.
    b. don't tell them, it will only encourage them to experiment with sex too soon.
    c. when they have a boyfriend, or a girlfriend during adolescence.

15. Your twelve-year-old daughter wants a pajama party. You:
    a. forbid it.
    b. allow it, but with supervision.
    c. leave the kids alone to have a good time.

16. Your thirteen-year-old daughter says she wants to wear provocative clothes, "like all the other girls." You:
    a. tell her that such attire is inappropriate even if others are wearing it.
    b. allow it so she doesn't feel rejected.
    c. tell her she is too young to wear such clothes.

17. Your fourteen-year-old daughter tells you she wants to go steady. You:
    a. encourage her to engage in other social activities.
    b. tell her she must wait until she is eighteen.
    c. talk to her about birth control.

18. Your teen-age son is gaining a reputation as a "ladies' man" or "swinger." You:

    a. feel proud he is so popular with the opposite sex.

    b. don't like it, but figure "boys will be boys".

    c. feel concerned about his need to see so many girls.

19. You find your sixteen-year-old daughter engaged in heavy petting. You:

    a. talk to her about birth control.

    b. have a frank discussion but suggest she not rush things.

    c. restrict her dating privileges.

20. When your teen-ager goes out on his or her first date, you feel:

    a. somewhat apprehensive.

    b. happy and proud.

    c. fearful and anxious over what might happen.

SCORING

1.	a–1. b–2, c–3	8.	a–2; b–3; c–1	15.	a–1; b–2; c–3
2.	a–2. b–3. c–1	9.	a–3; b–2; c–1	16.	a–2; b–3; c–1
3.	a–3. b–1. c–2	10.	a–1; b–2; c–3	17.	a–2; b–1; c–3
4.	a–1. b–3. c–2	11.	a–2; b–1; c–3	18.	a–3; b–1; c–2
5.	a–2. b–1. c–3	12.	a–3; b–1; c–2	19.	a–3; b–2; c–1
6.	a–1; b–2; c–3	13.	a–2; b–3; c–1	20.	a–2; b–3; c–1
7.	a–3; b–1; c–2	14.	a–3; b–1; c–2		

A socre of 20–33: You tend to be too rigid in your own attitudes to talk frankly about sex with your children. Try to communicate a bit more openly?

A score of 34–47: You have probably achieved a fairly healthy level of communication with your children about sex as well as other subjects.

A score of 48–60: You are perhaps too permissive in your dealings with your children about sex. Giving them more guidance would help.

Do Your Children Love You?

You may think that you are the ideal mother, and that your children adore you, but it may be that you are taking a lot for granted.

Answer the following questions truthfully and the result will prove most revealing!

Mark a. or b. and then check your score at the end.

1. a. Do you make a fetish of keeping your home spick and span?
   b. Or do you tolerate a certain amount of untidiness on the part of your offspring?

2. a. Do you try to look nice at all times?
   b. Or do you dress up only when you plan to go out?

3. a. Do you excell at cooking, sewing, etc.?
   b. Or do you just muddle along in that respect?

4. a. Do you try to buy your children's affection by overwhelming them with pocket money and gifts?
   a. Or do you believe in moderation in all things?

5. a. Are you the impatient sort?
   b. Or do you always keep your temper in check?

6. a. Do you encourage your children to take an active part in running the home?
   b. Or do you prefer to run things yourself?

7. a. When your children try to enlist your aid with their homework or other problems, do you tell them that you are much too busy or tired and advise them to stand on their own two feet, etc.?
   b. Or do you always assist them in every way possible?

8. a. Are you continually showering them with do's and don'ts without giving them a reason?
   b. Or do you try to explain to them why some things are permitted, and others not?

9. a. Do you try to keep cheerful even under the most trying circumstances?
   b. Or are you prone to nag when things go wrong?

10. a. Do you encourage your husband to tell the children about his job?
    b. Or do you think that children do not wish to be bothered with that sort of stuff?

SCORING

Score five points for each correct answer: 1–b; 2–a, 3–a; 4–b; 5–b; 6–a; 7–b; 8–b; 9–a; 10–a. Maximum score, 50.

If you have genuinely scored 40–50 points your children must think the world of you.

25–35 points means that your best is not quite good enough.

20 points and under would indicate only one thing—you are unwittingly building a barrier between yourself and your children.

Are You Living with a Compulsive Gambler?

Living with a compulsive gambler can be a devastating experience.

The first thing for you to accept is that the compulsive gambler suffers from an illness. The compulsive gambler is not a weak person, nor does he or she desire intentionally to hurt others. The compulsive gambler is caught in the grip of a progressive illness for which treatment is available in Gamblers Anonymous.

Just as there is Gamblers Anonymous for the compulsive gambler, there is Gam-Anon for the families and close friends of the compulsive gambler.

The following questions may help you to decide whether or not you are involved with someone who is a compulsive gambler:

1. Do you find yourself haunted by bill collectors?
2. Is the person in question often away from home for long, unexplained periods of time?
3. Do you feel that he or she cannot be trusted with money?
4. Does he or she promise faithfully to stop gambling; beg, plead for another chance, yet gamble again and again?
5. Does he or she borrow money to gamble with or to pay gambling debts?
6. Have you noticed a personality change in the gambler as his or her gambling progresses?

7. Have you come to the point of hiding money needed for living expenses, knowing that you and the rest of the family may go without food and clothing if you do not?

8. Do you search the gambler's clothing or go through his wallet when the opportunity presents itself, or otherwise check on his or her activities?

9. Does the gambler hide his or her money?

10. Does the gambler lie sometimes compulsively, avoid any discussion of his or her debts, or refuse to face the realities of the situation?

11. Does the gambler use guilt induction as a method of shifting responsibility for his or her gambling upon you?

12. Do you attempt to anticipate the gambler's moods, or try to control his or her life?

13. Do you feel that your life together is a nightmare?

SCORING

If you can answer "Yes" to at least six of these questions, Gam-Anon may be able to help you.

What is Gam-Anon? Gam-Anon is a fellowship of men and women who are husbands, wives, relatives, and close friends of compulsive gamblers.

You need not wait for the compulsive gambler to seek help before you can come to Gam-Anon.

Gam-Anon teaches effective ways of coping with the gambling problem. By seeking help for ourselves and gaining serenity and peace of mind, we find that we are better able to cope with our problems on a day-to-day basis and in some cases motivate the gambler toward seeking help for himself or herself.

How Much Do You Know about Your Parents As People?

You share a house and life with your parents for a good many years, then leave home, and the time you share turns into touching base every so often: Christmas, Thanksgiving, birthdays. For a few hours the family unit is close again . . . or is it? Frequently we start out with the best of intentions, but end up rerunning the same old quarrels.

This year, try something different: Try imagining your mother and father six years old and scared of the dark, or fourteen and overjoyed at the prospect of a first date. At what age was that first date? That first kiss?

Take the quiz here, then ask your parents to check your answers. It should lead to some new, startlingly different conversations, and, with luck, better understanding.

WHILE THEY WERE GROWING UP

1. As a child, your mother/father thought about being a _____ when she/he grew up.

2. What did your mother/father and her/his mother and father argue about most?

3. If your mother/father ran away from home as a child, where did she/he go?

4. What was your mother's/father's nickname?

5. What does your mother remember best about her father?

6. What kind of men would your mother have gone out with in high school?
   a. captain of the football team
   b. class comedian
   c. best dancer
   d. student-body president
   e. captain of the debating team

7. What is the childhood accomplishment your mother/father is most proud of?

8. Did your father have a childhood hero? Who?

9. If a bully hit your father as a child on the school playground, he would have
   a. fought with him

    b. told the teacher

    c. backed off and avoided it

10. In high school, your father dated
    a. the smartest girl in the class
    b. a cheerleader
    c. the class sweater girl
    d. Miss Congeniality
    e. no one; he was too short

11. When he left school and supported himself, your father's first job was _____ .

12. If your mother worked to support herself, her first job was _____ .

13. What is your mother's/father's strongest personal memory of World War II?

14. Does your mother/father remember her/his grandmothers' maiden names?

15. If your mother/father grew up in a home where a language other than English was spoken, does she/he still speak it? Understand it?

WHAT THEY ARE LIKE
AND WHAT THEY LIKE/DISLIKE

16. On trips, who drove most?

17. What is your mother/father allergic to?

1S. Does your mother/father *really* like the chicken wings and the end cut of the roast?

19. What was a big disappointment in your mother's/father's life?

20. If your father could be a sports figure, he'd like to be
    a. Reggie Jackson
    b. Bjorn Borg
    c. O. J. Simpson
    d. Jack Nicklaus

21. What is your mother's/father's most vivid family memory of the year you were seven? What is yours?

22. If you took your mother/father to a concert, she/he would rather hear
    a. a symphony

    b. Lawrence Welk
    c. Victor Borge
    d. Benny Goodman

23. What makes your mother/father feel misty?

THEIR COURTSHIP AND MARRIAGE

24. How many years have your parents been married?

25. What was your mother's favorite gift from your father?

26. Where did your father propose to your mother?

27. What song reminds them most of their courtship?

28. Where did your parents spend their honeymoon? How long was it?

29. How did your parents meet?

30. What does your mother wear to please your father (and vice versa)?

31. Did your mother and father like each other on their first meeting?

32. How long did your parents know each other before they were married?

33. Which years of their marriage do they have the happiest memories of?
    a. 1–5 years
    b. 5–15 years
    c. 15–25 years
    d. 25–35 years

34. What things do they argue about most?

WHAT THEY BELIEVE

35. How would your mother/father react to an unwarranted parking ticket?
    a. pay it and forget it
    b. take it to court and argue that it was unwarranted
    c. pay it but complain about the injustice of the whole thing

36. Does your mother/father support Proposition 13?

37. If you had an abortion, your mother/father would
    a. rather not know
    b. prefer to be told, even though she'd/he'd be very upset
    c. be sympathetic

38. Have your parents started saving for your wedding?

39. Their ideal wedding for you would be
    a. a big bash for four hundred
    b. a small family wedding in your backyard
    c. an elopement
    d. primarily for their friends and yours

40. Would your mother/father vote for the ratification of the ERA?

41. Your father would like to
    a. retire completely
    b. work full-time as long as possible
    c. retire but always work part-time

42. What luxury item is most important for your mother/father to have in the budget?

43. For the next President, your mother/father would most like to vote for
    a. Jimmy Carter
    b. Howard Baker
    c. Gerald Ford
    d. Ted Kennedy
    e. John Connally
    f. Jerry Brown
    g. Ronald Reagan

44. When your mother/father quarrels with a member of the family as adults, the cooling-off period is
    a. an afternoon
    b. less than six months
    c. six months to five years
    d. not over yet

45. Your mother's favorite book is _____ .

46. If you told your father you were moving in with your boyfriend, he would
    a. wish you well
    b. accept it but prefer you didn't mention it to his friends and family
    c. disapprove heartily

47. Which of your parents has stronger religious feeling?

48. Does your mother/father believe in life after death?

49. When your parents retire, they plan to
    a. sell the house and move to Florida
    b. buy a condominium
    c. buy a mobile home or RV and travel
    d. take a long trip to Europe or the Far East

SCORING

Give yourself a point for each similar answer, tally up the points, and find yourself below.

35 or over: Either you have ESP or you and your parents talk together a lot. Congratulations to both!

13–34: You may not take enough time to sit down and talk with your parents—not about you, but about them. It might also be useful to check to see which parent you seem to know less about.

0–12: Either your parents have been very closed about themselves, or you are continuing to cast them in the role of ''Mother'' and ''Father,'' even though you are all now adults. Talking about low-pressure information, such as in the preceding forty-nine questions, may be a good place to begin changing the way you all see one another.

YOU
AND YOUR
FRIENDS

Are You a Person
Who Makes Friends Easily?

Everyone likes to be liked. Those who don't are merely kidding themselves. Answer this quiz and see how you rate at the art of making friends.

1. Which of the four drawings of the swinging cat below reminds you most of yourself and your attitude toward others?

A

B

C

D

2. **In the following situations, which reaction is nearest to your own.** When traveling alone, you usually
   a. read.
   b. talk to those around you.
   c. silently study people.

3. You can name:
   a. three or more real friends.
   b. one or two real friends.
   c. no friends, only acquaintances.

4. If you attend a party and know only the host or hostess, you would:
   a. stay close to those who are giving the party.
   b. mingle and be happy to meet new people.
   c. feel uncomfortable.

5. If you enter a crowded, informal cafeteria or lunchroom and find only one seat available at a table with others, you would:
   a. wait until a table is vacant.
   b. leave.
   c. ask if you may join the others.

6. At a dinner party surrounded by unfamiliar faces, if you wished another helping you would:
   a. say nothing.
   b. help yourself.
   c. compliment your hostess and ask for another helping.

7. You find that you have chosen the wrong attire for a social gathering. You would:
   a. withdraw to a corner.
   b. act as you always do.
   c. make a big joke of it.

8. At a lecture with a large audience, you feel keenly opposed to a statement expressed. You would:
   a. speak up.
   b. gulp down your thoughts.
   c. make your point after someone else has broken the ice.

9. If you were to take a vacation alone at a resort, you would probably:
   a. remain alone.

    b. make friends and have fun together.

    c. find a couple of people and spend time with them.

10. You are at a dance where others are doing new steps, unfamiliar to you. You most likely would

    a. sit it out.

    b. watch carefully and then try the steps.

    c. be embarrassed but struggle along.

11. When there is a radical change in fashion, you would

    a. adopt the new style at once.

    b. hang onto your old wardrobe or hairstyle.

    c. wait until everyone else is wearing it.

12. When you read a newspaper, you usually

    a. confine your reading to one section, such as sports.

    b. read the entire paper.

    c. scan the headlines and read the items that catch your eye.

13. If a neighbor were to come for help on a minor matter at an inconvenient time, you would

    a. turn him or her down.

    b. suggest where to go for help.

    c. give your assistance.

14. In most situations, you

    a. do all the talking.

    b. like to listen to others and be silent.

    c. enjoy being a party to a conversation.

15. Most of your waking hours, you

    a. have time for others.

    b. have no time for others.

    c. have all the time in the world for others.

16. After an illness, you

    a. like to talk about it.

    b. say nothing until asked.

    c. refuse to discuss the matter.

17. When local or national politics come up, you

    a. register to vote, and vote.

    b. never vote.

    c. actively work for the candidates of your choice.

18. If you were to visit a town or country other than your own, you would probably
    a. think your surroundings at home are better.
    b. be interested in other ways of life.
    c. think it would be fun to revisit.

19. When you go to a mass sports event such as a football game, you
    a. enjoy the excitement of being there.
    b. feel apprehension about the crowds and traffic problems.
    c. wish you stayed home and watched it on TV.

20. If you were marooned with a group of people, you would
    a. relax and let them take care of you.
    b. try to organize group co-operation.
    c. take over complete leadership.

SCORING

HOW DID YOU SCORE?

1. a–2; b–2; c–4	8. a–6; b–2; c–4	15. a–6; b–2; c–4
2. a–2; b–6; c–4	9. a–2; b–6; c–4	16. a–2; b–6; c–2
3. a–6; b–4, c–2	10. a–2; b–6; c–4	17. a–6; b–2; c–6
4. a–4; b–6; c–2	11. a–6; b–4; c–2	18. a–2; b–4; c–6
5. a–4; b–2; c–6	12. a–2; b–6; c–4	19. a–6; b–4; c–2
6. a–2; b–4; c–6	13. a–2; b–4; c–6	20. a–2; b–6; c–4
7. a–2; b–6; c–4	14. a–2; b–2; c–6	

WHAT IT MEANS:

102–120: You can make friends any place, any time. You are gregarious to the point of being offensive—sometimes to the more introspective members of the group around you. This is a rousing good score for an "in" personality, and the chances are that you have the world on a string.

72–100: In all probability you pick and choose your time, your place, and the things you want to accomplish. You are friendly, charming, intelligent, and discriminating.

52–70: You are shy and reluctant to be an "in" person. If you feel the urge you can make the first move and find it rewarding.

40-50:   You are not "in" with groups but inside yourself. You probably feel lonely at times and want to make better contact with people. To be "in" with others, one must get "out" of his or her emotional shell.

Are You Losing Friends and Antagonizing People?

Friendship is like money—easier made than kept. There are many people in the world, and one makes many acquaintances, but true friends are rare. Friends are earned, and once found, they must be treasured. Friendship is a fragile relationship and requires as much care in handling as any other delicate and complicated thing. Here are some questions that may help you know whether or not you are losing friends and antagonizing people.

1.   Do you promise to do things and then forget about them?

Yes _____   No _____

2.   When a person is telling an incident or a story, do you always try to "top" it with one of your own?

Yes _____   No _____

3.   Do you have your own clique of friends from which you exclude others?

Yes _____   No _____

4.   Do you tell your friends what is wrong with them?

Yes _____   No _____

5.   Do you like to be the center of attraction at all times?

Yes _____   No _____

6.   If you make a loan to a friend, do you let everyone know about it?

Yes _____   No _____

7.   Can you keep a secret?

Yes _____   No _____

8. Do you often call on people to do trivial tasks for you?

Yes _____   No _____

9. Would you drop everything if a friend needed your help?

Yes _____   No _____

10. Are you generally in a good humor?

Yes _____   No _____

11. Is it easy for you to find good things about others?

Yes _____   No _____

12. Are you a person who drops in and forgets to pick yourself up?

Yes _____   No _____

SCORING

ANSWERS:

1. No. "He who promises and does not fulfill his word is like a ship with wind but no sail. A poor friend indeed." (Anon.)
2. No. "When one is belittled, he cannot be a friend because friendship is a two-way bridge with the handshake on an even level." (Japanese proverb)
3. No. "The only way to have a friend is to be one." (Emerson)
4. No. "Do not remove a fly from your friend's head with a hatchet." (Chinese proverb)
5. No. ". . . it requires a very fine nature to sympathize with a friend's success." (Oscar Wilde)
6. No. "Purchase not friends by gifts; when thou ceasest to give, such will cease to love." (Fuller)
7. Yes. "I set it down as a fact that if all men knew what each said of the other, there would not be four friends in the world." (Pascal)
8. No. "Excite them by your civilities, and show them that you desire nothing more than their satisfaction; oblige with all you soul that friend who has made you a present of his own." (Socrates)
9. Yes. "Be more prompt to go to a friend in adversity than in prosperity." (Chilo)
10. Yes. "Honest good humor is the oil and wine of a merry meeting, and there is no jovial companionship equal to that where the jokes are rather small, and the laughter abundant." (Irving)

11. Yes. "We love ourselves notwithstanding our faults, and we ought to love our friends in a like manner." (Cyrus)

12. No. "Friendship cannot live with ceremony, nor without civility." (Lord Halifax)

ANALYSIS:

11–12 correct answers: You have friends because you are one to the others. You are reliable, gracious, and outgoing, each a true art.

7–10 correct answers: You have friends, but some of them stick with you "in spite of everything." Hold close those you have and try to make one more true friend each year.

4–6 correct answers: You find yourself looking for friends, but unable to find them. Look at yourself, and we are sure they will come to you after you straighten out the kinks in yourself.

0–3 correct answers: Perhaps you like goldfish?

(P.S.: If you took time to read the quotations of the best minds of literature, give yourself an extra score for intelligence!)

Do You Have the Qualities of Friendship?

Friendship is a two-way business. To make friends you have to be a friend. The better friend you are, the more friends you are likely to have.

This test lists some of the qualities of friendship. Try it, and see how you score. Answer "Yes" or "No" to the questions before turning to the scoring key at the end.

1. Are people able to depend on you to keep your word?
2. Can they rely on you to respect their confidences?
3. Are you good at keeping the friends you make?
4. Do you often put yourself to trouble and inconvenience to oblige people?

5. Suppose they wanted to do something and you were not particularly keen, would you go along with them and do what they wanted to do?
6. Are you quick to pay your share of the expenses?
7. Are you generous with your praise and appreciation?
8. Do you show affection when you feel it?
9. Is it easy to forgive and forget?
10. Is it easy to give people the benefit of the doubt and make allowances?
11. There has been quite a difference of opinion. Would you speak first?
12. Do you own up when you are wrong and say you are sorry?
13. You may like somebody very much. But would it be the same if he, or she, became unpopular?
14. Are you quick off the mark to give sympathy and practical help when people need it?
15. Do you like to see others getting on and being praised and fussed over?
16. Can you agree to differ and stay on the best of terms?
17. Are you an attentive and sympathetic listener?
18. Are you always the same, not full of welcome today and too busy to bother tomorrow?
19. Do you mind people having other friends and interests that you do not share?
20. Could you say that you are much more interested in other people than in yourself?

SCORING

Count five marks for every "Yes." A score of 70 or over is good, and 60–70 is satisfactory. Under 60 is not satisfactory.

You are not likely to be a good friend if you are prone to dislike people. Usually, when we are like this we are wrapped up in ourselves. We like only those individuals who notice us and make a fuss over us, and dislike anybody who is not interested in us, or who will not do what we want.

If you desire to be a good friend, you will have to be more interested in other people than in yourself so that you put them first.

How "Good" a Friend Are You?

Most of us know many people, have close acquaintances, but when it comes to true-blue friends, we probably can count very few. We use the word "friend" erroneously many times because the true meaning is "confidant." In most cases friendship has to be earned and treasured to be kept. This quiz asks you to examine yourself to see if *you* are a good friend to those who rely on you.

1. An artist has made the two metal sculptures shown below and asks you to accept one for your home. Which would you choose?

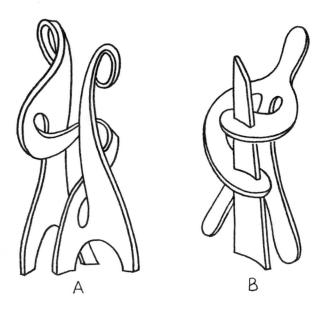

A   B

The following situations may have happened to you, or may happen to you in the future. In any case, give the response nearest your own with all the honesty you can muster.

2. A person whom you like very much has a child who is a complete brat. You are planning a party at home and know he/she will normally bring the youngster along. You would:
   a. tactfully say the party is one of those "for grownups only" affairs.
   b. grit your teeth, say nothing, and expect the worst.
   c. arrange for a companion or baby-sitter to take care of the youngster in your home.

3. A third party is continually making nasty remarks about a person whom you hold dear. You would:

a. pay no attention to the slurs.

b. demand that the attacker be silent about the person.

c. explain the behavior of your friend so the third party will understand him or her and refrain from being critical.

4. You feel reasonably sure that the date or mate of your friend is being morally disloyal. You would:

a. feel sorry but say nothing.

b. tell your friend about your suspicions.

c. tell your friend's date or mate to stop playing around.

5. Your friend has severe financial reverses, and comes to you for a loan. You would:

a. help him or her find a legitimate adviser, such as a banker or lawyer, with whom to discuss the matter.

b. money permitting, give him or her an outright loan, asking no questions and with no strings.

c. thoroughly investigate why the financial disaster happened.

6. Your friend is very chummy with a person whom you do not like. You would:

a. warn your friend about the other person.

b. arrange threesomes so your friend can make a comparison.

c. figure your friend knows what he or she is doing and it's none of your business.

7. Your friend has a tragedy in his or her family, such as a death, a serious operation, a fire, etc. At the same time, you are under great pressure of family or work. You would:

a. drop everything to assist your friend in any way you can.

b. assume your friend understands how hectic life is for you and do nothing.

c. phone or write and offer to help if really needed.

8. You know your friend has an unhealthy desire for something, such as candy and sweets, food in large quantities, alcohol, or drugs he or she should not have. You would:

a. make the ''forbidden fruit'' readily accessible because of the pleasure it gives him or her.

b. keep the temptation out of sight.

c. mete out small amounts if he or she asked for it.

9. A close friend of yours moves far away. You could:

a. assume your friendship will take up where it left off when you meet again, and leave it at that.

b. try to keep in touch with the person regularly by means of letters, phone calls, or messages delivered by mutual friends.

c. put him or her in the back of your mind except for special occasions such as birthdays, holidays, and anniversaries.

10. You are shopping for a gift for a friend. You would select

a. a practical gift you know he or she needs.

b. a gift that appeals to your taste even though you know it isn't quite what the recipient would pick out.

c. a frivolous thing he or she has admired in the past.

11. A friend constantly borrows from you but never repays or returns what you lent, such as books, the lawn mower, or a cup of sugar. You would:

a. inwardly gripe and write it off as a bad loss and a nuisance.

b. refuse to grant more loans.

c. jokingly ask him or her to sign an IOU and, if necessary, produce it as a reminder at a later time.

12. Your friend has uncouth, noisy bad manners. You would:

a. see him or her in places where his or her behavior makes no difference.

b. proudly present your friend to anyone, any time anyplace because of the value he or she has in other respects.

c. frankly discuss your discomfort with your friend.

13. This question requires *real* honesty. In your relationship with your friend or friends you:

a. are prepared and willing to go all out for them in any honorable way.

b. expect them to meet you halfway.

c. expect them to show their willingness to be a friend before you make a helpful, friendly gesture.

14. After careful evaluation, you feel you select your friends:

a. because whether they are right or wrong, you genuinely like them.

b. because they can be of help to you in business and in life.

c. because they are weak in some or many respects and you can help them.

15. A friend is having a minor problem, such as in his or her work or home life and asks you to lie so he or she can get out of it. You would:

a. lie if you had to.

b. flatly refuse to lie.

c. make up a story that evades the truth but isn't an outright lie.

16. If you were to have troubles and disappointments, you would:

a. keep a stiff upper lip and keep the problems to yourself.

b. use your friend as a sounding board.

c. expect your friend to come up with the right answers for you.

17. If a friend of yours were to die, you would:

a. express your affection for him or her by helping the family.

b. feel the loss, lick your emotional wounds, and do nothing.

c. observe the formalities of sorrow and let his or her family and his or her friends fade away.

18. A friend asks you to be his or her business partner. You would:

a. accept the offer if it seems mutually advantageous.

b. accept the responsibility out of friendship.

c. refuse in the belief it is unwise to mix business and friendship.

19. If your friend were to be away for a prolonged period of time, you would:

a. pay special attention to his or her date or mate.

b. entertain his or her date or mate only when you are in a group.

c. avoid his or her date or mate as much as humanly possible.

20. If you did something seriously wrong, you would

a. confess your error to your friend.

b. deny your responsibility in the error.

c. find a fall guy to take the blame or make up some pat alibis.

S C O R I N G

H O W T O S C O R E :

1. a–6; b–2
2. a–4; b–2; c–6
3. a–2; b–4; c–6
4. a–6; b–2; c–4
5. a–6; b–4; c–2
6. a–2; b–4; c–6
7. a–6; b–2; c–4

8. a–2; b–6; c–2
9. a–2; b–6; c–4
10. a–4; b–2; c–6
11. a–2; b–4; c–6
12. a–4; b–6; c–2
13. a–6; b–4; c–2
14. a–6; b–2; c–4

15. a–2; b–6; c–4
16. a–4; b–6; c–2
17. a–6; b–2; c–4
18. a–4; b–2; c–6
19. a–2; b–6; c–4
20. a–6; b–2; c–2

WHAT YOUR SCORE TELLS YOU:

100–120: You are a true friend, and those who share your attentions and loyalty are fortunate indeed. The problem is that there just isn't enough of *you* to go around and enough *like* you to supply the demand. You are a strong personality and a leader, the source of your power as a confidant to others. Your high moral standards keep you from being used by others but set you aside as a model.

80–98: Friendship comes easily for you because of your prevailing selflessness. It is easy for you to put yourself in the others' shoes, and you are empathetic when it comes to emotions. The few times when you let one friend down are very likely because you are busy helping another one.

58–79: People in this bracket are cautious about whom they attract and wary of their relationships. Their attitudes are tinged by self-interest and self-defense. When they give themselves, however, they can, if they want, be a stanch pillar.

40–56: This is a weak score. It is unlikely that many people consider you a true friend because you step on the toes and infringe on the rights of others. The tendency to be a know-it-all and a busybody hinders you, but a 180-degree change can be made . . . *if* you so desire.

YOU
AND YOUR
MENTAL HEALTH

How Relaxed Are You?

One of the evils afflicting us today is tension. We seem to be always in a rush, trying to do too much, and getting worked up over trifles.

This can make us ill as well as unhappy. It is wise to do something about it.

Here is a test that will help you recognize some of the factors that make you tense. Answer "Yes" or "No" to the questions before turning to the scoring key at the end.

1. Do you like people rather than dislike them?
2. Do you believe the majority of people you meet like you, or at least do not dislike you?
3. In the main, do you trust people and think of them as being on the level?
4. Do you find it reasonably easy to fit in with most people?
5. Can you adapt yourself fairly quickly to changes? (such as living in a new neighborhood, working under a different boss, being in a hospital)
6. Do you like explaining things and showing people how to do things?
7. Are you good with younger people, the very old, and with sick members of the family?
8. Are you a good patient when you are ill?
9. Can you take a vacation without getting upset if everything does not go according to plan?

10. Can you see people getting on without feeling the urge to work harder to keep up with them?

11. Are you pleased to see somebody else getting some of the attention?

12. Can you decide without making sure that other people agree with you?

13. Can you bear to be contradicted and, after agreeing to differ, remain on friendly terms?

14. Is it reasonably easy for you to forgive a hurt and forget a grievance?

15. Do you plan your day by selecting your priorities and doing these first?

16. Can you alter your plans without getting fussed?

17. Have you recognized that you are not indispensable and that one day people will have to manage without you?

18. Can you put up with somebody else's second best and the muddle made by others without becoming impossible to live with?

19. Are you firm about not allowing other people to flatter or persuade you into undertaking more than you should?

20. Do you have at least one easy, relaxed evening a week when you do what you want to do and get to bed early?

SCORING

Count five points for every "Yes". A score of 70 or over is very good; 60–70 is good, and 50–60 is satisfactory. Under 50 is not satisfactory.

Keep the test. Use it from time to time to check your "No" answers.

One way to become more relaxed is to learn about yourself and the way your mind works. Self-knowledge will enable you to reduce tension, as well as encourage you to become more tolerant of others.

Assist yourself physically by relaxing your muscles whenever your body feels tense. Stand or sit in any easy relaxed position, and try a few deep breaths.

Do You Need Psychotherapy?

If you're like most people, your life inevitably has its ups and downs. You may even have wondered if you need psychotherapy. How do you decide? What are the differences between normal ups and downs and the kinds of emotional problems that call for therapy?

Psychiatrists and psychologists say it's time to consider help when you feel so bad you can't function; when your problems start interfering with your daily life, your job, your marriage. "When this situation arises," says Dr. Thomas A. Williams, chairman of the department of psychiatry and behavioral sciences at Eastern Virginia Medical School, "the next question is: For how long? If it has been going on a couple of months or more, you probably could use some help."

But don't think you have an emotional problem just because you have occasionally felt or acted like this, especially if there's been a crisis—a death, divorce, loss of a job—that would upset anyone. With the person who could really use psychotherapy, these feelings occur frequently, usually over a period of months, and often for no apparent reason. Do you fall into this category? The following twenty questions should help you decide.

(These questions are based on the work of Dr. John S. O'Brien, psychologist, department of psychiatry, and Dr. John H. Brennan, director of psychiatric education, St. Elizabeth's Hospital, Boston.)

1. In new situations, such as a job interview, or a party where there are many strangers, are you afraid things will go badly for you?
   a. all or most of the time.
   b. frequently.
   c. occasionally.
   d. rarely or never.

2. When asked to do something you don't want to do, such as baby-sit for friends, or work late, can you say "No" when you really want to?
   a. all or most of the time.
   b. frequently.
   c. occasionally.
   d. rarely or never.

3. Do you ever completely lose your temper and realize afterward that you got much angrier than the situation deserved? For example, your spouse has been stuck in traffic and comes home late for dinner.
   a. all or most of the time.
   b. frequently.

   c. occasionally.

   d. rarely or never.

4. When you're with friends, can you get them to listen if you have a suggestion—like picking a restaurant or a movie?

   a. all or most of the time.

   b. frequently.

   c. occasionally.

   d. rarely or never.

5. Do you have a lot of difficulty making decisions—selecting a new coat, say, or deciding how to spend a weekend?

   a. all or most of the time.

   b. frequently.

   c. occasionally.

   d. rarely or never.

6. Do you hesitate to become involved in group activities? For example, do you find yourself standing alone at parties?

   a. all or most of the time.

   b. frequently.

   c. occasionally.

   d. rarely or never.

7. Do you seek approval or encouragement for things you do all the time, such as daily office tasks or preparing a meal for your family?

   a. all or most of the time.

   b. frequently.

   c. occasionally.

   d. rarely or never.

8. Can you express your displeasure when people take advantage of you—push ahead of you in line, for example?

   a. all or most of the time.

   b. frequently.

   c. occasionally.

   d. rarely or never.

9. Do you feel satisfied with your closest relationships?

   a. all or most of the time.

   b. frequently.

   c. occasionally.

       d. rarely or never.

10. Would you take a drink or a tranquilizer to give you confidence before a job interview or a party?

    a. all or most of the time.

    b. frequently.

    c. occasionally.

    d. rarely or never.

11. Are you bothered by habits, such as smoking or overeating, that you are unable to control?

    a. all or most of the time.

    b. frequently.

    c. occasionally.

    d. rarely or never.

12. Do you have fears—as of flying, or of small places—that you are unable to control or that keep you from doing what you want?

    a. all or most of the time.

    b. frequently.

    c. occasionally.

    d. rarely or never.

13. When you leave the house, do you have to go back to make sure the door is locked, the stove is off, etc.?

    a. all or most of the time.

    b. frequently.

    c. occasionally.

    d. rarely or never.

14. How often is sex unsatisfactory for you or your mate?

    a. all or most of the time.

    b. frequently.

    c. occasionally.

    d. rarely or never.

15. Does it take you more than an hour to go to sleep, or do you wake up more than an hour earlier than you want to?

    a. all or most of the time.

    b. frequently.

    c. occasionally.

    d. rarely or never.

16. Have you lost weight recently without a medical reason or a diet?
    a. very little, if any.
    b. more than five pounds.
    c. more than ten pounds.
    d. more than fifteen pounds.

17. Are you very concerned with cleanliness or contamination of yourself or objects you might touch?
    a. all or most of the time.
    b. frequently.
    c. occasionally.
    d. rarely or never.

18. Do you think the future is hopeless, or do you ever think of hurting yourself or committing suicide?
    a. all or most of the time.
    b. frequently.
    c. occasionally.
    d. rarely or never.

19. Do you ever see, hear, or feel things that nobody else is aware of?
    a. all or most of the time.
    b. frequently.
    c. occasionally.
    d. rarely or never.

20. Do you think you have superior powers or that other people are using superior powers against you?
    a. all or most of the time.
    b. frequently.
    c. occasionally.
    d. rarely or never.

SCORING

WHAT YOUR ANSWERS MEAN:

First of all, this is not a test involving right responses and wrong responses. We all lose our temper now and then over something trivial; we all occasionally feel dissatisfied with our closest relationships. In normal circumstances, however, the well-adjusted person will usually give the following answers:

1.	c or d	8.	a or b	15.	c or d
2.	a or b	9.	a or b	16.	a or b
3.	c or d	10.	c or d	17.	c or d
4.	a, b, or c	11.	c or d	18.	d
5.	c or d	12.	c or d	19.	d
6.	c or d	13.	c or d	20.	d
7.	c or d	14.	c or d		

Questions 1–10 evaluate how well you express your feelings and how much self-confidence you have. If many of your answers differ from the ones indicated above, it simply means you have problems expressing feelings or aren't very sure of yourself. If you want to change some of these feelings or behavior, psychotherapy would probably help you.

Questions 11–14 involve behavior that usually accompanies an emotional problem. If many of your answers differ from the ones listed, and if you think your problems are interfering with your daily life, it might be a good idea to see a professional and get an opinion.

Questions 15–20 deal with behavior patterns that could be important early-warning signs of a serious emotional problem. If some or many of your answers differ from the ones given here, you should get a professional opinion right away. If therapy is needed, it will be easier if you don't delay.

Are You Under Too Much Stress?

You can find out if there's too much stress in your life and do something about it before it's too late.

Your body has a number of "stressers"—primarily made up of adrenaline. But if your system is jolted frequently, the stressers lose their potency, making you susceptible to illness and possibly a premature death.

Here's a quick test to help you determine if there's too much stress in your life. (Note: Situations apply only to the past twelve months.)

1. Has anyone close to you died?

        Yes _____   No _____

2. Have you divorced or split with your mate?

        Yes _____   No _____

3. Have you had a serious accident or illness?

    Yes _____   No _____

4. Did you get married or start living with someone?

    Yes _____   No _____

5. Have you had trouble sleeping?

    Yes _____   No _____

6. Have you often felt you just couldn't cope?

    Yes _____   No _____

7. Are you pregnant or facing major surgery?

    Yes _____   No _____

8. Have you watched more than two hours of TV per day?

    Yes _____   No _____

9. Have you worried a lot about money?

    Yes _____   No _____

10. Have numerous people irritated or annoyed you?

    Yes _____   No _____

11. Have you used four or more tablespoons of sugar per day?

    Yes _____   No _____

12. Has jealousy occupied a lot of your time?

    Yes _____   No _____

13. Have you lived or worked in a heavily polluted area?

    Yes _____   No _____

14. Have you been dissatisfied with your sex life?

    Yes _____   No _____

15. Have you lived or worked in a very noisy area?

    Yes _____   No _____

16. Have you gotten more than two traffic tickets?

    Yes _____   No _____

17. Have you smoked more than three cigarettes per day?

    Yes _____   No _____

18.   Have you had more than one alcoholic drink per day?

Yes _____   No _____

19.   Have you been involved in at least one argument per week?

Yes _____   No _____

20.   Have your working hours drastically changed?

Yes _____   No _____

Give yourself a point for each "Yes" answer, then compare your score with those that follow:

SCORING

0–1   You are under very little stress and have nothing to worry about.

2–3   With continuous attention to diet, exercise, and a bright outlook, you'll be a picture of health in your golden years.

4–7   You're in good shape, but the stress you're under will make you susceptible to colds, coughs, and skin rash. You can avoid many of these by reinforcing your body with nutrition and rest. Try to eliminate some of the stresses over which you have control—like smoking, drinking, and eating junk foods.

8–15   The stress in your life is exposing you to illness or accident. It is vital that you cut out the traumas that are undermining your health. Remember that subtle stress—excessive TV, sugar, noise, and pollution—can slowly tear you apart.

16–20   You are a prime target for a major illness. It is still possible to rechannel your life if you seek professional help. You must also pay attention to protein intake, vitamins, rest, and physical activity.

Are You Depressed?

Are you depressed? You can find out if you or those close to you are depressed by using the Johns Hopkins depression checklist.

The checklist was developed after years of research and is designed to determine if the average person suffers from depression and if he or she should seek professional help, according to Dr. Lino Covi, head of the anxiety and depression research program at Johns Hopkins University and Gundry Hospital.

The checklist consists of eleven major symptoms of depression. Next to each symptom are four levels of involvement. Rate yourself (or anyone else you know well) on each symptom by putting a checkmark by "Not at All" (worth zero point), "A Little" (worth one point), "Quite a Bit" (worth two points), or "Extremely" (worth three points).

Add up all the points and divide by 11. This gives you your depression average. The average score for a normal person is .4.

"If you have a score of .70 or more, then that's an indication you need some type of treatment," said Dr. Covi. He emphasized that a score of .70 or more on a single day is not necessarily a cause for alarm. However, if the high score persists for several weeks, you should seek professional help.

JOHNS HOPKINS DEPRESSION CHECKLIST

	NOT AT ALL (0 Point)	A LITTLE (1 Point)	QUITE A BIT (2 Points)	EXTREMELY (3 Points)
Loss of sexual interest or pleasure	_____	_____	_____	_____
Thoughts of ending your life	_____	_____	_____	_____
Poor appetite	_____	_____	_____	_____
Crying easily	_____	_____	_____	_____
A feeling of being trapped or caught	_____	_____	_____	_____
Blaming yourself for things	_____	_____	_____	_____
Feeling lonely	_____	_____	_____	_____
Feeling blue	_____	_____	_____	_____
Worrying too much about things	_____	_____	_____	_____
Feeling no interest in things	_____	_____	_____	_____
Feeling hopeless about the future	_____	_____	_____	_____

Are You in Danger
of Having a Nervous Breakdown?

Are you in any danger of falling victim to a nervous breakdown?

Everyone has a breaking point, but some reach it much more easily than others. Some individuals can sustain great mental anguish without reaching the cracking point. Others require very little to reach that point.

There are symptoms that show whether you are skating on thin ice emotionally. Test yourself by checking "Yes" or "No" to the following questions.

1. Do you feel remote from people and things you used to like—your husband or wife, children, church, neighbors, sports, books?

    Yes _____   No _____

2. Has your attitude toward food changed—is it tasteless, hard to swallow, so that you do not care if you eat or not?

    Yes _____   No _____

3. Do you feel tired all the time, complain you do not get enough sleep, but wake up regularly during the night?

    Yes _____   No _____

4. Are you more critical of things these days, feel people are dull, movies no good, waiters rude, friends catty?

    Yes _____   No _____

5. Does your temper often get out of control easily, and have people remarked lately that you are harder to get along with than you used to be?

    Yes _____   No _____

6. Do you feel one or more persons are taking advantage of you, have it in for you, and are at the root of a lot of your troubles?

    Yes _____   No _____

7. Do you feel pessimistic about the value of life—that you are living in a jungle or a rat race?

    Yes _____   No _____

8. Are you conscious of your health, worrying about it? Do you feel that your work is suffering on account of it?

    Yes _____   No _____

9. Do you take other people's comments, suggestions, and criticisms as personal threats or rejections of you?

Yes _____   No _____

10. Have you let your appearance run down—care less about cleanliness, haircuts, beauty-parlor appointments, or new clothes?

Yes _____   No _____

11. Are you avoiding people you know well—old friends, relatives, business acquaintances?

Yes _____   No _____

12. Do you feel depressed for little reason, or suddenly elated with little real cause?

Yes _____   No _____

13. Do you anticipate commonplace situations with dread—do you not want to care for or play with your children, go to parties or business meetings?

Yes _____   No _____

14. Are you taking life more seriously, enjoying it less, and ready to argue hotly about insignificant details?

Yes _____   No _____

15. Is it harder lately to make small decisions like what to wear, what to talk about, what to order in restaurants?

Yes _____   No _____

16. Do you panic at the thought of having to attend to the things that have to be taken care of?

Yes _____   No _____

17. Are you afraid to be alone?

Yes _____   No _____

18. Have you thought of ending it all?

Yes _____   No _____

19. Do you feel at times that you are losing your mind?

Yes _____   No _____

20. Do you find it more difficult to concentrate?

Yes _____   No _____

21. Do you find yourself living more and more in the past?

       Yes _____   No _____

22. Are you tense and restless most of the time, unable to relax?

       Yes _____   No _____

23. Are you dependent on tranquilizers to carry you through the day?

       Yes _____   No _____

24. Do you worry about having a nervous breakdown?

       Yes _____   No _____

25. Do you feel sorry for yourself, thinking that you never get the breaks in life, that you could have had a better education, or that life has passed you by?

       Yes _____   No _____

SCORING

The twenty five questions you have just answered point to significant nervous-breakdown danger signals.

If you have given yourself the benefit of the doubt in answering but have come up with three or more "Yes" answers, you may be in emotional trouble.

But if you are one of the lucky few who can answer "No" to all twenty-five questions, it would seem that you have no emotional problems at all.

Does Life Drive You Round the Bend?

How do you face up to the pressure of modern living? Are you a bundle of nerves because today's lifestyle is driving you round the bend? Find out about yourself and your mate in this quiz. So get a pencil and your partner and see if your nerves are showing by answering the twenty questions. Then check your score to see what it means.

1. Glance at the three compositions of arrows below. Which best describes your feelings about your average day?

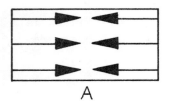 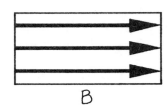 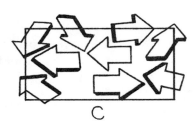

A   B   C

2. Do you have many projects going with no hope of completion in sight?
   a. yes.
   b. no.
   c. yes, but they don't "bug" me.

3. Are you satisfied with your material possessions?
   a. no; others have things I want.
   b. yes; I have adequate material goods in order to live comfortably.
   c. most of the time.

4. When you go to bed, do you fall asleep after a few minutes?
   a. yes.
   b. no; I roll and toss.
   c. usually.

5. Do you have attacks of indigestion or nausea?
   a. often.
   b. only when I am physically ill.
   c. occasionally, when faced with a tense situation.

6. Is your sex life satisfactory?
   a. very exciting.
   b. very dull.
   c. normal routine.

7. Do you have physical checkups?
   a. when I am ill.
   b. if others force me to do so.
   c. regularly, by my own volition.

8. When life doesn't run smoothly, do you blame yourself?
   a. if I think I made a mistake.
   b. seldom, because errors are usually caused by others.
   c. almost always.

9. Do you try to correct the external details of life that get you uptight, such as doors that creak, clothing that doesn't fit properly, etc.?
   a. no, because I don't have the time.
   b. I consistently try to eliminate irritants.
   c. I try to learn to live with them.

10. When lying down, can you feel your heart beating at a fast, strong rate?
    a. only after physical exertion.
    b. very often.
    c. very seldom.

11. Do you take medication, such as pep pills or tranquilizers, to control your moods?
    a. when I think I need them.
    b. only when and as prescribed by a reliable doctor.
    c. when people I know have had success with such medication.

12. Can you discuss your inner feelings with others?
    a. yes, with professionals.
    b. no, with no one.
    c. yes, with those who are near and dear to me.

13. Is there a balance in your daily/weekly routine between business and pleasure?
    a. no.
    b. yes.
    c. occasionally.

14. Are you content with your work?
    a. in general, yes.
    b. with reservations.
    c. definitely not.

15. Do you take care of daily, weekly, monthly, and yearly routines on time, such as renewing your driving license, paying bills, and filing income-tax forms?
    a. no.
    b. most of the time.
    c. yes.

16. Can you lose yourself in an enjoyable book, a hobby, walking?
    a. easily.
    b. no.
    c. it depends on what else needs to be done.

17. Are you competitive, wanting to be the best in any endeavor you attempt?
    a. highly.
    b. no.
    c. by fits and spurts.

18. Do you physically strike out against objects or people who have not directly offended you?
    a. yes.
    b. no.
    c. very seldom.

19. If you need help, do you have contacts such as bankers, doctors, or professional people who can assist you?
    a. yes.
    b. not sure.
    c. no.

20. In a day's living, is it important for you to do everything fast, such as eating, traveling, getting the job done?
    a. no.
    b. definitely.
    c. only in cases of emergencies.

SCORING

1. a–4; b–2; c–6. You'll note composition c is random, disorderly. This pattern is likely to create nervous feelings. Composition a is orderly but at odds, the arrows pointing aggressively at each other. Composition b is well organized, with objectives pointing in the same direction, hence ongoing.

2.	a–6; b–2; c–4	9.	a–6; b–2; c–4	16.	a–2; b–6; c–4
3.	a–6; b–2; c–4	10.	a–4; b–6; c–2	17.	a–6; b–2; c–4
4.	a–2; b–6; c–4	11.	a–6; b–2; c–6	18.	a–6; b–2; c–4
5.	a–6; b–2; c–4	12.	a–2; b–6; c–2	19.	a–2; b–4; c–6
6.	a–6; b–2; c–4	13.	a–6; b–2; c–4	20.	a–2; b–6; c–4
7.	a–6; b–4; c–2	14.	a–2; b–4; c–6		
8.	a–4; b–2; c–6	15.	a–6; b–4; c–2		

100–120: You are ruled mainly by your nerves. Learn to take life easy. Get plenty of rest and let tomorrow take care of itself. Dr. George E. Stevenson, internationally recognized psychiatrist, cautions: "The time to watch out is when tensions become frequent and persist."

80–98: This is a relatively uptight score, indicating some areas of stress. When the going gets rough, your nerves show.

50–78: You have good control over your nerves. Occasionally you are tense because life doesn't always run smoothly, but it is unlikely you have ever suffered from emotionally caused hives.

40–48: Dr. O. A. Battista, one of Pennsylvania's most respected research scientists, observes: "We need some tensions to stay alive. A jellyfish is completely relaxed but in no shape to dodge a speeding car."

YOU
AND YOUR
FINANCIAL
SENSE

Are You Headed
for Financial Trouble?

The rapidly escalating inflation rate has created numerous financial woes for the American public. Mortgage interest rates have made it difficult, if not impossible, for many people to purchase homes. Gasoline costs are increasing at an alarming pace. Budget meals are the rule rather than the exception in most homes as food prices continue to soar. As a result of these increases in the cost of living, many people now find themselves headed for serious financial trouble.

The American Bankers Association has identified ten warning signals that can help you spot trouble while there's still time to take corrective action. Answer each of the following questions and see whether you are headed for financial trouble.

1. Do you use credit today to buy many of the things you bought last year with cash?

2. Have you taken out loans to consolidate your debts, or asked for extensions on existing loans to reduce monthly payments?

3. Your standard of living has stayed pretty much the same, but does your checkbook balance get lower by the month?

4. You used to pay most bills in full each month, but do you now pay only the minimum amount due on your charge accounts?

5. Have you begun to receive repeated dunning notices from your creditors?

6. Have you been drawing on savings to pay regular bills that you used to pay out of your monthly paycheck?

7. You've borrowed before on your life insurance, but this time, are the chances of paying it back more remote?

8. Do you now depend on extra income, such as overtime and dividends, to get you through to the end of the month?

9. Do you use your checking account "overdraft" to pay regular monthly bills?

10. Are you juggling your rent or mortgage money to pay other creditors?

SCORING

Be honest with yourself. If you answered "Yes" to two of these questions, it's time to take a close look at your budget. If you answered "Yes" to three questions, you may be headed for difficulty. And if five or more "Yes" answers to these questions apply to you, you are definitely in trouble.

Do You Waste Your Money?

How are you facing up to these inflationary days? Are you realistic, or do you hide your head in the clouds? The spiraling cost of living is a bald fact. Do you make money stretch? Try this quiz to find out what your attitudes are about money and its meaning.

1. Consider your general attitude toward everyday living. Which of the pictures below would best describe your approach to life?

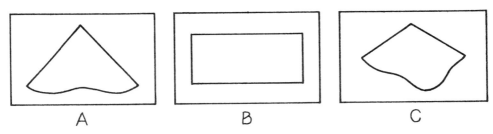

2. Do you race through tasks, find you made a mistake, and have to redo them?
    a. seldom.
    b. often.
    c. never.

3. Do your expenditures exceed your bank account?
    a. no.
    b. yes.
    c. on rare occasions such as emergencies.

4. If you need an item of apparel, do you keep an eye out and wait for a sale?
    a. usually.
    b. no.
    c. yes.

5. Do you overspend in order to impress people?
    a. yes.
    b. no.
    c. sometimes.

6. If you have a piece of equipment such as a television, a washing machine, or a car that fails, would you buy a new one rather than have it repaired?
    a. yes.
    b. I would figure relative costs.
    c. no, I would keep and repair the old piece of equipment.

7. Assume you were dining out with your family or close friends in an unpretentious restaurant. The food is excellent but you cannot eat all that is served. Would you ask the waitress or waiter to pack it so you can take it home?
    a. yes.
    b. no.
    c. probably not.

8. You have a pair of socks with a hole in one of them. You would:
    a. mend the hole.
    b. throw the pair away.
    c. find a way to use one or both.

9. You have a certain amount of money to spend on a suit. You would:

    a. buy one well-made garment.

    b. buy several inexpensive suits.

    c. repair and update the clothing you have in your closet.

10. In your living quarters, house, apartment, hotel, or motel, do you turn off gas and electricity and close water faucets when they are not needed?

    a. no.

    b. not if someone else is paying the bill.

    c. always.

11. When you speak with a person on the phone, by letter, or in general conversation, do you have a purpose?

    a. yes.

    b. no.

    c. most of the time.

12. Can you efficiently do several things at the same time?

    a. yes.

    b. no.

    c. most of the time.

13. If your living quarters were filled with old books or magazines, would you:

    a. throw them into the trash?

    b. give them to a collection agency?

    c. let them pile up?

14. If you felt you had a certain unexplored talent, such as writing, salesmanship, or in law, you would:

    a. take courses that might help you.

    b. just dream about your unfulfilled possibilities.

    c. brush aside your thoughts.

15. Do you use more things than are really needed? For instance, do you wipe your hands with four paper towels when one would suffice?

    a. yes.

    b. no.

    c. never considered the question before.

16. Do you have a tendency to overbuy perishable items, such as fruit, vegetables, or paints?

    a. yes.

   b. no.

   c. sometimes.

17. When it comes to food, are your eyes bigger than your stomach? Do you leave food on your plate?

   a. sometimes.

   b. no.

   c. yes.

18. Do you evaluate your living and working environment with the idea of saving yourself effort?

   a. yes.

   b. no.

   c. occasionally.

19. Are you as careful with the property of others as you are with your own?

   a. no.

   b. yes.

   c. more careful.

20. Following the suggestions of many experts who are concerned about our wasteful habits, can you list ten ways you can save or conserve natural energy?

   a. yes.

   b. no.

   c. perhaps four or five.

SCORING

1.	a–4; b–6; c–2	8.	a–6; b–2; c–6	15.	a–2; b–6; c–4
2.	a–4; b–2; c–6	9.	a–6; b–4; c–6	16.	a–2; b–6; c–4
3.	a–6; b–2; c–4	10.	a–2; b–2; c–6	17.	a–4; b–6; c–2
4.	a–4; b–2; c–6	11.	a–6; b–2; c–4	18.	a–6; b–2; c–4
5.	a–2; b–6; c–4	12.	a–6; b–2; c–4	19.	a–2; b–6; c–6
6.	a–2; b–6; c–4	13.	a–2; b–6; c–4	20.	a–6; b–2; c–4
7.	a–6; b–2; c–4	14.	a–6; b–4; c–2		

100–120: You are a very careful, thoughtful person who is aware that what we have today we may not have tomorrow unless we take care of it. Your thinking recognizes the potentials of time, energy, and materials.

80–98:   You are not wasteful but perhaps this quiz has tickled your brain a bit. Usually those who rate in this bracket are busy people who occasionally toss away something they need later, or make errors in a purchase.

58–78:   This is a score often made by people who can be thrifty one day and carried away by desires the next. "Waste not the smallest thing created, for grains of sand make mountains—seconds form eternities."

40–56:   Those who have this dubious score tend to be careless—and couldn't care less. They are often the same people who claim that life owes them a living and that life is unkind to them. Thus they waste themselves.

How Is Your Business Sense?

Business sense implies that we know what we are doing as well as knowing the best and safest way to do it. People without any business sense simply muddle along. They become tangled up in difficulties, fall unprepared into responsibilities, and get themselves overinvolved, without really comprehending what it is all about and what is going to happen next.

This test is designed to help you check on your business sense, or lack of it. Answer "Yes" or "No" to the questions before turning to the scoring key at the end.

1. Do you try to live within your income with something left over for an emergency?
2. Do you think that reasonable thrift is a good thing, rather than believe that money is only good for spending?
3. Do you keep a reasonably accurate record of your income and expenditures?
4. Do you check bank statements as they come in and read documents before you sign them?
5. Can you say about how much you are worth at the present moment?
6. Have you made a will?
7. Do you carry adequate but not excessive insurance?
8. Before buying an expensive item like a car, would you check your outgoings against your incomings to make sure you can afford it?

9. Would you ask for an estimate before ordering work done, say, on your house?

10. Are you careful about monthly payment purchases, noting the dates when payments are due?

11. Would you ask a knowledgeable friend to recommend someone to do a job for you, rather than pick a name haphazardly from the telephone directory?

12. Are you wary about acting on impulse?

13. Do you consider all the pros and cons before making an important decision?

14. Are you quick to spot promising opportunities, to weigh up the chances, and take advantage of them?

15. Before borrowing money, would you make sure that you knew exactly what is involved in the method and date or dates of repayment?

16. Are you a reasonably good judge of people? That is, can you usually tell when they are being frank and truthful?

17. Without being unfriendly or unduly suspicious, are you careful about involving yourself with strangers and casual acquaintances?

18. Do you encourage your friends to be frank with you?

19. Do you seek advice only from those fully competent to give it?

20. Do you know what is involved in consenting to become a guarantor or an executor (or executrix) for a friend?

SCORING

Count 5 points for every "Yes." If you score 80 or over, your business sense is good. You are likely to do well for yourself; 70–80 is unsatisfactory; 60–70 is fair. Under 60 is not satisfactory. We develop a good business sense by: (a) being orderly and methodical about our affairs—for example, by watching our spending and keeping an account of how we stand; and (b) by being strictly practical in our approach to problems—that is, by finding out exactly what and how much are involved, and the best method of dealing with the problems.

Are You a Smart Shopper?

To what extent can you reasonably expect to get satisfaction out of your everyday business transactions? You can measure your Quotient of Buymanship by checking your answers to shopping problems adapted from typical cases handled by the Better Business Bureau.

In some cases, the questions may be subject to different interpretations, which could make either answer correct. But for your score based on the answers the Bureau considers correct, please turn to the key at the end.

1. A stockboy marked some cans of nuts at $.15 instead of $.51. The cashier noted the mistake and advised the customer of the correct price. The customer insisted that the store was obligated to sell the nuts at the $.15 price as marked.

    Must the store sell the nuts at $.15?

    Yes _____   No _____

2. A dealer advertised a "Free Pool Table" with the purchase of a living-room suite for $398. When a BBB shopper objected to the price and said she didn't want the pool table, the dealer offered to let her have the suite itself for $328.

    Was the offer phony?

    Yes _____   No _____

3. A realtor showed a young couple a house that they liked but felt was too expensive. Two months later, they discovered the house was now for sale by the owner.

    Can this couple purchase the house from the owner without having a commission due the realtor?

    Yes _____   No _____

4. A lady purchased a refrigerator. Two days later, she saw it advertised by the same store at 20 per cent off. She complained to the BBB that the manager would not give her a 20 per cent discount on her purchase.

    Should the BBB handle her complaint?

    Yes _____   No _____

5. The BBB referred a complaint to a dealer about a burned-out transmission on a new car, still under warranty. The manufacturer's engineer reported that an inspection of the gears showed teeth had been broken, clearly by abuse (apparently drag racing), and the company refused to make a warranty adjustment.

    Was the company right in its position?

    Yes _____   No _____

6. A drugstore advertised a brand of toothpaste as $1.05 size, sale $.67. Although the manufacturer's list was $1.05, this brand and size regularly sells for $.89 at this store and at the majority of other stores in the market area.

    Is the advertised comparative price correct?

    Yes _____   No _____

7. A store advertises "Three Rooms of Carpet" for $169. The small print in the ad states, "Up to thirty Sq. Yds."

    Will thirty yards be enough for the average three rooms?

    Yes _____   No _____

8. The BBB questions all business-opportunity ads that make claims of large earnings for investors. If documented proof of actual earnings is not available, the Bureau suggests caution to inquirers.

    Should media also require proof of earnings before accepting such ads for publication?

    Yes _____   No _____

9. A retailer advertises "Wholesale to Everyone."
    Is this possible?

    Yes _____   No _____

10. A car dealer advertises that he sells his new cars "at cost." However, the dealer takes his invoice price from the manufacturer and then adds the cost of sales commissions, advertising, make-ready, and overhead in order to arrive at his final "at cost" figure.

    Is this a deceptive "at cost" offer?

    Yes _____   No _____

11. A woman received a trinket in the mail with a request for a $1.00 donation.

    Must she mail the donation or return the trinket?

    Yes _____   No _____

12. Two days after a bad robbery, a burglar-alarm promoter mails a letter to everyone in the neighborhood and frightens many with the warning, "You may be next!"

    Is this an illegal use of the mails?

    Yes _____   No _____

13. A customer complains to the BBB that the salesman was so insistent she finally signed the contract just to get rid of him.

Now, she asks, will the BBB help her cancel the contract?

Yes _____   No _____

14. One store has a promotional line of house paints that is constantly advertised at about 40 per cent off. The BBB checked these "sale" prices as being advertised thirty-nine different times in one six-month period.

Is this a phony sale?

Yes _____   No _____

15. A lady answered an ad for a $289 color TV combo. After she signed the purchase contract, the salesman warned her that she could not run her sweeper or even a fan on the same circuit. "He frightened me," she said, "into changing the order for a $625 set."

Was she a bait-and-switch victim?

Yes _____   No _____

16. The salesman says, "You can call the BBB. They recommend us."
Could this be true?

Yes _____   No _____

17. The salesman wrote, "As is" on the sales slip for the used car, but he assured Mr. Y that it was in fine running condition. The purchaser soon found that the car needed extensive repairs. He tried to get the dealer either to make the repairs or to take the car back. The dealer refused.

Can he force the dealer to make an adjustment?

Yes _____   No _____

18. Mrs. X called a TV repairman, but before he could arrive, her husband had corrected the trouble. When the repairman arrived, she sent him away. Later, she received a bill for $20.00 to cover the service call, and she protested that she owed nothing because the serviceman did absolutely no work.

Must Mrs. X pay this bill?

Yes _____   No _____

19. Five months after purchasing a health-insurance policy, the insured was operated on for gallstones, which had been troubling him off and on for several years. The company denied payment of the claim because the condition existed prior to the starting date of the policy.

Should the company pay this claim?

Yes _____   No _____

20. Mrs. New purchased some slacks for her husband's birthday. They were not to his liking, and she tried to return the gift and get her money back. The store manager offered to exchange the merchandise, but he informed her that store policy prohibited refunds.

Was the store manager within his rights?

Yes _____   No _____

SCORING

Give yourself 5 points for each of your answers that agree with the following:

1. No.   This was an honest mistake. The store is not obligated.
2. Yes.   The price of the merchandise had obviously been raised to cover the cost of the "free" item.
3. No.   The realtor has already rendered his service.
4. No.   The manager is within his rights. And this is obviously a bona fide reduction from a regular price.
5. Yes.   Car warranties cover normal wear, but not abuse.
6. No.   The list price is not a true selling price in the area.
7. No.   You can check this by measuring your own three rooms.
8. Yes.   It would be an enlightened step for the protection of readers.
9. No.   He can't sell at the same prices he pays for his merchandise.
10. Yes.   "At cost" should have the same meaning as "wholesale" in question 9.
11. No.   There is no obligation to return or pay for unordered merchandise that the recipient does not use.
12. No.   But the BBB condemns it as scare selling.
13. No.   Her signature commits her to her agreement.
14. Yes.   The true price is the continuously advertised figure.
15. Yes.   Bait has many forms. This is one of the worst.
16. No.   The BBB never recommends any company, product, or service. Instead, it reports a summary of its file information so that the inquirer can use the information to make up his own mind.
17. No.   "As is" means there is no guarantee.
18. Yes.   She is responsible for ordering the service call.
19. No.   The law does not require that pre-existing conditions be covered until the health-insurance policy has been in effect three years.

20. Yes. That's why it's important to know in advance about a store's policies on refunds and exchanges.

If you score 90–100, grade yourself as having an excellent Quotient of Buymanship. If you score 80–90, there's a risk that a really slick operator can mislead you. If you score below 80, you need help.

YOU
AND YOUR
CAPACITY FOR SUCCESS

Do You Have Initiative?

Some people have great initiative and are willing to "take the bull by the horns," while others wait to be told what to do and when to do it. Those possessing initiative are the trail blazers. This test will help you assess whether or not you have initiative.

1. Which of the diagrams below best depicts your attitude toward life?

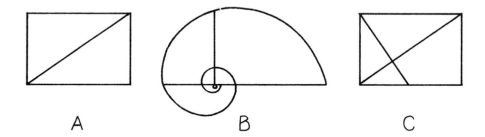

A   B   C

In the following, please select the reaction nearest your own:

2. I find myself bored with life.
   a. Never _____
   b. Sometimes _____
   c. Often _____

3. I wait for others to do things for me.
   a. Never _____

b. Sometimes ＿＿＿＿＿
c. Often ＿＿＿＿＿

4. I am interested in many subjects other than those that apply directly to my work.
   a. Never ＿＿＿＿＿
   b. Sometimes ＿＿＿＿＿
   c. Often ＿＿＿＿＿

5. I would enjoy being the chairperson, leader, or active working member of a social, educational, or religious group.
   a. Never ＿＿＿＿＿
   b. Sometimes ＿＿＿＿＿
   c. Often ＿＿＿＿＿

6. I plan ahead in my daily life and for my leisure time.
   a. Never ＿＿＿＿＿
   b. Sometimes ＿＿＿＿＿
   c. Often ＿＿＿＿＿

7. I see things that need to be done and do them without being told.
   a. Never ＿＿＿＿＿
   b. Sometimes ＿＿＿＿＿
   c. Often ＿＿＿＿＿

8. When there is a quarrel, I try to be the first to solve the problem and to "calm the troubled waters."
   a. Never ＿＿＿＿＿
   b. Sometimes ＿＿＿＿＿
   c. Often ＿＿＿＿＿

9. I try to upgrade my life in respect to such things as my clothing, my living environment, and my financial stability.
   a. Never ＿＿＿＿＿
   b. Sometimes ＿＿＿＿＿
   c. Often ＿＿＿＿＿

10. When I find bothersome things about my living or working conditions, I try to improve matters.
    a. Never ＿＿＿＿＿
    b. Sometimes ＿＿＿＿＿
    c. Often ＿＿＿＿＿

11. My life is basically ruled by an "I don't care" attitude.

a. Never _____

b. Sometimes _____

c. Often

12. Generally speaking, I would characterize myself as a shy and/or fearful person.

a. Never _____

b. Sometimes _____

c. Often _____

SCORING

1. a–5; b–10; c–0. Under psychological testing conditions those who possessed the greatest degree of initiative, the doers and the creative people, chose b, because they said the design had a greater challenge than a or c. A goodly number liked the directness of a, while those who tended to be withdrawn and timid about taking initiative selected c.

2. a–10; b–5; c–0

3. a–10; b–5; c–0

4. a–0; b–5; c–10

5. a–0; b–5; c–10

6. a–0; b–5; c–10

7. a–0; b–5; c–10

8. a–0; b–5; c–10

9. a–0; b–5; c–10

10. a–0; b–5; c–10

11. a–10; b–5; c–0

12. a–10; b–5; c–0

YOUR SCORE _____

90–120: Those in this bracket have great initiative and get things done. They instigate ideas and projects. There are some dangers in these independent, aggressive and self-assured personalities, however, for they often stifle the budding initiative of those with whom they live and work.

50–85: This is an average score, rated by those who can take initiative if and when they feel like it or when it is necessary. Many testees in this bracket seemed happier than those with higher scores because the former were willing to follow the decisions of others and to delegate responsibilities without taking the initiative.

0–45: This is a weak score, one usually made by those who are willing to let others do their thinking for them. Some have been browbeaten and have lost their powers of initiative. Others are merely physically or mentally lazy. Many are unhappy.

Are You Persevering?

It is easy to keep trying when we can see ourselves making progress, and when we are encouraged by people's appreciation of our efforts.

On the other hand, we can experience discouraging periods when we seem to be making no progress at all, when people are too busy to bother with us, or are not interested in what we are doing, or are critical and unfriendly.

We then need all the perseverance we possess to stick at it. Here is a test for you to try. Answer "Yes" or "No" to the questions before you turn to the scoring key at the end.

1. Are you able to stand firm in the teeth of criticism and disapproval?
2. Can you remain calm and refuse to be upset by unfriendliness and opposition?
3. Can you make your point and stick to it during a discussion?
4. Would you carry on if others ridiculed your principles or belittled your ability to do something?
5. Would you remain loyal to a friend who had become unpopular?
6. If you knew the odds were against you, like people withdrawing their support, would you carry on with a project you believed in?
7. Do you make a point of finishing anything you undertake to do, like staying with a job to the end even when it is long and tedious?
8. Would you put yourself to considerable inconvenience to keep a promise you had made?
9. Would you be willing to go back to school in order to master a new subject or method?
10. Do you patiently collect and consider all the relevant data and weigh the pros and cons before making an important decision?
11. Do you shoulder the domestic responsibilities that come your way, like doing your share of nursing a sick member of the family?
12. Are you good with difficult, moody people, like the old and the chronically sick?
13. Are you good at showing people how to do things, explaining to children, and training house pets?
14. Do you carry on for as long as possible when you are unwell?
15. Do you have another go and keep trying when you fail or when things go wrong?
16. Are difficulties and setbacks challenges and spurs to further effort?
17. Once you make up your mind, is it hard to stop you?
18. Possibly you take your time about making friends, but once you have made them, do you keep them for years?

19. Possibly things take you a long time to learn, but do you get it perfect in the end and never forget it?

20. Can you bear to be blamed and misunderstood and carry on in spite of it?

SCORING

Count 5 marks for every "Yes." A score of 70 or over is very good, and 60–70 may be counted good; 50–60 is satisfactory. Under 50 is not satisfactory.

We develop perseverance when we care intensely about somebody or something, and when we know what we want from life and what we want to make of ourselves.

What Are You Worth on the Job?

Has it been years since you received a raise or a promotion? If so, you may be unaware of your worth on the job. You are probably unable to demand the compensation your hard work deserves or to work toward bettering your performance. The following quiz is designed to help you evaluate your worth at work and to inspire you to set your sights on a more satisfying career.

1. In the last five years how many times have you asked for a raise?
    a. My employer may have offered me one but I did not ask.
    b. I am always trying to get raises and promotions because my work is good.
    c. Since my union makes sure I get raises, I never negotiate for bonuses, merit increases, or promotions.
    d. Even if I deserve a raise, I am too timid to ask for one.
    e. Since I do only what I have to at work, I really don't deserve a raise.

2. In the past five years how many times have you received a raise?
    a. none.
    b. one.

    c. two.

    d. three to four.

    e. five or more.

3. Over the past five years how much money did your raises total?
   a. 0–$100.
   b. $100–$500.
   c. $500–$1,000.
   d. $1,000–$5,000.
   e. $5,000 or more.

4. What are your chances of getting a raise within the next year?
   a. excellent.
   b. very good.
   c. good.
   d. poor.
   e. slim.

5. Next year what are your chances of asking for a raise?
   a. slim.
   b. poor.
   c. good.
   d. very good.
   e. excellent.

6. In the past five years how many times have you asked for a promotion?
   a. If my employer did not offer, I did not bother.
   b. Since I do good work, I am always in a good position to be offered or to ask for a promotion.
   c. No one gets promoted at my job, so I don't even try.
   d. Even if I deserve a promotion, I am too timid to ask for one.
   e. I have asked for a promotion or was approached by my boss for one, but hiring freezes and company layoffs have blocked my success.

7. In the past five years how many promotions have you received?
   a. none.
   b. one.
   c. one, substantial both in salary and in position.
   d. two, at least one of which was substantial in salary and in position.
   e. three or more.

8. What did your promotions offer you?

a. Just a title with little or no financial rewards.

b. Little or no financial rewards but a chance to move up in the company.

c. Financial as well as professional rewards. I see myself moving up in the company.

d. No promotions were offered, and I never asked to be moved up.

e. A chance to do more work, get the same pay, and stagnate for the next five years.

9. How would you rate your chances for getting a promotion in the next year?

   a. excellent.
   b. very good.
   c. good.
   d. poor.
   e. slim.

10. If you were your boss, how would you rate your work?

   a. excellent.
   b. very good.
   c. good/satisfactory.
   d. poor.
   e. unsatisfactory.

11. How would you describe your evaluations at work?

   a. excellent.
   b. very good.
   c. good/satisfactory.
   d. poor.
   e. unsatisfactory.

12. How would you describe yourself at work?

   a. I'm a procrastinator. I never manage to complete my work on time.
   b. I find as many excuses as I can to get out of doing work.
   c. I'm bored, but I'm too lazy to look for another job.
   d. I'm bored, but I find things to do that will ultimately make my work record look impressive.
   e. I love my job and am constantly trying to better my position.

13. How do you view your strengths at work?

   a. What strengths? I'm mediocre.

    b. I have clearly analyzed my strengths and can discuss them with my present boss or future employer.

    c. I think I know what my strengths are, but I'm not sure.

    d. I never really thought about strengths in relationship to work, but I am convinced mine are limited.

    e. I have clearly analyzed my strengths and will devise a plan and strategy to help them benefit me at work.

14. How do you view your weaknesses at work?
    a. I have clearly analyzed my weaknesses and have genuinely worked to improve them.
    b. I have analyzed my weaknesses and am beginning to work toward improving them.
    c. I have no weaknesses that I can think of.
    d. I have weaknesses but I refuse to do anything about them.
    e. I have weaknesses but they are not clearly defined or written down. I'll work until my boss brings them to my attention.

15. In the past five years how many times have you initiated job-related projects (extra work)?
    a. one.
    b. two.
    c. three.
    d. four.
    e. five or more.

16. If you were your boss, how would you rate your self-initiated projects?
    a. excellent.
    b. very good.
    c. good/satisfactory.
    d. poor.
    e. unsatisfactory.

17. How would you grade your self-initiated projects?
    a. excellent.
    b. very good.
    c. good/satisfactory.
    d. poor.
    e. unsatisfactory.

18. Which of the following best describes how you feel about your job?

a. I love it, but I'll never get anywhere as long as I remain in it.

b. I love it, but I haven't had a raise or a promotion in four or more years.

c. It's completely boring, but I'm too afraid to leave. After all, who would want me?

d. I find it interesting, have had some promotions and raises, but the job is just not applicable to my education and past work experience.

e. I love my job, find it interesting, and am moving up in the company at the right pace and salary rate.

19. Is your job related to your education and past work experience?
    a. No! I'm underemployed!

    b. My qualifications are perfect for the job. Yet I work far beyond my job-description duties and am not paid or recognized for this extra service.

    c. According to my background I'm in the right field, but I'd rather not be.

    d. I am in a job I love, in a field where there is growth and expansion, and I am positioning myself for advancement.

    e. I am in the right job and field, and if I push harder, I can expect additional opportunities.

20. How would you describe your attitude toward work?
    a. Highly motivated and ambitious. I'm always trying to improve my work life.

    b. I seldom think about promotions, raises, or my career.

    c. I think about promotions, raises, and my career, but in order to advance I have to leave my present job. I'm too afraid to do that!

    d. I don't deserve a better job, higher salary, or promotion because I feel worthless.

    e. I have tried to work toward a better salary, job, and a better life, and in the near future I will realize these goals.

21. When you made career goals last year, how many did you realize?
    a. I did not make any career goals last year.

    b. I forgot about the goals I did set.

    c. I set some goals, started to work toward them, but became involved in other projects.

    d. I developed goals and am presently working toward completing them.

    e. I realized all my career goals.
22. How many career goals can you set for the coming year? (List them on a separate sheet of paper.)

    a. five.
    b. four.
    c. three.
    d. two.
    e. one.

SCORING

Look up the value of each answer below, then add up your score.

1. a–3; b–5; c–4; d–2; e–1	12. a–2; b–1; c–3; d–4; e–5
2. a–1; b–2; c–3; d–4; e–5	13. a–1; b–5; c–3; d–2; e–4
3. a–1; b–2; c–3; d–4; e–5	14. a–5; b–4; c–2; d–1; e–3
4. a–5; b–4; c–3; d–2; e–1	15. a–1; b–2; c–3; d–4; e–5
5. a–1; b–2; c–3; d–4; e–5	16. a–5; b–4; c–3; d–2; e–1
6. a–3; b–5; c–1; d–2; e–4	17. a–5; b–4; c–3; d–2; e–1
7. a–1; b–2; c–3; d–4; e–5	18. a–3; b–2; c–1; d–4; e–5
8. a–3; b–4; c–5; d–1; e–2	19. a–1; b–2; c–3; d–5; e–4
9. a–5; b–4; c–3; d–2; e–1	20. a–5; b–3; c–2; d–1; e–4
10. a–5; b–4; c–3; d–2; e–1	21. a–1; b–2; c–3; d–4; e–5
11. a–5; b–4; c–3; d–2; e–1	22. a–5; b–4; c–3; d–2; e–1

82 points or more: Welcome to the upwardly mobile group of workers. You are career-oriented and ambitious. Thoughtful planning and hard work have already netted you raises and promotions, and you can expect to make even more advances in the future.

68–81 points: You're on the right track. You're curious at work, want the best for yourself, and actively try to improve your life. Although advancement seems slow, you have received most of the raises and promotions you've wanted. If you continue to persevere, better job opportunities await you.

57–67 points: You're very middle-of-the-road. You've had at least one raise in the past five years, but wage freezes, layoffs, and company restructurings have kept you in a lower-level position. Although you have a lot of talent, you refuse to explore other job possibilities and take control of your own career. Analyze your situation, decide where you would like to be in the next five or ten years, and immediately start working toward your goals.

47–56 points: Because you cling to security and don't take risks, you feel trapped in an unsatisfyung job. Whenever you try to help yourself out of your predicament, you tend to give up easily. Make a New Year's resolution to get out of your rut!

46 points or less: You're definitely not career-oriented. A job is just a job to you, and you couldn't care less about working toward promotions, raises, or bonuses. Don't blame your low salary or lack of promotions on others. If you want to be compensated, you'll have to improve your attitude toward work, assess your career goals, and work toward them.

Are You a Trustworthy Employee?

Can your boss turn his back on you without having to worry about whether you're going to steal him blind or cheat his customers? Are you an ethical employee who can be trusted, or an employee who requires close monitoring to guard against your committing illegal or unethical acts while on the job?

To gain insight into your trustworthiness as an employee, answer the following questions in this simple test.

HAVE YOU EVER . . .

1. Taken items of merchandise from your employer without his knowledge or permission?
   a. Yes.
   b. No.

2. Taken money from the cash register without your employer's knowledge or permission?
   a. Yes.
   b. No.

3. Kept money from a sale without recording the sale?
   a. Yes.
   b. No.

4. Falsified information while filling out an application form or report for your employer?
   a. Yes.
   b. No.

5. Purposely shortchanged a customer?
   a. Yes.
   b. No.

6. Permitted friends or relatives to take items of merchandise from your place of employment without payung for them?
   a. Yes.
   b. No.

7. Given friends or relatives "special discounts" without your employer's knowledge or permission?
   a. Yes.
   b. No.

8. Sold a damaged or used item of merchandise as an undamaged or unused item?
   a. Yes.
   b. No.

9. Attempted to get paid for time not actually spent working?
   a. Yes.
   b. No.

10. Deliberately overcharged a customer for a purchase?
    a. Yes.
    b. No.

11. Told a lie to your employer or made up a false excuse for not working?
    a. Yes.
    b. No.

12. Borrowed an item of merchandise from your place of employment without your employer's knowledge or permission and returned it at a later date?
   a. Yes.
   b. No.

13. Attempted to sell a customer an item of merchandise he did not want to purchase?
   a. Yes.
   b. No.

14. Lied to a customer about the availability of an item of merchandise so you could try to sell him an out-of-style or "slow turnover" item instead?
   a. Yes.
   b. No.

15. Manipulated customers into thinking they were getting a good deal on a purchase even though you knew they were being "taken"?
   a. Yes.
   b. No.

SCORING

If you answered "Yes" to one of the questions, you are basically a trustworthy employee but show occasional signs of being less than completely honest.

If you answered "Yes" to any two of the questions, you have demonstrated untrustworthy behavior that probably will be noticed by your employer. If discovered committing these misdeeds, you will most assuredly be out of a job.

If you answered "Yes" to three or more questions, you are definitely an untrustworthy employee who should be fired immediately. You may be getting away with your indiscretions for now, but it's just a matter of time before you are caught by your boss and summarily dismissed from your job. You must seek counseling to amend your ways or face the grim prospect of having your employment record forever marred by the fact that you were once fired from a job for committing illegal or unethical acts while performing your duties.

Can You Lead?

Not everyone wants the responsibility of being the boss. Others are cut out of leadership material. There are those situations when there are "too many chiefs and not enough Indians" and those when no one wants to make decisions. This test will help you assess whether you are managerial quality in your home or work or are better fitted to work under the guidance of others.

1. Glance at the two abstract drawings below. Which do you prefer?

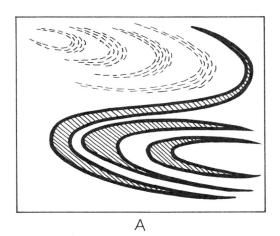

A

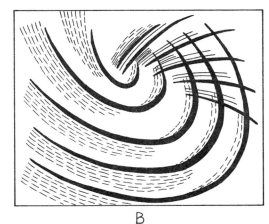

B

2. Look at the lines of figures below. If the figures in each line were added, which would have the largest sum? You have only *ten seconds* and must *estimate* the answer. (No fair cheating on time.)

    a. 0 8 3 6 0 1 5 7
    b. 5 1 9 0 0 3 5 1 4 0
    c. 4 1 9 0 5 0 1 4

3. TRUE _____ FALSE _____ Usually people need to know the reason they are asked to do something.

4. TRUE _____ FALSE _____ There are times when your decisions should not be questioned.

5. TRUE _____ FALSE _____ Those in the role of leadership should maintain a "buddy" relationship with those with whom he or she deals.

6. TRUE _____ FALSE _____ In order to be objective, one should turn a deaf ear to the problems of his or her associates.

7. TRUE _____ FALSE _____   Some people in a community are so weak or stupid that they will never be of any value.

8. TRUE _____ FALSE _____   A good boss should be more feared than respected.

9. TRUE _____ FALSE _____   To ask advice from your family or associates is a sign of weakness in leadership.

10. TRUE _____ FALSE _____   Praise is more conducive to good performance than criticism.

11. TRUE _____ FALSE _____   It is better to work out each day than to formulate long-range goals.

12. TRUE _____ FALSE _____   The emotional makeup of a boss has little bearing on the performance of those around him or her.

13. TRUE _____ FALSE _____   When a person is angry with a person or persons, he should show it in no uncertain terms.

14. TRUE _____ FALSE _____   A good boss should try to do most of the jobs himself.

15. In the match pattern below there are nine squares. By removing four matches, you can have only five squares. Which four matches would you take away?

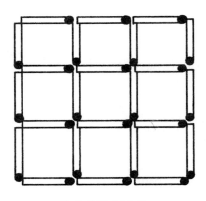

SCORING

1. a. 10 points; b. 5 points (Under psychological testing conditions it was shown that neither choice was "wrong." In both cases, people now in positions of leadership identified with the black portions of the drawings. Those who selected a. seemed to be more objective and outgoing in their relationship with others than those who preferred b.)

2. a. (The sum is 30.)   10 points

    This problem involves the ability to arrive rapidly at an estimate, a necessary talent for many facets of leadership.

3. TRUE   10 points

4. TRUE   10 points

    (You don't explain to a person standing in the path of an oncoming train.)

5. FALSE   10 points

6. FALSE   10 points

7. FALSE   10 points

8. FALSE   10 points

9. FALSE   10 points

10. TRUE   10 points

11. FALSE   10 points

12. FALSE   10 points

13. FALSE   10 points

14. FALSE   10 points

15.   10 points

This problem involves the ability to see the total and to change it into the desired. Most executives tested solved it usually in less than a minute.

ANALYSIS:

Highest possible score on this test is 150.

130–150: Whether you are managing your home or on the job, this is a fine score, provided you answered honestly. Many look to you for leadership, but you also have the ability to lead others into roles of responsibility. You have this talent, which you are willing to share by example.

60–125:   Those who rate in this wide range are not "born" bosses but they often *learn* techniques if they wish. Libraries abound in books and magazines that help to develop good, sound ways of constructively influencing others. Perhaps, however, you are one of those important people who prefer play in the line rather than to be the quarterback.

1–55:   Testees seldom rate so low a score, but those who do are in need of self-discipline and the guidance of others.

Are You Winner or Defeatist?

As individuals, we tend to divide into two categories.

We move forward, acting positively to overcome obstacles. Or we tend to retreat, refusing to face up to reality, and taking the easy way out.

Here is a test to help you discover which is your dominant attitude.

1. You have an inferiority complex regarding your appearance. Would you ask friends to advise you, and seek the aid of skilled people like a good hairdresser?

    Yes _____   No _____

2. You are nervous about speaking in public. Would you join a drama club, or discussion group, or a public-speaking class?

    Yes _____   No _____

3. You have suffered an illness or an accident, or acquired a physical disability. Would you concentrate on getting better as soon as possible and permit it to interfere with normal life as little as possible?

    Yes _____   No _____

4. Are difficulties and setbacks challenges that make you want to have another go and do better next time?

    Yes _____   No _____

5. Can you stand up for yourself and avoid being upset by awkward, rude, hostile, unhelpful people?

    Yes _____   No _____

6. You have a personal problem, like discovering that somebody you love does not love you that much. Could you face up to the hard reality of the situation and decide what action to take?

    Yes _____   No _____

7. A decision you should make will arouse criticism. Would you make it and stick by it?

    Yes _____   No _____

8. You need the support and co-operation of other people. Some are uninterested and some are unwilling to help. Would you persevere in your efforts to win them over?

    Yes _____   No _____

9. A friend does something wrong or adopts an unpopular attitude. You may not approve, but would you stand by him in the sense of remaining friendly and helpful?

    Yes _____   No _____

10. You have put your foot in it and made yourself generally disliked. Could you eat humble pie and apologize?

    Yes _____   No _____

11. There is an unpleasant job to be done. Are you the type who gets it done as soon as possible?

    Yes _____   No _____

12. A necessary job is long, hard, tedious, boring, monotonous. Would you stick at it until it was finished?

    Yes _____   No _____

13. You are interested. Your friends are not. Would you go it alone?

    Yes _____   No _____

14. Your friends are interested. You are not. Nevertheless, you are becoming involved. Could you say: "Sorry, there are other things I want to do."?

    Yes _____   No _____

15. People are taking you for granted. Could you say: "Sorry, I'm not available like that all the time."?

    Yes _____   No _____

16. You appear to be making no impression. Would this cause you to go out of your way to be extrafriendly and helpful?

Yes _____   No _____

17. An arrangement falls through. You are disappointed. Would you find something else you could do?

Yes _____   No _____

18. Old friends die or move away. Would you continue to go out among people and develop new friendships?

Yes _____   No _____

19. You have to change your job or move away. Could you adapt yourself to make the best of it?

Yes _____   No _____

20. You have been trying a long time but seem to have made little progress. Would you try even harder?

Yes _____   No _____

SCORING

Count five points for every "Yes." A score of 70 or more is very good. It shows that your dominant attitude is to overcome obstacles and not to retreat from them.

A score of 60–70 may be counted good; 50–60 is satisfactory.

Below 50 is not satisfactory.

Aim at being positive, constructive, and practical in your approach to life.

Do You Achieve Goals You Set for Yourself?

Are you an achiever, able to meet the goals you set for yourself? This quiz by Laurence Smalheiser, Ph.D, will help you understand your own achievement potential. Check each of the statements below to the best of your ability as True, False, or Uncertain; then score your achievement potential and see just how much of an achiever you are.

1. TRUE_____ FALSE_____ UNCERTAIN_____ I tend to be accused of making excuses.

2. TRUE_____ FALSE_____ UNCERTAIN_____ I tend to miss social events because of work commitments.

3. TRUE_____ FALSE_____ UNCERTAIN_____ I tend to give up on projects because of time or difficulty involved.

4. TRUE_____ FALSE_____ UNCERTAIN_____ I like to plan things well in advance.

5. TRUE_____ FALSE_____ UNCERTAIN_____ I tend to select easy goals.

6. TRUE_____ FALSE_____ UNCERTAIN_____ I carefully map out my plans to accomplish my goals.

7. TRUE_____ FALSE_____ UNCERTAIN_____ I often make sacrifices to get what I want.

8. TRUE_____ FALSE_____ UNCERTAIN_____ I tend not to know what I want out of life.

9. TRUE_____ FALSE_____ UNCERTAIN_____ I prefer to work on tasks that are difficult and challenging.

10. TRUE_____ FALSE_____ UNCERTAIN_____ I would rather engage in a sport or a game certain of victory.

11. TRUE_____ FALSE_____ UNCERTAIN_____ I tend to question my ability to accomplish things.

12. TRUE_____ FALSE_____ UNCERTAIN_____ I can get things done but usually have to be pushed.

13. TRUE_____ FALSE_____ UNCERTAIN_____ Why knock yourself out when you don't know what tomorrow will bring?

14.   TRUE_____ FALSE_____ UNCERTAIN_____   I would choose someone to play on my team because of friendship rather than ability.

15.   TRUE_____ FALSE_____ UNCERTAIN_____   I tend to lose interest in projects when they don't go right.

SCORING

SCORING KEY: Circle each number corresponding to the answers checked and then add to obtain your total score.

	TRUE	FALSE	UNCERTAIN		TRUE	FALSE	UNCERTAIN
1.	1	4	2	9.	2	0	1
2.	2	0	1	10.	0	4	1
3.	1	3	2	11.	1	4	2
4.	4	1	2	12.	0	3	1
5.	0	4	2	13.	0	4	2
6.	4	1	2	14.	1	4	2
7.	3	0	1	15.	0	3	2
8.	1	4	2				

Your total score: _____

36 points or more: You tend to be efficient and organized in your approach to tasks and to life in general. You plan ahead and are generally enthusiastic about the activities you are engaged in. You may be criticized at times for being overly competitive or so engrossed in what you are doing that you neglect the feelings of others.

16–35 points: You are capable of bringing much energy and determination into play. Your areas of interest may differ from time to time and you may allow yourself to be sidetracked by friends and family. Still, in important matters, you do what is expected of you in meeting your obligations.

15 points or less: Because you sometimes avoid facing problems and responsibilities, you may find yourself becoming anxious and dissatisfied. You need to become more aware of the major goals in life. Don't blame others for your problems—but examine what you have done yourself, or failed to do. You have a tendency to be careless and forgetful, but you have the potential to do better. If you make a real effort you will find that being an achiever is not so difficult.

Are You a Hard Worker?

When there is work to be done, some people moan and groan, while others accomplish miracles of hard work with apparently little effort and a maximum of enjoyment. In judging your merits as a worker, it is necessary to evaluate both your attitude toward work in general and toward your own job. This test will help you assess whether or not you are an efficient, hard worker.

1. In the illustration below, which of the four lettered squares in the bottom row fits into the white square in the top picture.

Answer the following questions "Yes" or "No":

2. Do you often try to find ways to simplify your job?

        Yes _____   No _____

3. When under a job pressure, do you think sleep is a waste of time?

        Yes _____   No _____

4. Do you usually know where your personal belongings are?

        Yes _____   No _____

5. Do you always try to find people who will help you with your duties?

        Yes _____   No _____

6. Do you cheerfully finish a job even if it means working overtime?

        Yes _____   No _____

7. Are you plagued by the fear that your work is not up to standard?

            Yes _____   No _____

8. Do you take time off for relaxation or to do something unrelated to your usual tasks?

            Yes _____   No _____

9. Is a relatively set personal schedule part of your living pattern?

            Yes _____   No _____

10. Does each day seem to bring more burdens than you are capable of handling?

            Yes _____   No _____

11. Do you resent suggestions from others about the way you approach your job?

            Yes _____   No _____

12. Are you smug when you are praised for a job that you know is not up to par?

            Yes _____   No _____

SCORING

1. Lettered square d. Under psychologically controlled testing conditions those who selected proved to be intent and hard workers. They were able to see small details and relationships and to arrive at a correct conclusion, regardless of the time required. They noted, for instance, the difference between the sizes of the partial handbags in c and d. Give yourself 2 points for the correct answer.

2. Yes. Simplification of a job is not laziness. 2 points.

3. No. Sleep is an important part of well-being. Fatigue often leads to errors and accidents. 2 points.

4. Yes. This is an important sign of your personal organization. 2 points.

5. No. The catchword here is "always." Some people spend so much time getting others to help that they could have done the job three times over. 2 points.

6. Yes. When possible it is psychologically sound to finish a task even if it means extra time. 2 points.

7. No. If you said "Yes," you are probably a victim of frustration, which in turn leads to errors. 2 points.

8. Yes. Psychologists agree there should be a rhythmical pattern between rest and relaxation, hence the establishment of on-the-job coffee breaks.   2 points.

9. Yes. Routine in daily living contributes greatly to competency in living.   2 points.

10. No. As in answer 7, the feeling of being overwhelmed can be avoided by done one or more things well until they become habits.   2 points.

11. No. Good suggestions now and then are appreciated by the wisest men.   2 points.

12. No. To collect compliments for a job you know is not up to par is a kind of mental dishonesty.   2 points.

Your total score: _____

18–24: Testees in this bracket are hard workers. Because of the skill they have in organization they often give the surface appearance of "breezing through" their job.

10–16: Those in this bracket often work to live, rather than living to work. They profit either by a careful evaluation of their approach to their jobs or, in some cases, by changing occupations if possible.

0–8: Testees who rate this score are few and far between. They are in need of the feeling of satisfaction that comes from working, and they often profit from being reminded that even the hobo on the road chops wood for a meal.

Are You Efficient?

You may think you are efficient and competent, but try answering the following questions truthfully and you may be in for a surprise!

Mark a. or b. and then check your score at the end.

1. a. Are you systematic?
    b. Or are you apt to let things slide?
2. a. At night do you generally turn in at a set hour?

b. Or do you often feel too lazy to go to bed?

3. a. Do you believe that things are always piling up on you?
    b. Or are you always able to cope with your everyday chores?

4. a. Do you enjoy meeting, and dealing with, the unexpected in your business and/or private affairs?
    b. Or do you easily panic and, so to speak, lose your grip?

5. a. Are you inclined to be careless in your dress?
    b. Or do you take care with your appearance, without necessarily overdoing it?

6. a. Do you ever get your dates mixed up?
    b. Or are you very careful in that respect?

7. a. Do you always think before you act?
    b. Or are you prone to rush in where angels fear to tread?

8. a. Are you always on time when meeting someone?
    b. Or do you feel that a half-hour difference one way or the other doesn't matter?

9. a. Are you always on the lookout for ways and means to improve your work?
    b. Or do you believe that it's too much bother and stick to a fixed routine all the time?

10. a. Are you careful in your speech?
    b. Or are you apt to slur your words?

SCORING

Score 5 points for each correct answer: 1–a; 2–a; 3–b; 4–a; 5–b; 6–b; 7–a; 8–a; 9–a; 10–a.

Maximum score is 50.

If you have genuinely scored 40–50 points, you have nothing to worry about.

A score of 25–35 points means that you're apt to be a little careless at times, but it's hardly catastrophic. Most likely you're a cheerful, live-and-let-live person.

Are You in the Right Job?

Is your job killing you? Many workers do feel disgruntled, frustrated, disappointed, and turned off by their jobs. Others are fulfilled and contented.

The following quiz will help you realize whether or not you are better off looking for another job. Just answer "Yes" or "No" to these questions:

1. Do you get up in the morning raring to get to your job?
2. Do you think you're appreciated by your superiors?
3. Are you fearful of losing your job?
4. Do you think the physical environment of your job is generally pleasing?
5. Do you feel you're underpaid?
6. Do you like the product or service that is the end result of your work?
7. Is there a fair degree of male-female sociability on the job?
8. Do you take pride in keeping the equipment you use in good condition?
9. Do you worry about your work while not on duty?
10. Do you work primarily for the money?
11. Would you stay if there were no fringe benefits?
12. Would you want a member of your family to do the same general type of work?
13. Does time go by rapidly during work hours?
14. Do you find yourself talking shop outside of work hours?
15. Are your ideas openly accepted?
16. Would you truly feel a loss if your job were discontinued tomorrow but you were guaranteed an income?
17. Do you have a sense of accomplishment on the job?
18. Would you strongly want to be in another job?
19. Do you often steal things at work to get even?
20. Do you loaf, watch the clock, daydream, take long coffee breaks, take long lunches, quit early, come in late?
21. Do you often feel tired about three quarters of the way through the day?
22. Do you think that your job puts most of your talents to work?
23. Is there room for creative advancement?

SCORING

Now score all your answers. Give yourself a point for each answer that matches the following:

1 Yes; 2 Yes; 3 No; 4 Yes; 5 No; 6 Yes; 7 Yes; 8 Yes; 9 No; 10 No; 11 Yes; 12 Yes; 13 Yes; 14 Yes; 15 Yes; 16 Yes; 17 Yes; 18 No; 19 No; 20 No; 21 No; 22 Yes; 23 Yes

21–23 points: You are really a fabulous addition to your company. You show a tremendous pride in your work and willingly give of yourself to whatever job you perform.

20 points: You do enjoy your work but sometimes you wish you had a little more energy left over to take part in some other aspects of your life.

19 points: Most of the time you are fairly satisfied, but there is a definite doubt in your mind, and you might be better off somewhere else. How about looking around—today.

15–18 points: You feel your job gives plenty of security for you and your family, but you often wish you were in another field. You're in the wrong job but are scared to switch.

13–14 points: You need to do some serious thinking about what you really want to do or you'll stay there forever.

11–12 points: You can't wait until the day is over and you can go home. Every minute on the job ties you down even more.

7–10 points: Better quit quick, to make something of your life.

0–6 points: You've been completely brainwashed to believe that any work is good work. Nonsense! Put your energies to fulfilling your potential.

POTPOURRI

Are You a TV Addict?

Do you sit glued in front of your TV set, pausing only long enough to go to the bathroom or grab a quick snack in the kitchen? Is TV the most important part of your life?

TV addiction is a serious malady. Those who are "hooked" find it difficult to function without watching television every day. TV addiction can lead to social introversion, failure to communicate with one's spouse, and, in some cases, even divorce.

Are you a TV addict? Take this simple test to find out.

1. Your TV set breaks down and must be taken into the repair shop. You are informed that it will take one week to fix your set. You would:
   a. rent or borrow a TV set for the week.
   b. watch as many of your favorite programs as you could at other people's homes.
   c. find some other form of entertainment to keep you occupied during the week.

2. How often do you keep the TV set on when you are preoccupied with other tasks around the house?
   a. often.
   b. sometimes.
   c. hardly ever.

3. You've been waiting all week to see a special TV program. At the last minute, however, you remember that you promised to attend a friend's party the very evening when the program is scheduled to air. You would:

a. call your friend, make an excuse for being unable to attend the party, and stay home to watch your TV program.

b. go to the party reluctantly, upset over having to miss the TV program.

c. forget about the TV program and go to the party expecting to have a good time.

4. How often do you watch TV while you are eating dinner?
   a. often.
   b. sometimes.
   c. hardly ever.

5. You are watching your favorite TV program when friends drop by unexpectedly for a visit. You would:
   a. finish watching the TV program before visiting with your friends.
   b. watch the rest of the TV program while you visit with your friends.
   c. turn the TV set off and visit with your friends.

6. You check your *TV Guide* and discover that the only programs on that evening are reruns you have already seen. You would:
   a. watch a full evening of TV as usual.
   b. watch some TV but find something else to do the rest of the evening.
   c. do something instead of watching any TV that evening.

7. How often do you plan your social activities around the TV schedule?
   a. often.
   b. sometimes.
   c. hardly ever.

8. You are watching your favorite TV program when a transmission problem results in the loss of your picture. The picture loss continues for several minutes. You would:
   a. angrily call the local TV station and complain.
   b. sit looking at the TV listening to the sound and waiting for the picture to reappear.
   c. find something else to do until the problem is corrected.

9. Are you able to tell what programs are on at a certain time without looking them up in *TV Guide*?

   a. often.

   b. sometimes.

   c. hardly ever.

10. How do you feel when another commitment prevents you from watching TV one evening?

   a. disappointed that I couldn't watch TV.

   b. I have no real feelings one way or the other.

   c. Relieved that I had something to do other than sit home and watch TV.

SCORING

Score 3 points for each a answer, 2 points for each b answer, and 1 point for each c answer.

If you scored 25 or over, you are a certified TV addict. It is obvious that "the boob tube" rules your life. If you don't break the viewing habit, life will pass you right by.

If you scored between 16 and 24, you spend far too much time in front of the TV set. But don't feel alone—the vast majority of the American public uses TV as their principal form of entertainment. Try cultivating some other interests like reading a good book, listening to music, or visiting with friends before you wind up a TV addict.

If you scored between 10 and 15, you have managed to keep your TV viewing in its proper perspective. Although you watch some TV, it is not the most important part of your life. Good for you!

How Good a Bluffer Are You?

What is bluffing? It's not lying, for lying is often destructive. It's not guessing, for the guesser has only a fifty-fifty chance of being right. It's not cheating, for cheating victimizes others. Bluffing is really a skill, an art, and a courtesy to others as well as a necessity to ourselves. As one psychologist puts it, it is "piecing together what one knows to cover a gap of ignorance."

We all bluff but we don't know how skillful we are because most of us deny that we bluff at all. There is the verbal bluff, the bluff of action, and combinations of both, and however upright a citizen you may consider yourself, you carry on some kind of a bluff every day in the year.

Our individual "bluffability" can be measured by our instinctive reactions to situations such as those described in the following test.

People call bluffing by other names—tact, deceit, bragging, flattery, optimism, or pretending. You can't take lessons in bluffing—it just sort of "comes to you"—but there's a natural kind of training period in everyone's life, which is the eight to sixteen years you spend in school. After a survey made at an Ohio high school some years ago, the faculty felt they had a grave situation on their hands. While many students answered the questionnaire with answers they thought their teachers would like to hear, one third expressed what the scandalized teachers called "a desire to deceive." Eleven per cent of the students said bluntly that success in life depends on one's ability to bluff. The Ohio teachers were convinced that the students who bluffed were forming bad habits that would ruin their chances of "getting ahead", later on. But the opposite viewpoint declares that the student who knows how to bluff is developing imagination, logic, ingenuity, and creative reasoning. A certain amount of bluffing is inherent in human nature. Life is full of surprises, unexpected developments for which we are not prepared, crises we have never met before, and problems for which we have no previously formulated answers. The need to bluff becomes apparent.

If you played poker for a living, you'd admit that your whole career depended on your ability to bluff. But there is no one who can hold a job without bluffing at all. And most of us would go farther and accomplish a lot more if we knew how to bluff better.

You couldn't be a good parent without bluffing. It's your bluff at being completely honest, completely wise, and completely good that carries your children through the first eight or ten years of their lives, when their sense of security is built on believing you're perfect.

You couldn't be a good wife or a good husband without bluffing; in fact, you wouldn't be married at all. Bluffing in marriage takes skill, because you have to put something over on the person who is better equipped than anyone else in the world to see through you. The good partner in marriage won't try to; that's part of his or her bluff. "Bluffing by consent," you might call it. If you could dissect an unhappy marriage you'd probably find that when love stopped, bluffing stopped, too.

Your success and happiness depend on your ability to bluff in little ways, every day, every week, every year, for after all, when you bluff you are pretending that you are braver than you are, that you know more than you do, or that you're happier than you feel. Bluffers usually try hard to become the kind of people they have claimed to be. The less you bluff, the lower your personal "standard of living."

Now take the test that follows to compute your own "bluffability." Circle the answer that is correct for you, but don't try to guess which answer indicates that you're a good, bad, or indifferent bluffer—because the order of the questions have been thoroughly scrambled.

1.   You have to make a speech before a club. Will you
    a.   write it out and memorize it?
    b.   make notes to refer to while you are making your talk?
    c.   talk extemporaneously?

2.   If a large gathering you spot someone you know you should speak to, but you've forgotten his or her name. Will you
    a.   avoid the person?
    b.   find someone else in the crowd who can tell you the name?
    c.   go to the person whose name you can't remember and engage him (or her) in conversation?

3.   You are looking for a job, but the better-salaried openings listed in the job-opportunities column of the newspaper are in fields in which you've had no experience. Will you
    a.   apply for the kind of work in which you've had experience, in hopes of doing so well you'll eventually work up to a better salary?
    b.   look into job openings in fields distantly related to your own?
    c.   apply for the high-salaried jobs regardless of your lack of training?

4.   The boss has handed you a tough assignment—so tough you know instantly that you have only one chance in a hundred of making good. Will you
    a.   suggest another assignment you might undertake instead?

   b. tell him you can't do the job?

   c. conceal your worry and accept the assignment with a show of confidence?

5.   You have been invited to a party that is very important (to you, or to your spouse) from a business point of view. Names of the important guests have been published in the newspaper in advance. Will you

   a. study the list to see how many people you've met before?

   b. read the list once or twice and then discard it?

   c. memorize the entire list?

6.   You are calling on a sick friend. Will you

   a. immediately ask how she (or he) feels?

   b. discuss her (or his) illness only when she (or he) brings the subject up herself (or himself)?

   c. quickly talk of something else whenever she (or he) refers to her (or his) illness?

7.   You are giving a swanky dinner party. You've hired a maid to serve it, and the menu includes broiled squab. But there are only twelve squab for twelve guests, and in serving at the table the maid drops one on the floor. Will you

   a. tell the guests it doesn't matter because you never eat fowl (doctor's orders) and the one on the floor was extra?

   b. confess the truth and get your wife (or husband) to divide a squab with you?

   c. say to the maid, "Take that one away and bring in another."?

8.   You have driven twenty miles to see a football game. When you get to the gate you find you left your money at home and haven't enough for the tickets. Will you

   a. turn around and drive home?

   b. try to find a side entrance where you could sneak in?

   c. go to the manager, tell him you've lost your tickets, and ask that he let you in?

9A. (For men only) You've lost your job. Will you

   a. take your wife out to dinner and a show, and tell her sometime later in the evening?

   b. tell her the facts as soon as you get home?

   c. keep it to yourself with the idea of telling your wife only after you've lined up another job?

9B. (For women only) You haven't been feeling well for some time, and now the symptoms seem to indicate something is gravely wrong. Will you
   a. consult a doctor but keep it secret from your husband until afterward?
   b. openly make an appointment with the doctor, but as if it were for something minor?
   c. tell your husband your fears and ask his advice?

10. You have heard a rumor that your spouse's favorite brother has been caught stealing but is making retribution and therefore will not be prosecuted. Will you
   a. tell your husband (or wife) immediately?
   b. get in touch secretly with the brother, with the idea of telling your husband (or wife) only if the brother admits the report is true?
   c. keep the matter entirely to yourself and try to forget it?

SCORING

Calculate your score by giving yourself the right number of points for the answer you circled:

1.	a–1	5.	a–1	9A.	(MEN ONLY)
	b–3		b–2		a–3
	c–2		c–3		b–2
2.	a–1	6.	a–3		c–1
	b–2		b–2	9B.	(WOMEN ONLY)
	c–3		c–1		a–2
3.	a–1	7.	a–1		b–3
	b–2		b–2		c–1
	c–3		c–3	10.	a–1
4.	a–3	8.	a–2		b–2
	b–1		b–3		c–3
	c–2		c–1		

Now add up your score and study the analysis that follows for your own case:

BLUFFER EXTRAORDINARY—25-30:

Anyone with a score of 30 is, of course, a champ, but if your score is 25-30 you qualify as a Grade A bluffer. You're the kind of person who believes you never get anywhere without taking risks; you like to bet, and you always bet to win. You're not reckless, for a good bluffer is not a wild bluffer. (For example, those who circled c of question 4 are not skillful bluffers, because it isn't clever to attempt a bluff that is doomed to instant failure; in this situation the good bluffer "pieces together what he knows to cover a gap of ignorance," and taking the positive approach, suggests an assignment for which he has at least a little background; the poor bluffer, always "negative," tells the boss flatly he couldn't do the job.) If you scored in this group, you have a deep sense of inner security, which makes it possible for you to attempt things for which you are only partially prepared. You don't feel the need of knowing beforehand that everything is going to come out all right; you have what your friends consider blind confidence that you can make it come out all right. You've been knocked down, suffered more defeat or failure than your careful friends, but you can take it better than they can. If you're a man, you've undoubtedly been fired at least once, and you've quit a job at least once; in both cases the next job was better. You're pretty nice to live with, and your friends describe you as interesting or "original." Your kids think you're a scream. It would be easier to embalm you than to take the bluffing out of you.

BLUFFER OF MERIT—20-25:

If your score is 20-25, you're not topflight, but you are a good bluffer. The difference between you and the man or woman with a score of 30 is one of technique only; your instinct to bluff is just as strong, but your artistic judgment isn't as good. Your personality is less stable than that of the Grade A bluffer; sometimes you attempt the impossible; sometimes you err in the other direction and bet a sure thing to place. You have been criticized for "not facing facts." On the other hand, friends often comment, "I don't know how you do it. . . ." You like to hear that, for though you appear to be the kind of person who doesn't care "what people think," actually you are motivated by a strong desire to please. You get along well with people, but you do your best in any project, social or professional, if you tackle it alone. You've got the makings of a Grade A bluffer; all you need is finesse.

BLUFFER WITH RESERVATIONS—15-20:

If you scored 15-20 points you are a mediocre bluffer. When you take a chance, you're painfully conscious of it; it's not that you don't believe in taking chances (you probably call them "well-considered risks"), but when you finally step up to the window, you always bet to show. You are easily embarrassed; if you could recall every situation in which you've bluffed, you'd find that nine out of ten times your reason for bluffing was to save yourself or someone else from embarrassment. The really good bluffer frequently bluffs without knowing it; you know when you're bluffing, even when you're doing it to be kind, and therefore you don't do it very well. Men in this group prefer to work for someone else; when they are in business for themselves they often worry themselves into poor health. Women in this group make wonderful committee members and poor club presidents. If you scored 15–20 points, you're conservative in your tastes, you prefer the company of people you've known for a long time, and you are often blunt when you mean to be nice. What you need is more self-confidence—then your "bluffability" rating will improve.

BLUFFER WITH DUNCE CAP:

And finally, you who scored only 10–15 points! Obviously you are a rotten bluffer, or else you think so little of others that you don't even try. Your favorite slogans are, "I'd rather be safe than sorry" and "I believe in calling a spade a spade." You're every bit as original as those sayings, too. You lack imagination, creative ability, and nerve; once or twice in your life you thought of crawling out of your rut, but someone talked you out of it and you were secretly relieved. You're the one who has suffered most from your inability to bluff, but others have been shortchanged by it too. Your family, for example; while you were calling spades spades, a lot of romance and fun and human warmth went out the window. A dull life is safe, all right—but you will be sorry!

What Kind of Decorating
Is Right for You?

Everything we do sends out some kind of message," says psychologist Dr. Syvil Marquit, "and all of us tend, subconsciously, to communicate messages in decorating." The furniture you select and arrange, the colors you choose, the pictures and the accessories all reveal your inner nature and fundamental needs. Everything you own is saying something about you, your frustrations, your dreams, your joys, even your hostilities. This quiz will not only help you become more aware of your inner thoughts (and help you capture messages in houses you visit) but also tell you what kind of decorating is right for you.

Every question in the quiz should be answered. In some cases, you may have to choose the answer closest to your own particular lifestyle; or you may have to use your imagination and check the answer that would be the ideal situation for you.

1. Suppose you were decorating your dream foyer or hall. Would you choose:
    a. a great light fixture that attracts attention the moment you enter?
    b. plants, a statue, or a little fountain?
    c. a floor of checkerboard tile or colorful ceramics?
    d. a display of art on the wall?

2. When you entertain, how do you seat guests in the living room? Do you:
    a. like to sit in the middle of the group so that you can talk to everybody?
    b. place a favorite guest close by in a seat facing you?
    c. put people near a chess table or another thought-provoking object such as an African sculpture or an abstract painting?
    d. seat friends in an unusual way—cushions on the floor?

3. Where do you place guests for a small dinner:
    a. you and your host at either end of a rectangular table with your special guest on your right?
    b. everyone seated at a candlelit table—shape doesn't matter?
    c. at a round table?
    d. at individual folding tables?

4. In your living room, what kind of seating do you prefer:
   a. sofas and chairs in casual fabrics or other interesting texture?
   b. lots of elegant chairs in velvet, silk, or other soft smooth fabric?
   c. director's chairs?
   d. new foam blocks or a carpeted platform?

5. Visiting your house, do people tend to:
   a. gather around a bar?
   b. sit in small groups?
   c. sit around a coffee table or two small tables?
   d. lounge on a low couch or sit on cushions?

6. Which of these objects do you prefer in your living room?
   a. sports trophies?
   b. treasured possessions, including antiques?
   c. controversial posters or graphics?
   d. stereo equipment, a piece of art or sculpture you did yourself?

7. What is your preference on the walls:
   a. mirrors or family portraits?
   b. landscapes, animal pictures?
   c. painting of a storm or a picture showing an Indian war, rodeo, hockey, or a football game?
   d. impressionist or modern painting in bright colors?

8. How are these wall decorations displayed?
   a. in large, rather ornate frames?
   b. in a perfectly balanced arrangement?
   c. in asymmetrical arrangements, unbalanced but orderly?
   d. at random?

9. How are treasured objects displayed on tables:
   a. standing alone, placed prominently?
   b. two objects placed together balancing each other?
   c. a mixture of several things on a bare surface?
   d. one unusual piece placed asymmetrically?

10. What kind of collections do you display?
    a. mementos from vacation trips, each with a personal story attached?
    b. the family's coat of arms and family photos, or china?
    c. handsome weaponry or unusual chessmen?

    d. things in natural materials—like shells or stones or baskets—grouped in an arrangement?

11. In general, do you prefer to live with:
    a. bright greens or blues?
    b. warm purples or reds?
    c. stimulating pinks or yellows?
    d. soft blues or browns and naturals?

12. How do you like to use color in your house:
    a. put bright colors together?
    b. blend lots of pastels?
    c. always look for unexpected combinations?
    d. use lots of shades of the same color?

13. Which would you prefer to have in your kitchen:
    a. something really dramatic that draws guests into the room, such as a fireplace, a wall of posters?
    b. plants, lovely ceramics, beautiful old jars?
    c. lots of electrical gadgets, a great mortar and pestle?
    d. indoor barbecue?

14. Which of these beds would you prefer:
    a. king sized?
    b. four-poster?
    c. twin bed?
    d. water bed?

15. What type of headboard would you want:
    a. something rather elaborate and custom-made?
    b. Victorian wicker, or an antique one with angels or flowers on it?
    c. very contemporary with lots of built-in gadgets?
    d. very inconspicuous or maybe none?

16. Which of the following is closest to the way you express your own creative ability in your house:
    a. a screen or some other object that you covered with photos and clippings from magazines, placed importantly in a room; a painting?
    b. a "found" object refreshed and put to new use, a thrift-shop rocking chair repainted, recovered?
    c. pieces of handcrafted pottery—they might be used as plant containers—or a metal-and-glass table you made yourself?

    d. a macrame wall hanging, huge paper flowers, pillows made from antique rugs?

17. For your bathrooms, would you choose:

    a. lots of mirrors?

    b. lots of wonderful towels?

    c. telephone?

    d. stereo outlet, a magazine rack?

SCORING

Each of us is many people, and we are a different person to everyone we know. Who are we really? To find out a little more about your character, write in the number of a's _____, b's _____, c's _____, and d's _____ you checked. If you checked six or more in any one category, this is your dominant trait. Second highest will tell you your secondary trait. (Most people are combinations of two or three.)

If you checked six or more a's you are rather an extrovert. You want, even insist, on interacting with other people. You are outgoing, like to enjoy and participate in life to its fullest. You want people to remember you, so you're always intent on making an impact, or a lasting impression. This is why your living room is arranged so that you are in the mainstream with your guests, whom you make subtly aware of your achievements—trophies, photographs with celebrities and other objects that show an ability to perform either as part of a team or on your own. You like to dominate dinner parties, sitting at the head of the table, and the bright colors all around your house denote your happy nature, your joyful verve for life. Even your choice of bed (king sized) reveals your expansiveness, and mirrors on the walls reflect an approval of self, and thus a general feeling of well-being.

If you checked six or more b's you are delightfully romantic. You wish to avoid all the ugliness and unhappiness in life and will strive to have deep and meaningful relationships. This is why you like to dine by the softness of candlelight and have special treasured possessions, with sentimental associations, all around you. Beautiful flower colors are your favorites, gentle fabrics, landscape or nature paintings arranged in perfect balance, graceful plants—everything indicates a need to elicit a feeling of peacefulness from things you live with. Rather than communicate with the world, like the extrovert, you prefer to devote yourself to one or two people when entertaining—which is reflected in your choice of placing a special guest near you, so that warm conversation can follow.

If you checked six or more c's you are a natural character. You think of life as a marvelous challenge and find great stimulation in competition, matching your strength, testing your abilities against others. An activist by nature, you reflect this throughout your lifestyle. The table you dine at is round so that all may enter into lively conversation. All the things you live with provoke comment—controversial posters, paintings, or sculpture, daring colors, the latest electrical gadgets. They may make the visitor feel insecure, but for you it's just another test, another way of learning another aspect of life.

If you checked six or more d's you are an exciting innovator. You are an explorer, always ready to try something new and probably very creative. Nothing you do is predictable, and so your house is likely to be full of unusual ideas—swinging seats, or no seats. No dining table, perhaps, but lots of cushions and little low tables. You have no fear about making a wrong choice, so you tend to experiment all the time, changing rooms around, constantly working out new ways to arrange things, and new color schemes. Naturally uninhibited, you will accept any new design instantly, where others might tend to be much more reluctant. Your house will never be dull.

What Does Your Closet Reveal About You?

There's more to your clothes closet than meets the eye.

What lies behind the closet door can tell more about your personality than you think.

In fact, says interior designer Michael Schachel, he can predict the type of person you are with 80 to 90 per cent accuracy from the way your closet looks.

He has a test you can take to find out what your closet reveals about you.

"I can tell from a closet whether people are rich or poor, neat or sloppy, neurotic or not, easygoing or nervous," said the Miami designer.

Here's Schachel's test. Give yourself 5 points for each "Yes" answer. Then tally your score and look to the bottom of this story for the personality traits you've uncovered.

1. Do you hang similar garments next to one another—shirts with shirts, dresses with dresses, etc.?
2. Do you arrange shirts by sleeve length?
3. Do you hang shirts together by color?
4. Do you remove winter clothes from your closet and store them when summer arrives?
5. If someone hung something out of place in your closet, would you be upset?
6. Do you have fewer than five garments in your closet that you haven't worn in the past year?
7. Do you use hangers of just one type—either all wood, all metal, or all plastic?
8. Do you have more than ten pairs of shoes in good condition?
9. Do you vacuum or sweep your closet once a week?
10. If someone asked to look in your closet, could you be certain that clothes for the cleaners were not piled in a corner?
11. Do you know, without looking, how many pairs of shoes you own?
12. Is your closet lighted?
13. Does your closet hold only wearing apparel?
14. Would you be pleased if someone gave you a garment bag for a birthday present?
15. Do you have only ties on your tie holder, only belts on your belt holder?
16. If you bought a new coat, could you part with the old one without trying it on one more time?
17. Are your shoes, hats, wigs, or handbags neatly boxed?

18. If your roommate or spouse draped your new suit over the rod, would you feel compelled to tell him or her you didn't appreciate the gesture?

19. Is every garment in your closet ready to be worn—no broken zippers, ripped seams, or missing buttons?

20. Are you absolutely certain there's no wad of paper stuffed in that pair of shoes that pinches your toes?

SCORING

If you scored 0–25 points, consider yourself either a slob or a free spirit. Other things are more important to you than closets. You are creative, impulsive, and would just as soon live out of a suitcase as a closet. As a lover, you walk on the wild side; as a parent, you're permissive. Where others get a feeling of satisfaction and peace from being orderly, you only feel annoyance at the pettiness of it all.

If you scored 25–50 points, you are a secret nonconformist. You would chuck the establishment existence and be totally happy if it weren't for a puritanical streak that keeps you straight.

You care what others think. You might feel more comfortable in jeans, but you'd never risk being the only one there so casual. As a lover, you make sure the blinds are drawn, the cat is out, and the kids are asleep.

If you scored 50–75 points, you put on a convincing front that you're just one of the guys—free-wheelin' and happy-go-lucky. But behind the quick little laugh, you're a frazzled bundle of nerves. Loud music makes you jump. Dog hair offends you. You look better in a polyester leisure suit than you do in dungarees. You are precise and semirigid. You blame your compulsive habits on your upbringing.

Love is something you enjoy in proper privacy.

If you scored 75–100, you're so uptight you'd come totally unglued if a wet puppy climbed in your lap. You like your pencils sharp, your hair down flat, your bed turned down, and your cuffs turned back. You make schedules and stick to them.

What lies within the closet door . . . doesn't lie, Schachel says.

Are You Miss Neat or Mr. Slob?

It takes all sorts to make the world . . . some folks lead exceptionally disciplined lives, other are so disorganized it's a wonder they survive. Which category do you fall into? And what about your family and friends? Try this fun quiz. You'll be surprised at the answers.

FOR WOMEN ONLY:

1. At this moment, are any of your clothes held together by safety pins?
   a. none.
   b. some.
   c. many.

2. Do you enjoy lounging around in your robe with your hair up in curlers?
   a. always.
   b. never.
   c. occasionally.

3. Is your kitchen sink filled with unrinsed, unwashed dishes?
   a. seldom.
   b. never.
   c. most of the time.

4. Do friends remind you that something is awry in your dress, such as a slip showing, shoulder strap hanging, a run in your hose, smudged makeup?
   a. often.
   b. sometimes.
   c. never.

5. Before you retire to bed, do you straighten your living quarters, (clean ashtrays, pile up papers, ready the sink for the waking meal)?
   a. no.
   b. yes.
   c. about half the time.

6. Do you let your ironing pile up for more than a week?
   a. often.
   b. seldom.
   c. never.

7. If the lights were to go out in your living quarters, could you grope your way to things you need for the emergency (candles, flashlight, correct doors, medicine cabinet, etc.)?
   a. yes.
   b. no.
   c. doubtful.

8. Do you follow the rule, "A place for everything and everything in its place."?
   a. strictly.
   b. no.
   c. for some items.

9. Do you store seldom-used clothing, equipment, blankets, etc., in plastic bags, bottles, or labeled boxes?
   a. no.
   b. yes.
   c. some items.

10. Do you sort, file, select, and weed out your possessions?
    a. quite often.
    b. never.
    c. once in a while.

FOR MEN ONLY:
1. Is a chair your favorite place to hang your coat and trousers?
   a. no.
   b. occasionally.
   c. yes.

2. Are your pockets filled with trash, such as bits of paper, loose tobacco, paperclips, broken pencils, etc.?
   a. yes.
   b. no.
   c. sometimes.

3. If a neighbor were to ask you for a specific article that you possess—such as a rake, a pencil, a hammer, nails—could you get it for him or her?
   a. immediately.
   b. after some search.
   c. no.

4. Can you repair and do you have available equipment to sew on buttons, mend a rip, iron a shirt?

    a. yes.

    b. no.

    c. in a makeshift way.

5. Do you send your items of clothing to the cleaners or laundry when they are soiled?

    a. no.

    b. sometimes.

    c. always.

6. Do you leave newspapers and magazines scattered around your living room?

    a. usually.

    b. sometimes.

    c. always.

7. Do you expect others to clean and pick up after you?

    a. of course.

    b. of course not.

    c. sometimes.

8. Is a good physical appearance important to you?

    a. no.

    b. yes.

    c. most of the time.

9. Do you rely on others in your family or on the job to find things for you?

    a. seldom.

    b. occasionally.

    c. often.

10. When you have to write mathematical problems, do you place the digits in correct, straight columns?

    a. no.

    b. sometimes.

    c. yes.

FOR MEN AND WOMEN:

1. Do your keys elude you?

    a. sometimes.

    b. often.

    c. almost never.

2. When you dry your hands after washing them, do you leave the towel smudged and soiled?

    a. yes.

    b. no.

    c. only slightly.

3. Were, or are, your parents untidy?

    a. no.

    b. yes.

    c. moderately so.

4. Do you have a scientific "bent"—an interest in and knowledge of such things as medicine, mathematics, chemistry?

    a. yes.

    b. slight.

    c. no.

5. Do you have as much concern about the cleanliness and quality of your undergarments as you do about your outer clothing?

    a. no.

    b. yes.

    c. sometimes.

6. After a meal, is your place scattered with crumbs and spotted by food?

    a. almost never.

    b. occasionally.

    c. often.

7. If you noticed a large spot on your blouse or shirt just as you were leaving the house, would you change if time permitted?

    a. yes.

    b. no.

    c. perhaps.

8. Do you make an effort to keep the entrance to your living quarters clean and attractive?

    a. no.

    b. yes.

    c. only on special occasions.

9. Do you save a clutter of things for which you have no need, such as old magazines, letters, cans, bottles, or bits of fabric?
   a. no.
   b. sometimes.
   c. very often.

10. Do people complain that they cannot read your handwriting?
    a. yes.
    b. sometimes.
    c. no.

11. Do you conscientiously replace tops and lids to bottles and tubes?
    a. no.
    b. about half the time.
    c. sometimes.

12. After using equipment such as eggbeaters, pots, paint brushes, cameras, etc., do you carefully clean and ready them for next use?
    a. always.
    b. seldom.
    c. sometimes.

SCORING

CHECK YOUR SCORE:

For Women:
1. a–8; b–4; c–2
2. a–2; b–8; c–6
3. a–6; b–8; c–2
4. a–2; b–4; c–8
5. a–2; b–8; c–6
6. a–2; b–6; c–8
7. a–8; b–2; c–4
8. a–8; b–2; c–6
9. a–2; b–8; c–6
10. a–8; b–2; c–6

For Men:
1. a–8; b–6; c–2
2. a–2; b–8; c–4
3. a–8; b–4; c–2
4. a–8; b–2; c–4
5. a–2; b–4; c–8
6. a–2; b–6; c–8
7. a–2; b–8; c–4
8. a–2; b–8; c–6
9. a–8; b–6; c–2
10. a–2; b–6; c–8

For Men
and Women:
1. a–4; b–2; c–8
2. a–2; b–8; c–4
3. a–8; b–2; c–6
4. a–8; b–4; c–2
5. a–2; b–8; c–4
6. a–8; b–4; c–2
7. a–8; b–2; c–6
8. a–2; b–8; c–6
9. a–8; b–4; c–2
10. a–2; b–4; c–8
11. a–2; b–4; c–8
12. a–8; b–2; c–2

WHAT YOUR ANSWERS REVEAL ABOUT YOU AND YOUR FAMILY:

150-176:   People who rate this are usually so neat and well organized they make others uncomfortable. They are the tie straighteners, the dandruff flickers, the ashtray cleaners, the pillow plumpers. At this point, orderliness becomes an obsession, an end rather than a means for an efficient way of living.

A recent advice column cited a true case of such a person: A hostess, before giving a dinner party, asked each person for his or her shoe size. She had just bought white carpets and in order to avoid soiling the rug planned to ask her guests to wear slippers in the house. Only a few accepted the invitation. Those who went were nervous all evening.

110-148:   This is a fine score, one deserved by well-organized people who appreciate the value of putting things away when not needed, or keeping equipment clean and their environment attractive.

Their example is often followed by others and the people in this score range waste little valuable time floundering in search for things they know they have.

60-108:   This indicates those who are not necessarily dirty or slovenly but who could do well with new, more precise habits. Begin with your clothing.

Hang up your clothing preferably in the same place each day and night. Keep your clothes neat, mended, and clean. Tackle one by one each point where you are weak on this quiz and consciously set a positive pattern.

Start with the important points first, the items that frustrate you most. If, for instance, you always mislay your keys, establish a place for them.

44-58:   Your lack of neatness must confuse you and upset your family and friends. You and your environment give the impression of having been hit by a cyclone.

If you have any inner peace it comes in spite of and not because of your way of life. The happy thing is that you can make the hours easier for yourself if you use your God-given good judgment and establish automatic habits of neatness.

Can You Cope with
a Medical Emergency at Home?

Do you have the know-how to cope with a medical emergency at home?

The country's leading organization of family doctors compiled a special medical quiz to test your first-aid knowledge—and to improve it. The quiz lists ten medical emergencies and asks what you would do in each case. "All these situations happen frequently at home," said family physician Dr. John S. Derryberry, a director of the American Academy of Family Physicians.

1. Your husband develops unusually sharp chest pains after a meal. Do you
   a. give him a big dose of soda?
   b. tell him not to worry?
   c. call your doctor or take him to a hospital emergency room?

2. An electric shock knocks your child unconscious. Do you
   a. prop up his head and let him come to gradually?
   b. lay him flat, ensure that his jaw is raised and that he is breathing okay?
   c. give him a sharp blow on the chest?

3. Your child starts to choke at mealtime and cannot breathe. Do you
   a. grip him from behind with your clenched arms and squeeze sharply upward under his upper abdomen?
   b. give him a drink to wash the food down?
   c. give him a sharp pat on the back?

4. You spill boiling water on your arm. Do you
   a. put butter over the scald?
   b. apply oil or dry mustard?
   c. apply cold water?

5. Your child swallows some bleach. Do you
   a. administer lemon juice or diluted vinegar?
   b. give soda?
   c. give warm water and induce vomiting?

6. Granny falls and complains of back and hip pains. Do you
   a. help her into a chair or bed to rest?
   b. make her comfortable and send for an ambulance?
   c. help her walk around to loosen up?

7. Your child swallows half a dozen birth-control pills. Do you
   a. give orange juice to dissolve the pills?
   b. conclude he didn't swallow enough of the pills to do harm?
   c. induce the youngster to vomit?

8. Your child crashes through a glass door and opens up a deep gash on his arm. Do you
   a. apply a tourniquet?
   b. apply first-aid cream and bandage the wound?
   c. wrap the gash firmly with a clean towel and take him to a hospital?

9. Your child swallows two dozen of Granny's iron pills. Do you
   a. induce the child to vomit, then see your doctor?
   b. give the youngster a laxative?
   c. conclude that the pills cannot do any harm?

10. Your child swallows gasoline or kerosene. Do you
    a. give him warm water to lessen the effects?
    b. make him vomit?
    c. get him to a hospital?

SCORING

Here are the answers:

1. c. If the pain is severe and lasts longer than a few minutes, it is probably more than just indigestion, so don't take any chances.

2. b. It is vitally important to determine if the child is breathing. If he is not, administer mouth-to-mouth resuscitation and send for emergency help.

3. a. It is called the Heimlich method and has proved to be the most effective first-aid technique for dealing with choking.

4. c. Cold water will help ease the pain. Then get medical attention.

5. a. Lemon juice and vinegar are acids, and they will neutralize bleach, which is alkaline. Then take your child to your family doctor or hospital emergency room to see if further treatment is necessary.

6. b. Old people are particularly prone to broken hips. Helping Granny into a chair or bed, or making her walk could aggravate a fracture.

7. c. Induce the child to vomit by either making him drink a lot of warm water, or by sticking a spoon handle down his throat.

8. c. Wrapping the wound firmly will help stem the bleeding. Direct pressure is better than a tourniquet.

9. a. Iron pills in large doses can be fatal to a small child. He must have his stomach emptied by a doctor.

10. c. Vomiting could make the situation worse, and warm water will hasten the absorption of the gasoline or kerosene into the body. The child must have his stomach emptied by a doctor.

A SPECIAL TEST
FOR OUR READERS

Did You Like This Book?

We thought it only fitting and proper that we conclude the book with our own test designed especially for you, the reader. We'd like to find out if you liked our book. The mini-test below will provide both of us with the answer.

1. Did you enjoy taking most of the tests?

2. Were the tests generally interesting, entertaining, and thought-provoking?

3. Did you learn anything about yourself from the book?

4. Did the tests answer some of the important questions you often ask yourself?

5. Were you influenced to reconsider your behavior, attitudes, or opinions based on what a particular test or series of tests revealed about yourself?

SCORING

If you answered "Yes" to at least one of the questions, you have indicated that reading and "playing" this book was a pleasurable and rewarding experience. You have been entertained, informed, and stimulated by the variety of tests offered.

We sincerely appreciate your interest in reading our book. We'd now like to learn even more about how you felt about taking the tests. Which tests did you enjoy taking most? Which tests did you enjoy taking least? What other test topics or specific titles would you enjoy seeing in *The Book of Tests II*?

We encourage you to send us any ideas you may have for new tests to be included in *The Book of Tests II*. We are interested in knowing what else you want to find out about yourself. To get in touch with us, just write to:

The Book of Tests
Doubleday & Company, Inc.
245 Park Avenue,
New York, N.Y. 10017

THE EDITORS

Notes